"As new contexts emerge, new questions arise. We all recognize that times are a-changin'. But changing times demand wise guides. I can think of few better guides to help us navigate this period than Mike Goheen and Tim Sheridan appropriating Lesslie Newbigin. If you are a leader feeling rumblings in your soul about church, culture, and the world overall, you should read this book! And as you read, ask the Holy Spirit to apply these truths to your life and church."

—**Tyler Johnson**, lead pastor, Redemption Church (AZ)

"'Faithful are the wounds of a friend' (Prov. 27:6). This saying came to mind repeatedly as I read this appraisal of three contemporary efforts to reenergize the church in its missionary identity and mandate. There is warm appreciation for how all these 'friends' (for they are, especially the highly esteemed Tim Keller) long to reach and impact our culture for Christ and the gospel, combined with sharp but respectful critique of shortcomings and dangers that become apparent in the wider light of the whole Bible narrative and its implications. The authors' exposition and application of the missionary life and theology of Lesslie Newbigin is a master class of clarity and illumination, repeatedly offering eye-opening insights as to how we have come to be where we are in the Western world (and wherever the toxins of Western idolatries have penetrated). Any church that is praying for a fruitful missionary encounter with their surrounding culture will find here a rich resource of biblically rooted priorities, characteristics, and practices that align with the whole-Bible gospel, center on the cross and resurrection of Christ, and glorify the God of all creation."

—**Christopher J. H. Wright**, Langham Partnership;
author of *The Mission of God*

"Few grasp Lesslie Newbigin's magisterial contributions to everything that is essential to Christianity—the universal story of Scripture, the comprehensiveness of the gospel, the mission of the church—as well as Goheen and Sheridan do. *Becoming a Missionary Church* offers riches for both the Newbigin beginner and veteran. It persuasively articulates an invigorating Newbigin-inspired vision for renewing the culturally captive North American church that is more compelling than contemporary alternatives. Its critique of those alternatives is careful and fair-minded, managing to leave readers both more appreciative of the wisdom they contain while also more clear-eyed about their shortcomings. Both my understanding of what is necessary for renewing the church and my passion for deeper engagement in that task have grown because of this book, and I am grateful."

—**Amy L. Sherman**, author of *Kingdom Calling* and *Agents of Flourishing*

"This book is overflowing with rich insights regarding the missionary nature of the church. Goheen and Sheridan engage in conversation with past developments in missionary ecclesiology as well as recent trends like the missional church movement, the emergent church conversation, and Tim Keller's center church. In each case, the authors allow Lesslie Newbigin's seminal vision of the church in mission to provide a welcome and needed corrective. Readers will value the book's balanced perspective, which spotlights both the strengths and the gaps in the influential movements it evaluates. This isn't just a 'theory' book; it teems with practical implications for how the church can participate in God's mission more fully and faithfully today."

—**Dean Flemming**, MidAmerica Nazarene University;
author of *Contextualization in the New Testament*

"A fresh look at Newbigin's wisdom for the Western church. We have much to gain from Goheen and Sheridan as they draw us into the profound and often overlooked insights that Newbigin offers for the church today. This book is for all who take seriously God's mission and the call to be a missionary church."

—**Jim Mullins**, lead pastor, Redemption Church Tempe

"Ironically, much of what has passed for 'missional church' has been untethered from the careful theological reflection and wisdom of its forefather, Lesslie Newbigin. Goheen and Sheridan re-tether the church to mission by grounding the whole life of the church in its true missionary identity. They call us to embrace suffering, cultural exile, vocation, and Sunday gatherings as an intended part of God's mission. Their critiques are incisive, even-handed, and charitable. The nuanced missiological reflection in this book is a priceless gift to readers. I was inspired to continue leading churches into God's mission while trusting the results to him."

—**Jonathan Dodson**, founding pastor, City Life Church;
author of *The Unbelievable Gospel*

Becoming a
Missionary
Church

Lesslie Newbigin and
Contemporary Church Movements

Michael W. Goheen
and Timothy M. Sheridan

Baker Academic
a division of Baker Publishing Group
Grand Rapids, Michigan

From Michael:
To Len and Evelyn Noort, Nick and Nelly Noort,
Hank and Renie Van Ryk, and John and Margaret Vegt
with love and gratitude

From Timothy:
To Andrea, my best friend and loving wife

© 2022 by Michael W. Goheen and Timothy M. Sheridan

Published by Baker Academic
a division of Baker Publishing Group
PO Box 6287, Grand Rapids, MI 49516-6287
www.bakeracademic.com

Printed in the United States of America

Library of Congress Cataloging-in-Publication Data
Names: Goheen, Michael W., 1955– author. | Sheridan, Timothy M., 1973– author.
Title: Becoming a missionary church : Lesslie Newbigin and contemporary church movements / Michael W. Goheen and Timothy M. Sheridan.
Description: Grand Rapids, Michigan : Baker Academic, a division of Baker Publishing Group, [2022] | Includes index.
Identifiers: LCCN 2021049817 | ISBN 9780801049279 (paperback) | ISBN 9781540965578 (casebound) | ISBN 9781493436552 (ebook) | ISBN 9781493436569 (pdf)
Subjects: LCSH: Missions—theory. | Newbigin, Lesslie. | Church.
Classification: LCC BV2063 .G5675 2022 | DDC 266—dc23/eng/20211130
LC record available at https://lccn.loc.gov/2021049817

Baker Publishing Group publications use paper produced from sustainable forestry practices and post-consumer waste whenever possible.

22   23   24   25   26   27   28   7   6   5   4   3   2   1

Contents

Part 4 Center Church

Preface

This is primarily a book for pastors and congregational leaders. It is offered with the hope that it might foster a deeper commitment to and understanding of what it means to become a missionary congregation. Recovering our missionary identity is urgent because our missionary identity is central to our biblical identity.

Our primary concern in this book is to hear Lesslie Newbigin's voice. He is considered by many to be the father of the now widespread concern for the church's missionary nature. To hear his voice, we do two primary things in this book: First, we set his missionary understanding of the church in its historical context of the early twentieth century. Second, we set him in dialogue with three important church conversations or movements that have developed his missionary vision—the missional church, the emergent church, and center church. We do so not by way of a deep dive, either historically or analytically, into these conversations. Rather, we offer our overall sense of the main themes in each conversation and their helpful contributions to a missionary church. But we also reappropriate Newbigin's voice of critique and enrichment and inject it into each conversation.

We had limited space. This often kept us from the kind of nuance and detail we would like to have given. Yet we have read widely in these areas—between us, all of Newbigin's published (and many unpublished) writings; all of Tim Keller's published (and some unpublished) writings, as well as video and audio materials; and the majority of missional and emergent literature. What is covered in this book is the subject of both of our PhD dissertations. We have attempted to distill the main themes of these conversations and interact with them in light of Newbigin's thought. Some may feel that we are unfair in our criticism or that we neglected certain books and authors or that we have not provided enough nuance. And it may be true. But we have not done so deliberately.

This book contains two primary sections: (1) the historical context of Newbigin's missionary ecclesiology from 1938 to 1998 and (2) the three contemporary church conversations—missional, emergent, and center. We bracket these with a personal appeal to become a missionary church and a closing summary of what that might look like in view of our journey through this book. Originally, we intended to include a section on Newbigin's missionary ecclesiology presented as a whole in its systematic unity. But this became a book on its own[1] and provides much of the background for our discussion.

At times it has been emotionally difficult for us to write this book. There is more criticism in this book than either of us is used to offering in our writing. And these critiques are not just of theological positions but of people who hold those positions, including people we respect and appreciate as brothers and sisters in Christ. But we pray this would be for the sake of the kingdom and faithfulness to Scripture.

Writing this book has also been a great learning experience for both of us. We understand Newbigin more deeply as we set him in dialogue with others who share similar concerns. We have deepened our insight by listening to the voices of so many from each of these conversations. Most important of all, we believe that we grasp Scripture's teaching more fully because of the voices of brothers and sisters in Christ. Indeed, the love of God revealed in the gospel is so wide, so deep, so high, so broad that it is only together with all God's people that we can understand it (Eph. 3:18).

---

1. Michael W. Goheen, *The Church and Its Vocation: Lesslie Newbigin's Missionary Ecclesiology* (Grand Rapids: Baker Academic, 2018).

Acknowledgments

Mike dedicates this book in love and gratitude to four couples who, through their generosity and kindness, have played an important role in his ministry: Len and Evelyn Noort, Nick and Nelly Noort, Hank and Renie Van Ryk, and John and Margaret Vegt. The church is made up of faithful people who faithfully use the various resources God gives them for the sake of his kingdom. Our participation in God's mission is often in unrecognized and hidden acts of love that sometimes have a wide ripple effect on the lives of many. So it is with these four couples.

Tim dedicates this book in love and gratitude to his loving and supportive wife, Andrea. It has been a long, winding journey filled with many joys, setbacks, and challenges to see this book finally published. Without her continued encouragement, support, and sacrifices, it would have never happened.

1

Becoming a Missionary Church

An Invitation

The Book's Title and Our Quest

The title of our book describes accurately our primary concern: *becoming a missionary church*. This has been a life quest central to both of our lives in pastoral ministry, teaching, speaking, and writing. And we believe it is urgent, not as the next new path to success, but because it is only when the church is missionary in its very nature that we are faithful to what God has called us to be. Or, to put it another way, this quest is about fully recovering a central component of the Bible's teaching about God's people—something essential to the Christian faith.

If the title expresses *what* we want to see the church become, the subtitle indicates *how* we want to contribute: *Lesslie Newbigin and contemporary church movements*. This book is primarily an exercise in contemporary historical theology. We discuss three significant church conversations that have emerged in the first decades of the twenty-first century—missional, emergent, and center. But we do so in dialogue with Lesslie Newbigin and his missionary ecclesiology. It is especially this last sentence that is important: we want pastors to return to Newbigin, who is the source of much of the discussion. There remains a richness to his missionary ecclesiology that is desperately needed today.

The popular language of "missional" in North America finds its origins in the book *Missional Church*.[1] Its authors' stated goal was to contextualize Newbigin's vision of a missionary church into the North American setting. In many ways the book achieved its purpose, and this has borne much fruit. However, there were two things about that translation that have impacted subsequent development. On the one hand, there are significant aspects of Newbigin's missionary ecclesiology that did not feature in the book. This set a certain trajectory during the past two decades in subsequent efforts to shape a missionary church. On the other hand, the book does not make it clear that the authors' missional ecclesiology is part of a much larger story reaching back to the early twentieth century. Newbigin's ecclesiology developed as part of a lengthy and rich theological discussion to which the *Missional Church* authors were returning. The cumulative effect of these two factors has been a loss of some of the robust theological work of Newbigin and of his contemporaries.

When traditions evolve and move into new settings, it is inevitable that some elements will feature more prominently while others recede. That is simply the creational and contextual nature of traditions. *Missional Church* captured much in Newbigin's missionary ecclesiology that was relevant for the North American setting. We are grateful for the vision expressed in that book and for the biblical elements of missionary ecclesiology that have been recovered in the two subsequent decades because of its publication. Yet we also believe there is much that is valuable for our context, both in Newbigin and in the early twentieth-century development of a missionary ecclesiology, that has not received sufficient attention. We thus seek a missionary understanding of the church that both embraces the healthy developments of these ecclesial movements and attempts to recover insights that have been neglected.

A fair question would be, Why proceed in this way? Shouldn't we simply assess all these church movements *and* Newbigin in the light of Scripture? Yes, indeed! But there is good historical reason for our approach. It is generally recognized that Newbigin is in some sense the father of a missionary understanding of the church as this understanding has been appropriated in North America. It was his books, primarily in the 1980s and 1990s, along with his tireless work in promoting a missionary encounter between the gospel and Western culture, that injected the notion of a missionary church into the bloodstream of the North American church. So a legitimate historical question to ask is how his vision has been carried forward into our present context. Most authors believe they are doing so—but how?

1. Darrell L. Guder, ed., *Missional Church: A Vision for the Sending of the Church in North America* (Grand Rapids: Eerdmans, 1998).

In tackling the subject in this way, we have found that, on the one hand, we are able to appreciate many insights within these conversations. Many have grasped, developed, and contextualized Newbigin in fresh ways that have contributed to a biblical missionary ecclesiology. We have also found, on the other hand, that there are biblical and central aspects of Newbigin's missionary ecclesiology that have been overlooked. We need to recover these insights.

The Urgency of This Quest

This is not purely for academic interest. We are not primarily concerned to set the historical record straight or defend one man's theology or correct others'. Rather, both of us feel a certain urgency in this matter—an urgency, no doubt, that we share with others with whom we engage in the following pages. Recovering the missionary nature of the church is urgent because *this is what the church is in its biblical identity*. If the church is to faithfully be the church of the New Testament, it must be a missionary body. This is not an optional extra or something that might enrich the church. Mission is about the *esse* (essence or being) of the church, not its *bene esse* (well-being). Nor is this a formula for growth or success. It is not just for young, hip, entrepreneurial-style church planters. Rather, this is about being faithful. This is for all church planters and pastors who want to be faithful to Scripture. It is for all churches in all traditions and in all settings.

But when *faithful* is connected to *missionary* so strongly, it becomes imperative to come to terms with what the latter word means. It is possible for the words *missionary* and *missional* to be filled with a meaning that does not come from the biblical story. And so our concern in this matter is to struggle toward a vision of the church as missionary—a vision that is shaped by Scripture.

Perhaps this urgency can be illustrated by an anecdote from Newbigin's life. When Newbigin "retired" from missionary service in India at the age of sixty-five, he and his wife, Helen, decided to travel from India to England over land using local transportation and hitchhiking. It took them two months to make the trek. During their journey, only one time were they were unable to find other Christians with whom to fellowship. That was in Turkey, one of the very earliest and greatest centers of the Christian faith, with a Christian tradition stretching back to biblical times. But when the Newbigins arrived in the late twentieth century, they found that the lampstand of the church in that region had been dismantled. This shook them, and they struggled to come to terms with the fact that a great living church can be completely destroyed.

That story serves as a salutary warning. There is no reason to think that the same thing cannot happen here. From Newbigin's standpoint, one of the things that will prevent such a catastrophic future is the recovery of a full-orbed missionary ecclesiology. A missionary ecclesiology is far more than simply being reminded that we must evangelize or be involved in issues of mercy and justice. It is much more than finding novel structures or church growth. It is certainly more than making the gospel relevant to our culture's despisers or attractive to a youthful generation that is departing the church. These all have their place, but a missionary ecclesiology is much bigger than any of these. It is nothing less than a recovery of the public and creation-wide truth of the gospel of our Lord Jesus Christ, a commitment to the Bible as the true story that narrates the meaning and purpose of the whole world, an embrace of the calling of the church to be the new humankind who tell and embody that story across the whole spectrum of their lives amid cultures that live by different stories, and a comprehensive missionary encounter with the religious core of culture. It is this kind of missionary ecclesiology and missionary encounter with culture—and these are of necessity two sides of the same coin—that we pursue in writing this book.

Our Shared Stories

Something of our concern can be made clear in our shared stories and experiences. Both of us are dual citizens of Canada and the United States. We have pastored and taught in both countries. In both countries the church is in deep trouble. Statistics show steep decline. But even more troubling is the fact that both the US and the Canadian churches fit well Newbigin's severe indictment of the Western church for being "an advanced case of syncretism."[2] The churches in these two countries have quite different histories and face considerably different challenges. Yet each is deeply compromised by the religious vision of its culture.

Canada is much further down the path of secularization or, better, neo-paganism. The church is smaller and on the margins of public life. It is characterized by a timid syncretism, is sometimes unsure of its identity, and often is quick to accommodate itself to the powerful winds blowing in Canadian culture. The challenges the Canadian church faces are more akin to those of the church in Europe, which is thin but alive. Both of us have church-planted

2. Lesslie Newbigin, *A Word in Season: Perspectives on Christian World Missions* (Grand Rapids: Eerdmans, 1994), 67. See also Newbigin, *The Other Side of 1984: Questions for the Churches* (Geneva: World Council of Churches, 1983), 23.

and pastored in Canada. We have found that the approaches used in the United States simply do not work in the hard soil of Canada.

In the United States, on the surface the church seems to be much bigger, stronger, and more alive. However, appearances can be deceptive. The United States faces the seductive challenge of civil religion. The United States is the only nation founded amid the Enlightenment, and so the Christian faith has been woven into its national identity from the beginning *as a privatized religion*. Thus Christianity has played a role in the American story that is unthinkable in Canada. While this has had some positive effect, it also brings the deadly danger of wedding the gospel to and domesticating it by many of the religious spirits that shape American life. The pronounced privatized and individualized faith, commonly accepted in the American church as the normal expression of Christianity, is a truncated version of biblical faith. This cultural captivity makes the church vulnerable to the anti-Christian religious public doctrines shaping American culture. This is more than a potential threat: as has been made clear in recent political events, it is a tangible reality doing great harm to the church's witness.[3]

In both countries, the recovery of a robust missionary church that takes the posture of a missionary encounter would go a long way toward restoring the church to biblical wholeness. Both need a fresh grasp of the gospel and the biblical story as a comprehensive vision that casts a different vision of public life than the Right or Left options. Both need a renewed vision of the church, not as a voluntary society tucked away in a private religious realm, but as the new humanity restored to their Adamic vocation under the lordship of Christ. Both need a new set of eyes to see the religious faith that is shaping their culture so they can shake the false assumption that they are either a neutral or a semi-Christian culture.

Both of us completed PhD work in the subject area of this book. Mike did his PhD at Utrecht University on Newbigin's missionary ecclesiology.[4] Tim did his PhD at Stellenbosch University on the missional and emergent church movements in light of Newbigin's thought. It is significant that both of us were motivated to pursue PhD studies because of our church-planting and pastoral ministries. Both of us began our PhD studies to reflect on the challenges we faced as we planted churches in the challenging context of Canada.

3. For more on differences between the United States and Canada, see Michael W. Goheen, *Introducing Christian Mission Today: Scripture, History and Issues* (Downers Grove, IL: InterVarsity, 2014), 217–23.

4. Michael W. Goheen, *"As the Father Has Sent Me, I Am Sending You": J. E. Lesslie Newbigin's Missionary Ecclesiology* (Zoetermeer, Netherlands: Boekencentrum, 2000), available at http://dspace.library.uu.nl/handle/1874/597.

Our research was driven by one question: What does it means to be a faithful church in North America today?

Both of us worked alongside another pastoral colleague, Andrew Zantingh, in an older inner-city Canadian church, a church that had dramatically declined and was about to close its doors. Over the next decade we saw the Holy Spirit dramatically revive this church in remarkable ways that still fill us with wonder. One of our first steps toward renewal was to articulate what Newbigin's missionary ecclesiology would look like in this inner-city setting.[5] So we can say that one of the tools the Spirit used was the insights of Newbigin's missionary ecclesiology to bring renewal to a dying church. We stress immediately that this was a work of the Spirit and not the fruit of theological insight or structural renovation. It was due, we are sure, much more to prayer and the power of the gospel than to retrieving our missionary identity. But this retrieval was an important part of the story. We struggled together to foster a missionary identity in that congregation, guided to some degree by the insights gained from Mike's doctoral work. And Tim had the joy of planting a daughter church out of that congregation years later. So we have experienced the difference these insights can make, even in an older, traditional church. And the life we saw the Spirit give contributes to the urgency of our quest.

Both of us have also worked within traditional churches in the following decades where we did not see the same kind of explosive growth or striking renewal. The work of the Spirit was much more organic and gradual. We know that the work to form missionary congregations is hard and slow; the kind of renewal of that first experience is unusual and certainly cannot be engineered or predicted. But slow and gradual growth is not a negative thing: we were both privileged to subsequently lead healthy congregations in which nurturing a missionary congregation is a long obedience in the same direction. This is just the reality of most ministry. It is likely the primary situation in which most reading this book will find themselves: neither in a dying church nor in a church with explosive growth. Rather, leadership is the daily (joyful and often difficult) task of forming disciples to follow Jesus across the spectrum of their lives. In this experience, we have learned from our colleague Zack Eswine that even though the American church wants things fast, large, and famous, the kingdom of God comes slowly, in small and mostly unnoticed ways.[6] This is the way that most churches will be renewed in their missionary

5. For thirteen goals that guided our pastoral work, see "What Might This Look Like Today?," chap. 9 in Michael W. Goheen, *A Light to the Nations: The Missional Church and the Biblical Story* (Grand Rapids: Baker Academic, 2011), 201–26.

6. Zack Eswine, *The Imperfect Pastor: Discovering Joy in Our Limitations through a Daily Apprenticeship with Jesus* (Wheaton: Crossway, 2015), 1, 21–22, 26.

calling. We long for more of this. It may be a long obedience, but it must be in the right direction.

Both of us have been working in theological education to train missional leaders for the past decade. Dissatisfied with the kind of theological education available, a group of church leaders in Phoenix invited Mike to pioneer a creative experiment in theological education that aimed to implement the insights of missionary and non-Western church leaders of the 1960s–1980s. The result was Missional Training Center (MTC), where we offer a fully accredited MA in missional theology as an extension site of Covenant Theological Seminary, St. Louis. Over the past decade, the central question we have asked is what it might look like to train leaders who can lead missionary churches in Phoenix. We have worked to fashion a missional curriculum—along with a pedagogy, structures, assignments, and evaluation—that breaks with the university model of theological education so that we can more effectively disciple missionary leaders.[7] We have seen the results of our modest efforts in ways beyond our expectation. A robust and full-orbed missionary vision shared ecumenically by a group of church leaders who live for the good of the city *can* make and *has* made a difference in the life of Phoenix.[8] And in the same process we have also seen that a missionary encounter with culture can bring suffering for faithful leaders in their battle with deep-rooted idolatry often embedded in local congregations. This too can bring a certain kind of blessing that other forms of "successful" pastoring cannot (Matt. 5:10–12).

Our work at MTC has expanded to formal partnerships with churches, church-planting centers, and theological seminaries in Brazil, Chile, and Hungary. We have had the opportunity to return there often to train leaders and translate a missional curriculum into these three very different cultural settings over the past decade. This has included intensive discipleship as well as master's and doctoral programs for pastors. Our own North American prejudices and capitulation to unchristian spirits have been exposed to us in the process. Seeing and hearing how a hearty missionary ecclesiology can be translated into different cultural contexts and what it can do to renew the church fills us with hope and a desire to see this vision move beyond the borders of North

7. See Michael W. Goheen, "A Missional Reading of Scripture for Theological Education and Curriculum," in *A Missional Reading of Scripture*, ed. Michael W. Goheen (Grand Rapids: Eerdmans, 2016), 299–329.

8. See Michael W. Goheen and Jim Mullins, *The Symphony of Mission: Playing Your Part in God's Work in the World* (Grand Rapids: Baker Academic, 2019). Mullins was one of the first participants in and graduates of MTC. He works as lead pastor of Redemption Church, Tempe, in Arizona. In this book we tell many stories of how a missionary understanding of the church has made a difference in Phoenix. Many of the people Mullins profiles are participants in or graduates of MTC.

America. And as we have experienced already to a significant degree—and this cannot be stressed too strongly—we in North America have much more to learn in the process than to teach, if we are willing to take the posture of humble learners.

Both of us would describe ourselves confessionally as missional neo-Calvinists. We identify self-consciously with Dutch neo-Calvinism,[9] a tradition probably best known by the names of those who have formed us most deeply—Herman Ridderbos, Herman Bavinck, J. H. Bavinck, and Abraham Kuyper. Neo-Calvinism is not simply the recovery of orthodox sixteenth-century Calvinist theology but emerged in the context of the growing hegemony of Enlightenment humanism in European life. The Enlightenment marked the conversion of a whole civilization to a new religious faith. This secular humanist faith reached its pinnacle during the late nineteenth century, subjugating the public life of Europe to its control. Christ and his church were relegated to the private realm and stripped of cultural power. Neo-Calvinism arose in direct response to this threat to the Christian faith.

Thus neo-Calvinism from its outset was molded by the conviction that the church must witness to the lordship of Jesus Christ in every part of cultural life. The gospel, if it is to be biblical, cannot be reduced to a message of individual salvation but announces the restoration of God's rule over the whole creation and entire spectrum of human life. The church is not a private religious community but the new humanity that exercises cultural power through ordinary Christians in their vocations.

The only defense against the formidable Enlightenment tide was to recover a robust understanding of the Christian faith capable of matching humanism's scope and power to equip Christians for faithful witness in the whole of life. Thus neo-Calvinism articulated the core of the Christian faith in terms of the comprehensive restoration of the good creation from the creation-wide effects of sin through Jesus Christ and by the Spirit. What is striking is the comprehensive scope of each key term: the *whole of reality* is God's creation, is distorted by sin, and is being restored to its original goodness. This all-encompassing vision of the Christian faith offered an alternative to the reigning humanism as a basis for a culture-wide mission.

What we have found most attractive in neo-Calvinism—a tradition that neither of us grew up in—is precisely that it is a historic and orthodox Christian tradition that was recontextualized after the Enlightenment to respond to the comprehensive religious power of humanism. Sometimes proposals for church renewal are not very deeply rooted in the past. North Americans love

9. This is also known as the reformational tradition or the Kuyperian tradition.

what is new and shiny. But neo-Calvinism is a recontextualized version of a historic tradition that takes place *after* the monumental conversion of the West to a secular humanist faith. It elaborates the historic Christian faith in a way that resists the power of confessional humanism to relegate the Christian faith to a private realm. Thus, it offers rich resources for the task of a creation-wide witness today.

Neo-Calvinism arose in a certain historical context in Europe at the end of the nineteenth century. It cannot be imported wholesale to North America but itself needs recontextualization to find new forms of life on this continent at this time. And this is where we have found Newbigin's work quite helpful.

Newbigin shares much in common with neo-Calvinism. In 1994 he affirmed the way that neo-Calvinism had "obviously been at work long ago spelling out concretely in the various spheres of society what it means to say 'Jesus is Lord'" and expressed his fervent wish that it "would become a powerful voice in the life of British Christianity."[10] In our experience, we have found that a dialogue between Newbigin and our own neo-Calvinism has been an enriching and correcting exercise. Newbigin wrote a century after the emergence of Dutch neo-Calvinism, when the missionary situation of the West was becoming even more obvious. His own cross-cultural missionary experience privileged him with valuable insight for a new neopagan era. His missionary vision has enriched us. That is what leads us to add "missional" to "neo-Calvinism" in our own self-description.[11] This is the theological and missiological tradition that shapes our vision in this book. And it is a tradition that propels our quest for a missionary church—a quest shared at different times and in different ways by Kuyper and Newbigin. What does a missionary church in twenty-first-century North America look like if it takes seriously Jesus's own gospel of the kingdom that includes the whole of public life?

We share our journeys and background not to offer qualifications for writing this book. Rather, we hope that opening a window on our varied ministries in a variety of settings will enable readers to see something of the urgency we feel about the topic—and will perhaps spark in others a similar concern. Further, it will help to explain the kind of ministry experience and theological formation that has led to the approach we have taken.

10. Quoted in Michael W. Goheen, "Mission and the Public Life of Western Culture: The Kuyperian Tradition," *The Gospel and Our Culture Network Newsletter* 26 (Autumn 1999): 6, available at https://missionworldview.com/wp-content/uploads/2020/06/ea8a85_4800e24267914982ab4a1112d42802d6.pdf.

11. See Goheen, "Mission and the Public Life."

Outline of This Book

In this opening chapter we have described our goal of seeking a missionary church. We hope you share our conviction about the need to become a missionary church, and so now we invite you into our journey and conversation. It will be helpful, then, to make clear how this book is structured and how to read it.

In the next four chapters we offer a rather detailed historical narrative of the development of the missionary ecclesiology that developed from the 1930s until the end of the twentieth century. We set Newbigin in the context of that story. In so doing, we hope to achieve two things. First, we hope to provide a window into the robust theological thinking that produced the notion of both God's mission and the missionary nature of the church. This history is not well known and will set many conversations today in historical context. For the patient reader, there are profound insights into the missionary congregation that have accrued from the rich conversation among Western missionaries and non-Western leaders. Some may be surprised to find how much of a missionary ecclesiology was already in place before the middle of the century. Moreover, there are areas of missional ecclesiology within that historical conversation that have disappeared from our discussion but could be recovered today.

The second thing we hope to do in these chapters is to show how this history forged Newbigin's missionary ecclesiology as he participated in, contributed to, and was shaped by the discussion. Indeed, Newbigin's vision can be understood only as part of this history. It may also be helpful to note that Newbigin (and others) engaged many issues similar to ones we face today. Some of the issues he encounters in his earlier debates reveal similar dangers that appear today in new garb. For example, the specter of Johannes Hoekendijk has returned repeatedly in both the missional and emergent church conversations. Attending to that conversation may head off the doom of repeating that history.

After the historical section, in the chapters that follow we set three contemporary church conversations in light of this historical trajectory. Each of these offers a theological vision for the missionary church in North America and, in one way or another, is connected to Newbigin. There are, of course, many more movements and traditions that have been influenced by this history that we could have engaged. But we have chosen the missional church, the emergent church, and center church.

Our reason for treating the missional church conversation is probably the most self-evident: many in this movement see themselves as the direct heirs of the Newbigin legacy. Treating the emergent church might appear initially to be outdated, since it seems that its day is past. But leading voices from the movement continue to raise questions and speak to issues that resonate with many in the younger generation. Their vision is diffused through podcasts, blogs, events, networks, and publications. And so they still have an important voice to engage if we seek a missionary ecclesiology.

We focus on center church for four reasons. The first is its widespread global influence. The second is the interesting and perplexing relationship of Tim Keller to Newbigin. By Keller's own account, he was influenced early by Newbigin, and this is clear in his theological vision. Yet Keller later unfairly lumped Newbigin together with theological perspectives of liberal Protestantism and distanced himself from Newbigin, all the while continuing to use Newbigin's insights. Third, our interest in Keller is also motivated by the fact that his theological vision for a missionary church is broader and closer to ours than are many of the other visions we treat in this book. Keller was deeply influenced by Harvie Conn, who was the most consistent advocate of neo-Calvinism at Westminster Theological Seminary. Conn also influenced both of us as students at that institution. However, we are confounded by many aspects of Keller's theological vision, not least his mischaracterization of neo-Calvinism. And we know we are not alone in our bewilderment: we have often been pressed by others with questions concerning various tensions in Keller's thought. Finally, it seems to us surprising that a theological vision of such influence has not been the subject of much more literary and critical interest. We see little in the way of searching analyses that are both appreciative and critical of Keller's vision of a missionary church.

Our treatment of each of these visions of a missionary church will involve description, appreciation, and critique. Our primary concern is to set the different movements in dialogue with Newbigin, observing with appreciation the helpful paths along which a missionary ecclesiology has traveled and providing a critique that draws out Newbigin's voice in the way of enrichment and correction.

We are not attempting a full-scale mapping and description of each movement. That would be impossible in the short space we give to each. Rather, our goal is to offer a sketch and portrait of some of the main lines of these conversations as they participate in the historical trajectory of Newbigin's vision of a missionary church. Thus we will not offer a nuanced or exhaustive analysis of various books and authors.

We hope to carry out this analysis in ways that are humble, generous, and fair. In this process, we sometimes find ourselves filled with thankfulness for what the Lord is doing and teaching us. At other times, we are in sharp disagreement with what we have read and deeply concerned about some proposals that appear to have accommodated themselves significantly to North American idolatry. At still other points, we are concerned about how much of Newbigin's own missionary ecclesiology is absent from these conversations. But we attempt to avoid a contentious or dogmatic posture because we are aware that we too are subject to many of the same cultural winds as the movements we have studied. Yet it is important to engage these issues for the sake of a faithful church. In so doing, we are sure our own description, analysis, and proposals will be subjected to the same scrutiny.

We are also acutely aware that many have built their reputations, speaking ministries, book publishing careers, and consulting businesses on specific theological stances taken on this topic. This is not, of course, all wrong. We ourselves are not totally exempt from such entanglements. Sometimes this is captive to economic motives, but certainly not always. But we do wonder whether this is the best matrix out of which to struggle toward a missionary church and whether it lends itself to a discussion that humbly pursues a missionary congregation. All of this makes us more aware of the difficulty and sensitivity of the task.

In the final chapter, we draw our analysis of these movements together and sketch Newbigin's legacy for a missionary church. We believe it offers a rich theological vision for the missionary church that remains much needed today. Our prayer is that this book will stimulate the contemporary church to deeper faithfulness.

One more thing about the outline and structure of the book remains to be said. When the book was originally conceived almost ten years ago, we assumed there would be four sections. We anticipated a section of two or three chapters on Newbigin's missionary ecclesiology, placed between the twentieth-century historical section and the contemporary church section. As the writing proceeded, those chapters on Newbigin turned into a book of their own, which was published by Baker Academic in 2018 as *The Church and Its Vocation: Lesslie Newbigin's Missionary Ecclesiology*. A promise was made in the preface that this book would follow. It was well on its way to completion already at that point, and we anticipated that it would follow within a year or two. Unfortunately, as a result of some very difficult circumstances, including Tim's involvement in a rather serious car accident in which he sustained critical head injuries, this book has taken longer to come to press than we anticipated. The gap between the two books is now about four years.

For this reason, throughout this book there are numerous footnotes to *The Church and Its Vocation* to orient the reader to the more detailed elaboration of Newbigin's missionary ecclesiology that sets the stage for the ongoing dialogue. It certainly would be preferrable to read that book first—that is how we envisioned the process, for Newbigin's vision needs to be understood in its unity. And if that summary drives readers back further, to Newbigin's own books, even better!

What Word?

There is a tricky terminological issue we had to wrestle with as we wrote this book. Do we adopt *missionary* or *missional* as the word for our normative vision of the church? Newbigin consistently described his ecclesiology with the adjective *missionary*, and this was the standard practice throughout the twentieth century. The problem with this word, of course, is that it designates the nineteenth- and twentieth-century cross-cultural missionary movement. Missions at that time was shaped by colonialism and reduced to cross-cultural expansion—activities that took place from the West to the non-Western world. The word *missional* was helpfully introduced by the writers of *Missional Church* for the sake of distinguishing the *identity* of the church as it participates in God's mission rather than *activities* of outreach, including crossing geographical boundaries. For a variety of reasons, this word has struck responsive chords and its use has proliferated. Today it means many things—from the profound to the trivial, from the deeply theological to the crassly pragmatic. And so it could be said, echoing a British newspaper's editorial quip about the word *postmodern*, "The word 'missional' has no meaning; use as often as possible."

And so, what to do in this book? We could adopt the word *missionary*. This would connect us to Newbigin and the riches of twentieth-century theological reflection as well as to other confessional traditions such as Roman Catholicism, which speaks of the church as "missionary by her very nature."[12] But this would risk readers misunderstanding *mission* in connection with its traditional usage, as overseas missions or as certain outreach activities, such as evangelism. This is not an empty danger: we have found this to be a continuing problem in some wings of the evangelical church.

We could adopt the word *missional*. This would connect us to much of the ongoing conversation through commonly accepted terminology. But it would risk the suspicion of many we have met, who view this conversation as a novel

12. "Decree on the Mission Activity of the Church" (*Ad Gentes*, 1:2), in *The Documents of Vatican II: With Notes and Comments by Catholic, Protestant, and Orthodox Authorities*, ed. Walter M. Abbott (New York: Guild, 1966), 585.

trend. It appears to them to be a new fad disconnected from the history of the church or another pragmatic attempt to prop up a declining church or a managerial ecclesiology that offers strategies to grow a successful church. For these onlookers, the word *missional* carries little biblical and theological weight. Whether or not this is fair is beside the point. The point is that the word *missional* could connect us to many things—things we are happy to be associated with and other things not so much.

We have both used the word *missional* often in our writings and in the work of theological education. (After all, we chose the designation *Missional* Training Center and the degree master's is in *missional* theology!) But there comes a time to ask whether a word has outlived its usefulness and should be abandoned for another or whether it still captures something essential to Scripture and therefore needs to be kept—and, of course, continually refilled with scriptural content. We do not believe there is a clear answer to the question of what word to use. But the question for us is, in this particular book and its argument, is *missional* the best word?

The only other option is to find another word altogether. Hendrik Kraemer, for example, along with others, speaks of *apostolic*.[13] Or we could join some who want to speak of the church's identity in terms of *witness*, or of the church as a "witness-bearing body"[14] or "community of witness."[15] Darrell Guder suggests that *witness* may be seen as the "overarching description of the church's missionary vocation."[16] There is a lot to like about both of these words. Or, finally, we could coin another new word alongside the many other adjectives offered up in today's supermarket of proposals for church renewal.

We decided in the end to primarily employ the word *missionary*, following Newbigin, since a big part of this book is about the recovery of neglected aspects of his vision. Normally we will use the word *missional* to describe a particular conversation taking place today in North America.

An Invitation

We are aware that church leaders are busy people. A cacophony of voices compete for time in books, conferences, podcasts, and more. And so a fair

13. Hendrik Kraemer, *The Christian Message in a Non-Christian World* (London: Edinburgh House, 1938), 2.

14. Kraemer, *Christian Message*, 2.

15. Darrell L. Guder, *Be My Witnesses: The Church's Mission, Message and Messengers* (Grand Rapids: Eerdmans, 1985), 48.

16. Darrell L. Guder, *The Incarnation and the Church's Witness* (Harrisburg, PA: Trinity Press International, 1999), 6.

question is whether this book is worth the investment of time. We recognize we are asking you to take time to come with us through a historical journey that began almost a century ago. And we're aware we are asking you to listen to our description and evaluation of influential conversations around the missionary or missional nature of the church. Is it worth it?

What is most important is not this book but that the church grows in faithfulness to its missionary vocation. To achieve this goal, we might encourage you to simply read Newbigin's vision, summarized in *The Church and Its Vocation*, or to return to Newbigin's work itself, which would demand more time. The thing is that his vision has been diffused into the North American church by many voices, and the word *missional* is pervasive today. Many want to know what that means and whether it is important. Questions from pastors and even scholars in various parts of the world ring in our ears. Moreover, the past twenty years have brought growing insight into what a missionary church might be in the North American setting.

This book can help clarify the historical origins of a missionary church and how it has developed. We are especially interested in Newbigin—the rich biblical and theological insights of the man whom many consider to be the father of the missionary church. We believe that understanding Newbigin, the historical context of his thought, and its contemporary development can help you be more faithful to the biblical call to be a missionary congregation. And so we invite you to invest the time to wrestle with where this all began, how its primary exponent articulated it, and how his vision has developed in the past twenty years in North America. This historical theology may help move us toward faithfulness to our vocation.

Yet we are quite aware that theology by itself simply cannot produce a missionary church, any more than new structures or better programs can; it must be the work of the Spirit. As Wilhelm Andersen puts it, the "missionary enterprise has not come into being through conscious theological reflection on the self-revelation of God in Jesus Christ, but through the descent upon certain men or groups of men . . . of a compulsion of the Holy Spirit to undertake the proclamation of the Gospel overseas."[17] The lack of a missionary spirit in a congregation can be remedied only by the work of the Spirit in response to fervent prayer and through the power of the gospel breathing new life. Yet that does not exempt us from faithful theological work. Bad theology can quench the Spirit's work. But a biblically faithful missionary

17. Wilhelm Andersen, *Towards a Theology of Missions: A Study of the Encounter between the Missionary Enterprise and the Church and Its Theology* (London: SCM, 1955), 13.

theology of the church can be one of the means the Spirit uses to guide us into growing faithfulness.

May the Lord grant that the lampstand of the church will not be removed in North America but that we recover the role and identity God has for us in his redemptive purpose unfolded in the biblical story and finally disclosed and accomplished in Jesus Christ.

PART 1

The Historical Development of a Missionary Church

2

The (Re)Birth of a Missionary Church (1938–1952)

Someone once wryly observed that much of the problem with music in today's worship is that many worship leaders believe that hymnology began with Hillsong. Analogously, for some, the missional church discussion began in 1998 when the book *Missional Church* was published,[1] or perhaps with Lesslie Newbigin in the decades previous. No doubt 1998 was a watershed for the discussion of a missionary church in North America. And it is without question that Newbigin's publications from the early 1980s onward played a catalytic role. Yet these occasions had a rich history, beginning at least as early as 1938 at the meeting of the International Missionary Council (IMC) conference held in Tambaram, India. Perhaps we can identify this as the place where the journey began toward a theologically rich notion of a missionary church.

This history is important in itself and thus worthy of our attention (since it is not well known). But it is also significant that this history deeply formed Newbigin's own missionary ecclesiology. And so, as *Missional Church* was written, the authors were not offering some novel theological idea or simply appropriating Newbigin's later work for North America. They were returning to a long-standing theological discussion that had been pushed off the rails by a variety of historical forces. To understand Newbigin's notion of a

---

1. Darrell L. Guder, ed., *Missional Church: A Vision for the Sending of the Church in North America* (Grand Rapids: Eerdmans, 1998).

missionary church, and to understand its revival in our day, we must return to this time period.

This chapter sketches the roots of this story, beginning with the rebirth of a missionary church in the 1930s. We will pay particular attention to the meeting of the IMC in Tambaram in 1938, where the elements of a missionary ecclesiology emerged that then developed in the ensuing decades. We will also attend to the relationship of Newbigin to this history. He was an integral part of this story. He read all the reports of the missionary conferences, and it is instructive to read his interpretations of the history. He was shaped by it and had a hand in shaping the conversation at key junctures. So his own intertwinement in these developments requires us to return to this history if we are to understand Newbigin's missionary ecclesiology and the ongoing developments in North America today.

Recovering the Centrality of the Church in Mission at Tambaram

On the first page of his volume written in preparation for Tambaram, Hendrik Kraemer poses the question that would occupy missionary thinking for the next twenty-five years: "The church and all Christians . . . are confronted with the question, what is the essential nature of the church, and what is its obligation to the world?" This could only be answered, he believed, as "the Church becomes conscious in a new way of its mission in the 'Christian' and the non-Christian world." The church is an "*apostolic* body" not because its authority is derived from the apostles but because "it ought to be a bearer of witness to God and His decisive creative and redeeming acts and purposes." It is only as we become aware of this apostolic character that we can "take hold of its real essence and substance." Kraemer then issues a challenge to Tambaram participants: grasping this apostolic nature of the church "as a witness-bearing body in the modern world" must "be the object before us." He calls the matter "urgent."[2]

Living almost eighty-five years later, we might wonder what made this so urgent. How was mission and church understood before? We can only answer these questions by noting the assumptions that were held about mission and church at the beginning of the twentieth century. As these assumptions came crashing down, the church moved to the center of mission and a missional understanding of the church emerged.

2. Hendrik Kraemer, *The Christian Message in a Non-Christian World* (London: Edinburgh House, 1938), 1–2.

The Separation of Mission and Church

At the beginning of the twentieth century, mission was primarily an enterprise of Christian geographical expansion understood to take place from the Christian West to the non-Christian world outside the West. It was carried out by mission societies, which sent missionaries to these mission fields to accomplish the task. The church in the West supported this enterprise with money and personnel; the church in the non-West functioned as a container into which freshly caught converts were placed to be nourished in the Christian faith.

There are serious problems with this notion of mission. And it is precisely these problems that stand in the way of a thoroughly missionary understanding of the church. As these assumptions were dismantled in the next quarter of a century, the biblical notion of a missionary church emerged.

The biggest problem is that mission and church are separated. Mission is a task carried out by a missionary society, an organization parallel to the church but separate from it. The church may well get behind the missionary enterprise as a supporter (in the West) or as the body that nourishes new converts (in the non-West). But the scandal is that mission has been removed from the church and entrusted to another body. In spite of theological developments, the problem still haunted mission two decades later, leading Newbigin to say that the separation of mission and church "which God has joined together must be judged one of the great calamities of missionary history, and the healing of this division one of the great tasks of our time."[3] The way to a missionary church runs along a path where this division is healed and mission belongs to the very nature of the church.

Why is this so important? Why did Kraemer see this reorientation of mission as urgent? Why did Newbigin speak of a great calamity? As we observe the problems that flow from this division, we see why it was such an important step for Tambaram to return the church to the center of missionary thinking.

The first problem is the reduction of mission. Mission is limited to certain activities in non-Western parts of the world. Mission consists of activities of evangelism, church planting, and social action designed to erect a cross-cultural witness in places of the world where there is no church. This remains a valid and indispensable part of the church's vocation; yet mission is much more than this. And when mission is reduced to the non-Western world, it no longer belongs to the church in Western culture. Meeting on the brink of the Second World War, the participants of Tambaram were well aware of the neopaganism sweeping Western Europe. Europe was hardly a Christian

3. Lesslie Newbigin, *One Body, One Gospel, One World: The Christian Mission Today* (London: International Missionary Council, 1958), 26.

territory anymore, if it ever had been. Later, Newbigin reflected on the fact that at Tambaram there was a "direct repudiation of this attempt to domesticate the gospel" within Western Europe and North America. Those churches "had become domestic chaplains to the nations, rather than bearers of the word of God *to* the nations." Kraemer's powerful voice at Tambaram challenged this "disastrous syncretism between Christianity and the values of nation and of western civilization." Kraemer's "deepest concern was for the integrity of the Christian message . . . and therefore for its sharp separation from the contemporary confusion between the gospel and the values of western civilization."[4] Along similar lines, Bishop Coorilos comments about Tambaram, "For the first time, North America and Europe were also considered as mission fields, marking a departure from the colonial understanding of 'mission from the West to the South.'"[5] If a missionary church was to be recovered, then mission had to be seen as the vocation of the church in every part of the world—and that included the West.

The second problem is the depreciation of the church. When mission and church are separated, not only is mission misunderstood, so is the church. When the church simply supports mission or nurtures its converts, then mission is removed from the church's life, and the calling of the local congregation is reduced to its pastoral role. The church turns inward and is concerned only with matters of its gathered and institutional existence. For a missionary ecclesiology to emerge, it is necessary to restore mission to the very being and identity of the church and heal the breach between mission and church.

Reconnecting Church and Mission at Tambaram

The healing of this breach began in earnest at Tambaram. Most discussions of this conference focus on Kraemer's remarkable challenge to the prevailing theology of religions. No doubt that was a significant legacy of Tambaram. But this focus ignores both the opening pages of Kraemer's book and the conference statement itself. The most significant accomplishment of this conference was that it recovered the centrality of the church for mission. William Richey Hogg correctly observes that Tambaram "made the church its central concern, and a new sense of its reality runs through every statement produced

4. Lesslie Newbigin, "The Significance of Tambaram—Fifty Years Later," *Missionalia* 16 (1988): 81–82.
5. Metropolitan Coorilos Geevarghese, "Towards and Beyond Edinburgh 2010: A Historical Survey of Ecumenical Missiological Developments since 1910," *International Review of Mission* 99, no. 1 (April 2010): 9.

there." He continues, "One point they made preeminently clear: the mission is not a segment of the church's life. On the contrary, the church exists to fulfill a divinely ordained mission."[6] A new approach to mission dawned. "In contrast to the language of both [early twentieth-century global missionary conferences in] Edinburgh and Jerusalem, we find here a new way of speaking about mission. At every point the Conference speaks of the mission of the Church. . . . The Church is the subject of almost every significant sentence about mission. . . . Tambaram signalled the beginning of the long period of Church-centered missiology."[7]

A remarkable historical anecdote jolts us to a fresh realization of just how significant and surprising this shift was. Attending Tambaram was veteran missionary Alfred G. Hogg, who was principal of the renowned Madras Christian College. Hogg was a distinguished missionary theologian who had spent many years in India. He admits that Tambaram brought a theological shift "that did not come to him until almost the end of his missionary career." What had he missed? The cosmic and communal dimensions were constitutive of the Christian faith. The community of God's people holds a central place in the biblical story as a bearer of a gospel that is cosmic in scope. He recognized that he had been betrayed by an individualistic approach to the Christian faith that had eclipsed just those dimensions. "I began to realise how persistently in regard to the whole issue of redemption from evil the Bible tends to think socially and corporately rather than individualistically. For it [the Bible] individual salvation is a sharing of corporate human redemption and indeed of cosmic redemption. The Divine purpose of the Bible announces it as a morally transformed humanity which shall be fit to be trusted with a transfigured world-order [of which] the Church is the nucleus and nursery."[8]

What led to such a shift that brought the church to the center—something that such a distinguished missionary scholar as Alfred Hogg realized for the first time? One of the overlooked factors that contributed to this new emphasis was the makeup of the Tambaram conference itself. The majority of the almost five hundred delegates from sixty-nine countries came from outside the West. Those from the Southern and Eastern hemispheres outnumbered Western delegates more than three to one. There were over twice as many delegates from Asia as from North America and Europe combined. But it was not just numbers. The non-Western delegates shared full partnership in

6. William Richey Hogg, *Ecumenical Foundations: A History of the International Missionary Council and Its Nineteenth-Century Background* (New York: Harper and Brothers, 1952), 297–98.

7. Lesslie Newbigin, *Sign of the Kingdom* (Grand Rapids: Eerdmans, 1980), 9–10.

8. Quoted in Carl F. Hallencreutz, "Tambaram Revisited," *International Review of Mission* 77, no. 307 (July 1988): 357n24.

influence and decisions, in leadership and participation, in a way they had not before. Even further, it was the makeup of these third-world delegates that contributed so heavily to an emphasis on the church. In keeping with past tradition, Western participants were sent primarily by mission organizations. By contrast, representatives from the younger churches were sent by the churches. Moreover, in this number there were fewer scholars and more pastors and church leaders who shared in the concrete ministry of the local congregations. No doubt all these demographics were a major factor that moved the church to a more central place.

Newbigin also attributes the turn to the church at Tambaram to a recovery of the gospel that had been eclipsed by either the social gospel of a nauseating liberalism or the individualistic gospel of evangelical pietism.[9] The dominant liberal view of mission had more confidence in the progress of science, education, medicine, and technology than in evangelism, conversion, baptism, and church planting. The kingdom of God was the goal of mission, but kingdom was altered to mean allegiance to a general benevolent "spirit" at work in the world, illustrated in the person of Jesus. Mission joined this spirit, which looked suspiciously like Enlightenment optimism, the primary spiritual resource of Western civilization. However, the neopaganism and totalitarian ideologies arising in Europe—spiritual forces that led to World War II—forced the conference to become clear about both its identity and its message. It was no longer adequate to strip down the gospel to either a gospel of individual and otherworldly salvation that ignored cultural forces or a social gospel that uncritically joined them.

An Emerging Missionary Church

The Tambaram report, titled *The World Mission of the Church*, reflects this new direction. It begins with a section on the gospel: "The Faith by Which the Church Lives."[10] Aware of the bitter disillusionment of so many in the West and of faith in "new gods," including "science and man's power to redeem himself," the statement seeks to "repossess" the heart of the gospel (13). The "Church's faith" is articulated in a narrative structure that looks very much like an updated Apostles' Creed. The work of Christ is set in the context of the kingdom of God, but—unlike in the liberal version of the kingdom offered in the preceding decades—the church is central in its task to "continue Christ's saving work in the

9. Newbigin, *Sign of the Kingdom*, 7–8.
10. *The World Mission of the Church: Findings and Recommendations of the International Missionary Council, Tambaram, Madras, India, December 12th to 29th, 1938* (London: International Missionary Council, 1939), 13. In this section, page numbers in parentheses will be from this book.

world" (14–15). This notion of continuing Christ's mission is found throughout the document. According to Christ's commission in John—"As the Father hath sent me, even so send I you"—the conclusion must be that the "Church exists to continue the work Christ began" (79). The church is sent to the world both as a "Message" and as a "Movement." The "Message" comes to the world in word and deed. As a "Movement," the church is summoned to "become in itself the actualization among men of its own message" and to be a "foretaste of the redeemed family of God which He has purposed humanity to be" (16). Only as the church is understood in terms of its witness to the kingdom can it guard against becoming an end in itself and hold true to God's purpose for it.

The gospel, and the church's vocation to make it known in life, word, and deed, is immediately set over against other "faiths." Significantly, of the four "faiths" mentioned, three are Western, including scientific skepticism. There is a growing awareness of the religious and idolatrous faith shaping Western culture.

On the heels of the first section on the gospel comes the second: "The Church—Its Nature and Function." This section "lays the main emphasis on [the church's] active and witness-bearing character" (22). It does not ignore the inner life of the church, which has traditionally been the primary focus of ecclesiology. Indeed, it strongly emphasizes the "perennial need of renewal" provided by the means of grace in the institutional and gathered life of the church. But this is for the purpose of building up the church for its mission. "The Church cannot fulfill its task as herald, exemplar and builder of the Kingdom of God unless it exercises constant penitence and experiences constant renewal in the Holy Spirit. For this purpose, it has received the Word and the Sacraments, the wellspring of the saving and renewing power of God in the lives of men" (23).

It is striking, in light of the marginalization of the church by mission societies, to read the words, repeated for emphasis, "It is the Church and the Church alone" used to describe who has the task of transmitting, proclaiming, and witnessing to the gospel from one generation to the next (24). The essential task of the church is to be an ambassador of Christ, to proclaim his kingdom, to witness to the kingdom "through its very existence," and to be a signpost to Christ as the Savior of all peoples and of human society. The place where this task is centered is the local church or congregation, which is a "living congregation," rooted in worship, Word, sacraments, prayer, and intercession. The marks of "being alive" are worship, sacrificial love, reading Scripture, devotion to serving society, and a missionary spirit (26).

The report goes on to detail the mission of the church. Six noteworthy emphases continue to challenge us today. The first is the plea to recognize evangelism as a God-given task that is inherent in the nature of the church as the body of Christ (35–39). It is an "expression of [the church's] loving devotion to Christ" and is an "essential characteristic of the Church" (35). The "evangelistic enterprise derives directly from the *congregation* or local church." It is "when its corporate worship and the life of the members glow with the presence of God" that "evangelistic gifts are developed among the members of the congregation" (36).

The second emphasis is the witness of the church to non-Christian religions, new paganisms, and the varying cultures of the world (40–47). There is a bold call to evangelize adherents of other religions and invite them into the church. The report rejects religion as a private domain of human life and recognizes it as a central and comprehensive power that affects the whole way of life of a culture. Thus the church must understand other religions as total systems of life. Moreover, the church, while being firmly rooted in its Christian faith and in fellowship with the church universal, is to appropriate all the riches of the many cultures so that the gospel is "expressed and interpreted in indigenous forms, and that in methods of worship, institutions, architecture, etc., the spiritual heritage of the nation and country [is] taken into use" (45).

The third emphasis is an entire section—in a report regarding world mission—on the "inner life of the church" (55–65). It is remarkable how the importance of nourishing the new life of Christ in congregations pervades this document. Early on, it identifies "one indispensable thing demanding special attention today" as the "continuous nourishing of its life upon the Bible" in studying it "together in prayer, meditation, and the guidance of the Holy Spirit." Only then "will they [congregations] be able to fulfill their calling amidst the confusion and unbelief of this age" (15). The section on the inner life of the church stresses the importance of worship, fellowship, sacraments, preaching, teaching and reading the Word, prayer, and music for the church in its mission. And in a striking section, there is a strong statement on the crucial importance of "The Christian Home" for the church's mission. This theme is not found with such emphasis in any other official missionary document. For the sake of the church's mission, Christians must develop homes where "Jesus Christ is the center and all its members seek to obey His law of self-denying love," where "it is the parents' supreme privilege to lead the children to Jesus Christ," and where "regular corporate family worship [is] practiced as a fundamental part of home life" that, in turn, blesses the family and is a powerful witness in the community (58).

The fourth emphasis is the considerable stress put on the mission of the church in society—the healing, economic, social, international, and political calling of the church. Since the church exists to continue the work that Christ began, like Christ, the church must identify itself with the need and suffering of the world so that God's love might be mediated to the world. The social calling of the world belongs to the essence of the gospel to restore the divine image in humanity, and so it is an integral part of the mission to which Christ has called his church (79). Throughout the report, we hear two concerns: How does the church engage the political, economic, and social systems of its particular culture with the gospel in public life? At the same time, how can the church itself by its very existence show what the kingdom would look like in these various areas of human life? Both distinctiveness from and solidarity with its neighborhood are essential for the church in mission.

On the one hand, this means that the church interprets the kingdom of God to the world "as it lives by the power of the Holy Spirit and demonstrates in its own life the principles of the heavenly kingdom" (106). It must build its own life on what the kingdom demands even as it calls society to conform itself to the kingdom. A church that condemns economic inequalities must seek to eliminate such evils from its own life; a church that proclaims a gospel that transcends all distinctions of race, class, and nation must not deny the gospel by allowing such distinctions into its own life; a church that proclaims the necessity of social care for the vulnerable must take care of its own (109). And so on.

On the other hand, the church must not only wait for the kingdom or seek to embody it in its own life but also work for expressions of it within its own cultural setting (109). This will mean, among other things, knowing well the social, political, and economic order in which it lives, stimulating and preparing its own members for social action in the world, and bringing this social calling into its worship so as to give members of Christ's body a sense of being coworkers with God in seeking the kingdom (110).

The fifth emphasis is the unity of the church and its importance for mission. On the basis of Jesus's high priestly prayer for the oneness of his followers so that the world may believe that God has sent him (John 17:20–23), the report ends with a stirring cry for unity and for an end to the divisions of Christendom. William Richey Hogg says, "Never before had so stirring an appeal been rung out by the younger churches."[11] And it is no accident that this call for unity came from churches outside the West. As they made clear in their summons, it was these churches whose mission to an unbelieving world suffered most when their contemporaries saw scandalous division. These churches were painfully aware of the contradiction and scandal of a divided church called to preach the gospel in which God's will is to "bring unity to all things in heaven and on earth under Christ" (Eph. 1:10).

11. Hogg, *Ecumenical Foundations*, 302.

The sixth and final emphasis is the unfinished evangelistic task in areas of the world that are wholly unevangelized. There is fresh emphasis on the evangelistic and missionary calling of the church in its local area, as we have seen. Moreover, the strong focus on the idolatry and neopaganism of Western culture made clear the call of the church to bear good news in the "so-called Christian countries" of Europe and North America (29). However, bringing the gospel to areas where it has never been heard remains indispensable to the missionary calling of the church (28–34). The report sets out a biblical mandate and a theological foundation for missions as a task "of the whole Church for the whole world" (31). There is fresh reflection on the new context in which missions to unevangelized areas must take place, as well as affirmation that there is still a need for missionaries and particularly evangelists from the older churches. The call to action and urgent appeal to complete the unfinished task of evangelism is extended not to mission organizations and agencies but to the local churches.

Summarizing Tambaram

This summary of Tambaram has been lengthy for good reasons. First, this conference is not so well known, in spite of its foundational importance for the development of a missionary church. It is remarkable that in 1938 much that is touted as new in missional church literature today had already been expressed. Second, as it highlights significant features of a missionary church, it has much to teach us today. Essential themes on missional ecclesiology have been eclipsed in much of today's literature. For example, rarely today does one see such emphasis on the family and its worship or on the importance of cross-cultural missions to places where the gospel has not taken root or on the structural idolatry of the West as religious. And finally, this conference had a formative influence on Newbigin. Even though he was in the United Kingdom in 1938 and did not return to India until 1939, he carefully read all the volumes of the Tambaram conference and affirmed the significance of this gathering for his own thinking. He observes, for example, that the Tambaram "message had implications which it took years and decades to translate into practice." With its recovery of the centrality of the church in mission, it was clear that an "unmissionary church and an unchurchly mission are both, from the standpoint of the gospel, absurdities."[12]

12. Lesslie Newbigin, "A Sermon Preached at the Thanksgiving Service for the Fiftieth Anniversary of the Tambaram Conference of the International Missionary Council," *International Review of Mission* 77, no. 307 (1988): 329–30.

Others made equally strong statements. For example, Karl Hartenstein, whose important theological labors would play an increasingly significant role in the development of a missional ecclesiology, comments on Tambaram: "Whoever says church says mission. And vice versa: Whoever says mission says church."[13]

But thinking about the missionary role of the church in every setting was in its infancy. Significant insights into the missionary character of the church lay scattered about like so many bricks with no theological framework to hold them together. It required a redemptive-historical and eschatological structure to assemble these insights into a unified edifice. And this would finally emerge at Willingen, Germany, fourteen years later.

Important Developments between Tambaram and Willingen

The years 1938 and 1952 bracket a historical development that brought the church to the center of God's redemptive purpose and defined its nature as missionary. Of course, these years are chosen because of the two significant IMC conferences at Tambaram and at Willingen. In the years between, significant developments would usher in a more consistent missionary ecclesiology at Willingen.

The first was the growth of the churches in the Southern and Eastern hemispheres. This was reflected in another, smaller, meeting of the IMC in Whitby, Canada, shortly after World War II. Tambaram's stress on the centrality of the church in mission was left intact at Whitby.[14] Yet, during the ten-year period before the Whitby conference, the non-Western church had grown significantly, and respect for it by the Western church had grown apace. Churches from the global South and East had not only survived the loss of Western missionaries during the war years but, in fact, had matured considerably in situations where it was costly to confess Jesus Christ. They were now adult churches, full participants in the missionary calling, and thus to be treated as full "partners in obedience."[15]

A second important development was the shift in thinking about Western culture and its supposed Christian character. Already at Tambaram Western missionaries and non-Western church leaders were questioning the notion of a Christian culture in Europe and North America. Tragic events overwhelmed

13. Quoted in Jürgen Schuster, "Karl Hartenstein: Mission with a Focus on the End," *Mission Studies* 19, no. 1 (2002): 66.
14. Hogg, *Ecumenical Foundations*, 335.
15. Wolfgang Günther, "The History and Significance of World Missionary Conferences in the 20th Century," *International Review of Mission* 92, no. 367 (2003): 528.

Europe in the following period. A world war engulfed the European continent, and that—along with the catastrophic damage inflicted on the world by totalitarian ideologies such as National Socialism, Fascism, and Marxism— shattered any shred of confidence that Europe was a Christian continent. The conviction that the West was as much a mission field as anywhere else in the world gained considerable ground.

The combination of these two things led to a dismantling of the distinction between the Christian West and the non-Christian non-West. This growing conviction suffused the entire Whitby conference. The whole world was considered a mission field, and the missionary "tasks which face the churches in all parts of the world are the same."[16]

Throughout this period there were also developments within mission theology, often fueled by the disciplines of theology and biblical studies, that would prove fruitful for a missional ecclesiology. Karl Hartenstein was a key figure. Hartenstein draws heavily on the theological work of Karl Barth and Emil Brunner, and on the biblical scholarship of Oscar Cullmann. Hartenstein's legacy was significant: his "work in the early thirties reoriented mission thinking for the next twenty-five years."[17]

Hartenstein was concerned to root mission in both solid biblical exegesis and rigorous theological reflection.[18] Hartenstein speaks of mission as first and foremost an activity of God and already refers to this in 1934 as the *missio Dei*. He refers to John 20:21 as the source of this terminology: "As the Father has sent me, I am sending you."[19] It is the double sending expressed in these verses that occupies his attention: the Father sends the Son, and the Son sends the disciples and the church of all times to continue his mission.

Hartenstein sets this sending firmly in the eschatological context of the coming of the kingdom. Jesus announces the coming of the kingdom, but in his mission it is both already fulfilled and not yet consummated. We live in an interim period between the coming of the kingdom in Jesus and the expectation of his return to complete his work. It is precisely mission that gives meaning to this redemptive-historical period between the resurrection and the return of Christ.

16. Charles W. Ranson, *Renewal and Advance: Christian Witness in a Revolutionary World* (London: Edinburgh House, 1948), 174.

17. John G. Flett, *The Witness of God: The Trinity, Missio Dei, Karl Barth and the Nature of Christian Community* (Grand Rapids: Eerdmans, 2010), 130.

18. Hartenstein believes that mission is subject to the temptation of aiming at success through "secure methods"—that is, as Flett explains, "formulating strategies according to givens in local cultures that will produce direct successes." *Witness of God*, 129. See also Karl Hartenstein, "Adaptation or Revolution," *Student World* 28, no. 4 (1935): 308.

19. Quoted in Flett, *Witness of God*, 131.

Here Hartenstein draws on a half century of New Testament scholarship that had rediscovered the centrality of the kingdom to Jesus's mission. He is especially indebted to Oscar Cullmann, about whom it was said in 1964 that "no other theology was so determinative on the European continent for the . . . grounding of mission than that of O. Cullmann's understanding of *Heilsgeschichte*."[20] Cullmann stresses the "eschatological character of mission, which must take place precisely in the intermediate period and which *gives to this period its meaning*."[21] The greatest weakness of the church, Hartenstein believes, is to not see itself as located within this redemptive-historical narrative, called in this interim period to carry on the mission of Christ.

In this era, the church is sent to continue the life of Christ in the world. The role it plays in this redemptive-historical era is to serve the world as a sign and pointer to the kingdom. Thus, says Hartenstein, it is equipped with the Spirit "through whom the Lord wills to equip his messengers, and without whom the mission remains a noisy gong or a clanging symbol."[22]

Hartenstein had captured much of the heart of a missionary church already in the late 1920s and early 1930s. His eschatological and redemptive-historical framework establishes the church as "a missionary, apostolic church."[23] "Mission is the decisive sign of her life, and the expression of her God-given existence."[24] There is no split between mission and church: "Basically the two words 'church' and 'mission' say the same. Mission is the church in movement, the church on her preaching journey in the whole world."[25]

Hartenstein's voice was a lonely voice, especially in the 1930s. His insights likely influenced Tambaram, but it would not be until Willingen that much of his theological work would bear fruit. It would be then that a theological framework would be established that would incorporate both the growing insights about church and mission since Tambaram and the new experience of the world church. But it would take the dramatic events in China at the end of the 1940s to dislodge the colonial framework and make clear the need for a new theological basis for mission.

20. Quoted in Flett, *Witness of God*, 150.
21. Oscar Cullmann, *Christ and Time: The Primitive Christian Conception of Time and History*, trans. Floyd V. Filson (Philadelphia: Westminster, 1949), 162–63 (emphasis in the original); cf. Cullmann, "Eschatology and Missions in the New Testament," in *The Theology of the Christian Mission*, ed. Gerald H. Anderson (London: SCM, 1961), 42–54.
22. Quoted in Flett, *Witness of God*, 132.
23. Quoted in Flett, *Witness of God*, 151.
24. Quoted in Flett, *Witness of God*, 132.
25. Quoted in Jürgen Schuster, "Karl Hartenstein: Mission with a Focus on the End," *Mission Studies* 19, no. 1 (2002): 66.

3

God's Mission and the Missionary Church (1952)

While the Tambaram meeting of the International Missionary Council (IMC) is not so well known, such is not the case for the Willingen gathering. The prevalent notion of the *missio Dei* or the mission of God emerges and becomes central to mission theology. Lesslie Newbigin expresses what many believe: "subsequent history has shown that [Willingen] was in fact one of the most significant in the series of world missionary conferences."[1]

Certainly, this conference is important for the subject of the missionary church. It was able to bring together a growing number of insights into a coherent vision of mission with the church central. There had been many developments in the global church, in missionary theology, and in biblical and theological studies. The church in the global South and East was maturing and exerting more influence on theological reflection. Insight into the missionary nature of the church that emerged during the Tambaram conference continued to evolve. New Testament studies had revived the centrality of eschatology, and there was an important ripple effect on mission. Significant theologians—to mention only the names Karl Barth, Emil Brunner, and Hendrikus Berkhof—were beginning to address mission in their theological writings. But all these areas were parallel streams unrelated to one another.

1. Lesslie Newbigin, "Mission to Six Continents," in *The Ecumenical Advance: A History of the Ecumenical Movement*, vol. 2, *1948–1968*, ed. Harold Fey (London: SPCK, 1970), 178.

Willingen was a moment in history—and this is its significance—when all these various tributaries flowed together into a single river of missionary theology that would define the church as missionary. Or, to change the image, it was the time when the scattered bricks from the global church, from missionary theology, and from biblical and theological studies were gathered and built into a unified framework.

The participants at the time certainly did not think of the conference in this way. In fact, the diversity and disagreement led many to conclude that the compromise statement of Willingen was a failure, a thin veneer masking deep division. But subsequent history has proved otherwise.

Lead-Up to Willingen

Perhaps one of the more important decisions the small gathering at Whitby made in 1947 was to instruct the ongoing research committee to give "immediate consideration" to the urgent need for further theological reflection on the missionary calling of the church.[2] The committee took up this task in 1948, when it was felt that "in the fields of Biblical and theological studies there had been taking place, for some years, movements that were proving deeply significant" and at the same time that "these studies and movements of thought had not become related, with sufficient explicitness, to the missionary calling of the church."[3] The title "The Missionary Obligation of the Church" was formulated by the committee.

But it was only at the committee's second meeting in 1950 that the urgency of the topic became quite apparent. It met in the wake of Mao Tse-tung's 1949 victory, which was followed soon after by the expulsion of all foreign missionaries from China. Since China hosted the majority of Western missionaries at this time, this dealt a significant blow to the whole missionary enterprise. Moreover, the end of colonialism was clearly in sight. Colonialism had provided the framework for missionary theology and practice for centuries. Now, with one-third of the world cut off from Christian mission and with the end of colonialism imminent, the whole missionary enterprise appeared to be in jeopardy. What theological foundation could provide a new basis for mission?

2. Minutes of the Enlarged Meeting of the International Missionary Council and of the Committee of the Council, Whitby, Ontario, July 5–24, 1947, 63.

3. *Missions under the Cross: Addresses Delivered at the Enlarged Meeting of the Committee of the International Missionary Council at Willingen, in Germany, 1952; with Statements Issued by the Meeting*, ed. Norman Goodall (London: Edinburgh, 1953), 10–11. In the next sections, page numbers in parentheses will be from this book.

A number of papers were prepared for the conference. Deeply divergent views of mission characterized this work, and the task at Willingen was to sift through them and draft a new theological framework for the mission of the church. The competing proposals were wildly discordant. But somehow they were finally stitched together by Newbigin into a compromised joint statement at the end of the conference. As it would turn out, Willingen would be highly significant for the birth of a missionary ecclesiology.

The Church Participates in the Mission of the Triune God

The final statement adopted by the assembly is the fruit of the history since Tambaram as well as eleven days of discussion by over two hundred mission and ecumenical leaders. But two men deserve special mention: in God's marvelous providence, it would be Karl Hartenstein and Lesslie Newbigin who would give expression to the final statement. Newbigin was the final craftsman,[4] but Hartenstein joined Newbigin on the drafting committee and Hartenstein's theological fingerprints are all over the final statement. It is hard to think of two better men for such a time as this.

The adopted statement was titled "The Missionary Calling of the Church." It begins, "The missionary movement of which we are a part has its source in the Triune God Himself" (190). Here is the most important legacy of Willingen: the concept of the mission of the triune God. While this is not developed here, it provides a redemptive-historical and eschatological framework for gathering and relating many biblical, theological, and missiological insights that had emerged in the first half of the twentieth century into a consistent missionary ecclesiology. Mission has its source in the love of the Father, who sends his Son to reconcile all things to himself. The Son sends the Spirit to gather his church together and empower it for mission. The church is sent by Jesus to continue his mission in the power of the Spirit, and this defines its very nature. The section ends with Willingen's most memorable and oft-quoted words: "There is no participation in Christ without participation in his mission to the world. That by which the Church receives its existence is that by which it is also given its world-mission. 'As the Father has sent Me, so send I you'" (190).

It should be noted that the "mission of God"—that exact terminology is not used until later—is elaborated in a five-point narrative structure beginning

4. A. W. Blaxall, "Willingen, 1952: The Calling of the Church to Mission and Unity," *Christian Council Quarterly* 34 (1952): 2.

at the opening of the biblical story and concluding with its end: creation; alienation by sin; the sending of Jesus as Savior and Redeemer; the sending of the Spirit to gather, nurture, and empower the church for its mission; and hope for consummation. On this basis we are taken up into the narrative of God's redeeming mission: "We who have been chosen in Christ, reconciled to God through Him, made members of His Body, sharers in His Spirit, and heirs through hope of His Kingdom, are by these very facts committed to full participation in His redeeming mission" (190).

Though the mission of the triune God is the most enduring legacy of Willingen, the conference touched on many other themes important for a missionary church. Here we note only three: the local congregation, unity and mission, and the comprehensive mission of the church.

The Local Congregation

The church-centered understanding of mission initiated at Tambaram continued at Willingen. Although this was vigorously challenged by prominent participants, the final reports remain in continuity with the earlier trajectory. The local church is the primary carrier of God's mission. The future of the gospel depends on the "'Church being the Church,' on its being a redeemed fellowship and a channel of God's redeeming grace, in the place and country where it is" (195).

We observe three characteristics of the local congregation. First, the congregation must identify with the place where it is set; it must be an indigenous church. The gospel demands local articulation in the language and life of the people if it is to be relevant and not foreign. There must be a deep solidarity with the world if the church is to fulfill its mission. Yet it is not solidarity that has priority, but the gospel. Put another way, the church is *rooted* in Christ but *related* to its cultural context. And so there is not just solidarity but foreignness as well. The church should "take a positive yet critical attitude" to its cultural context (196). It is thus important for the local congregation to see itself as part of the church universal that expresses a gospel that cannot be captive to any one culture.

A second characteristic is an emphasis on the inner life of the congregation. The missionary witness of the church depends on a healthy communal life, which depends on the Holy Spirit, who is the source of new life. Thus a fuller appropriation of this new life in Christ will come by prayerful study of the Bible in groups and as individuals, by formation of small prayer groups, by cultivation of the Christian home to nurture children in the faith, by a

concentrated effort to minister to the spiritual needs of the younger generation, by the nurture of the laity for their witness in the public life of the community, and by common worship. Not only will the church be equipped for
its mission in the world, but "non-Christian neighbours [will] see evidence
of the reality of the Christian fellowship in the church's corporate witness
and its impact on society" (198).

A final characteristic highlights the need for an adequately trained ministry.
Healthy congregations require good training for their leaders. Missionary
congregations require theological education aligned to the missionary vocation of the congregation. Willingen registered its concern that "theological
education throughout the world should be much more radically oriented to
the total missionary task of the church" (214). This means not simply the
addition of subjects normally associated with mission but "an emphasis on
the missionary obligation of the Church" in all theological subjects.

Unity and Mission

The importance of unity for mission is "one of the dominant concerns of
Willingen" (15). The statement on the calling of the church to mission and
unity closely links the two throughout. It speaks of a threefold response of the
church: worship, unity, and mission. These components are interdependent
and may not be isolated from one another without dangerous repercussions.
The calling of the church is to be one family in Christ and thereby to make
known the gospel of the kingdom to the world. Christ prayed for his disciples'
unity so that the world might believe that the Father had sent him. Since
Christ is not divided, the church "must demonstrate the Gospel in its life as
well as in its preaching, it must manifest to the world the power of God to
break down all barriers and to establish the Church's unity in Christ." Negatively, "division in the church distorts its witness, frustrates its mission, and
contradicts its own nature" (193).

Comprehensive Mission

As Willingen elaborated the "total missionary task" of the church, there
were tensions about the meaning of *mission*. These are reflected in the joint
statement. Yet it is precisely in a negotiated statement that sought to affirm
the different concerns that we find much insight into the total missionary
task.

Mission to Those Near at Hand and to Those Far Off

First, mission is both "in its immediate neighbourhood" and "to the ut-termost parts of the earth" (190). There was sensitivity to the imperialism of cross-cultural mission in the colonialist paradigm. And so the question was raised about whether this was a legitimate part of the church's mission and, if so, how it should be reoriented. A minority was racked by guilt and embar-rassment at the injustices of colonial missions and wanted to focus the church's mission exclusively on the immediate neighborhood. But the mind of the ma-jority was otherwise. And so, along with the affirmation that the church is to proclaim Christ's kingship to the ends of the earth, there was much struggle concerning how to reimagine the cross-cultural enterprise after colonialism.

This is reflected, for example, in the section "The Role of the Missionary Society" (201–7), where it is affirmed that "a church cannot divest itself of its missionary obligation and remain a church." What then is the place and role of the missionary society that has been the primary carrier of mission for years? How do such societies relate to the church? The role of the "for-eign missionary" is put in the context of a much broader view of mission: "Foreign missionary responsibility can be truly seen only in the setting of the total missionary responsibility of the Church and must never be isolated from it" (209). Cross-cultural missions is authentic only as it is part of the answer to "What is the mission to which God calls His Church today?" (208). The pattern of missionary responsibility must be reshaped in light of the gospel, the church, and the context: "The challenge of modern life forces Christians back to fundamentals: What is the Gospel? What is the Faith? What is the Church? What is God saying to us in this situation?" (215).

There is much here from which we can still learn, but much more that is irrelevant to our day. The point is that while there was a growing concern for the mission of the local congregation in its own neighborhood, this did not eclipse missions in other parts of the world, as has often happened today. Mission is at home: "Wherever there is a local congregation there is a com-munity which, by its very existence, is witnessing—however imperfectly—to the Gospel. To it comes God's call to fulfill that part of the Church's total missionary responsibility which lies in its immediate environment" (208). Mission is also to the uttermost parts of the earth: "The mission to the ends of the earth is the responsibility of the whole Church" (209).

Mission in Culture

The church is sent into the public life to bear witness to Christ's lordship over all of human life. The Willingen participants saw themselves as living in a revolutionary time. This was interpreted differently by various people: most saw the times as a challenge to Christian faith "more searching than any it had faced since the rise of Islam" (188). It was a time when false faiths were winning swift and sweeping triumphs, a time of battle between God's kingdom and evil spiritual forces that lure people toward hollow hopes. Thus the rousing challenge: "There is no room for neutrality in this conflict. Every man must choose this day whom he will serve" (189). Yet some were more positive: they saw the work of the Spirit in these revolutionary movements and urged the church's mission to join God in what he was doing.

Even in these disagreements, the participants were one in affirming that the church may not seek safety behind the walls of the church and preoccupy itself with its institutional life. It must "identify itself with the world, not only in its perplexity and distress, its guilt and its sorrow, but also in its real acts of love and justice" (191). That is, the church could not remain detached but must take up a stance of solidarity with the world. Sadly, "the Church [is] in complete retreat from the real battlefields of our time" (47). Submerged in its own institutional life, the church becomes "stagnant in mere activity," "indulging in reflections on itself," and "pondering over itself" (47, 50). It wastes "precious time striving introvertedly for an intellectual securing of its dogma" (47). Such a "pious Church has no answers for the needs and issues of the world, since it is not at all aware of the actual nature of the world's problems and questions" (47). The church in this situation must not think "only of its own sheep" but must "meet with genuine solidarity all those who have lost their way in the maze of this world" (54).

To be in solidarity with its culture and yet not compromise with the culture's idolatry, the church must *know* its culture: "Faithfulness to Christ will require the Church to come to grips with the social, political, economic and cultural life of the people to whom it is sent" (190). Moreover, it must learn to discern the signs of God's sovereign rule to bear witness to the mighty works of the Spirit (192). And finally, the church must recognize that "the special responsibility of laymen is to bear such witness in the public life of the community, to set up signs of the Kingdom in social righteousness and economic justice" (199). This theme of the vocation of the laity was gaining momentum and would gain even more in the next few decades.

Mission in Every Moment and in Every Situation

Discerning the signs of the times and bearing witness to the work of the Spirit in the revolutionary events of the times was an issue that caused controversy. After Willingen it would take the whole missionary movement in a different—and mistaken—direction. This issue is so important that we will deal with it in the next chapter. It is an issue that still plagues the church today, both in the ecumenical and in the evangelical traditions. At this point we can note that the compromise statement provided much insight into the missionary calling of the church. "The Church is sent to proclaim Christ's reign in every moment and every situation" (190). Discerning the times was not simply positive—that is, joining the Spirit in what the Spirit was doing. Nor was it simply negative—that is, discerning the idolatry and tumult of the times. It was both: "At one and the same moment opportunities for advancing the mission of the Church lie alongside the catastrophic destruction of that mission. . . . The Church is bidden in its mission to seek out the moments of opportunity and to interpret the catastrophes as judgments of God" (190–91).

The Witness of the Church in Its Words, Works, and Whole Life

The all-embracing mission of the church can be summarized in a sentence: "The Church's words and works, its whole life of mission, are to be a witness to what God has done, is doing, and will do in Christ" (191). Great stress was put on the involvement of the church in deeds of justice, compassion, and love in the world. But the church's witness is not only in deeds but also in words and in the life of the church. Evangelism and the witness of the church's life were not lost amidst the call to justice and compassion—witness in life, word, and deed.

Theological Girders for a Missionary Church in Willingen

Sometimes we treat mission theology as a separate and hermetically sealed subdiscipline little affected by the prevailing insights of other theological disciplines. This is a grave mistake. It is essential to observe that this missionary ecclesiology is deeply dependent on a number of scriptural and theological assumptions that give fuller context to the notion of God's mission. The *missio Dei* is like a puzzle put together with many exegetical and theological pieces that all contribute to the whole picture. We briefly mention six here that affected mission theology at this time.

Scripture

The first is a doctrine of *Scripture*. It is sometimes forgotten that Willingen coincided with the ascendency of the biblical theology movement—a redemptive-historical approach to Scripture in the ecumenical movement. This approach to Scripture is characterized by four major elements of consensus: (1) theocentric: the main character in the Bible is God, who is acting in history to work out his plan; (2) narrative unity: the Bible narrates one unfolding story of God's redemptive work, and all books, characters, and events must find their meaning within this narrative context; (3) history: the redemptive work of God is revealed in his mighty acts in history; (4) eschatology: God's redemptive work in history begins in Israel and reaches its eschatological climax in Jesus Christ.[5] All these components are present in a World Council of Churches (WCC) report issued three years before Willingen, titled *Guiding Principles for the Interpretation of the Bible* (Oxford, 1949). This report affirms that "the unity of the Old and the New Testaments is . . . in the ongoing redemptive activity of God in the history of one people, reaching its fulfilment in Christ."[6]

Thus, as Willingen speaks of the sending activity of the triune God, it is not simply a theological sending formula, but the expression of a long narrative. God's mission is the summary of a historical record of God's long redemptive journey in the biblical story. The participation of God's people in his mission must also be articulated in this narrative context. Their missionary identity stems from the role they play in this story as they participate in God's mission.[7] The Bible as a narrative of redemptive history provides the unifying framework for all the other theological components of the *missio Dei* paradigm. When this is missed, the fundamental nature of both God's mission and the missionary nature of the church is given a different unifying framework, and the meanings of both are modified.

We can demonstrate the central importance of understanding the Bible as a story for understanding both the mission of God and the missionary church by reference to Johannes Blauw. The IMC and WCC commissioned a book that would survey biblical theology and mission. The purpose of the book was to provide a discussion of the issues Willingen had raised in the context of a worldwide forum. Johannes Blauw was asked to undertake the task. His mandate was to draw together into one volume the recent work in biblical and theological studies that provided a foundation for the missionary character of the church. His book, finally finished in 1962, represents a summary of sorts of the way the missionary tradition used the Bible to interpret the missionary

---

5. Brevard Childs, *Biblical Theology in Crisis* (Philadelphia: Westminster, 1970).

6. Ellen Flesseman-Van Leer, ed., *The Bible: Its Authority and Interpretation in the Ecumenical Movement*, Faith and Order Paper No. 99 (Geneva: World Council of Churches, 1980), 14.

7. See Michael W. Goheen, *A Light to the Nations: The Missional Church in the Biblical Story* (Grand Rapids: Baker Academic, 2011).

nature of the church.[8] What distinctively and fundamentally marks the whole book is that the Bible tells a story, and it is this story that gives a missionary identity to the church. Two chapters are given to the Old Testament, one to the intertestamental period, and two to the New Testament; a final chapter addresses a theology of mission. This book remains a very fine narrative theology of mission.

We can also refer to Konrad Raiser, former general director of the World Council of Churches (1992–2003), to highlight the importance of the Bible as a single story in this emerging paradigm of the mission of God. Decades after Willingen and the publication of Blauw's book, in a theological skirmish with Lesslie Newbigin during the 1990s, Raiser looks back on this period with a critical eye and observes that it was a narrative and eschatological framework that bound together and gave fundamental shape to what he calls the classical ecumenical paradigm. God's triune mission and the missionary nature of the church were given expression and meaning in the context of the biblical story. He rightly recognizes that to change the paradigm of mission to be more suitable for a pluralistic context—something he wants to do—it will be necessary to find a new, unifying framework to replace the biblical story. To understand Willingen rightly, it is essential to take account of the narrative nature of Scripture that forms the *missio Dei* and the participation of the church in God's mission.

Eschatology

The second area emerging out of biblical and theological studies that nurtured a missionary ecclesiology is *eschatology*. One of the remarkable characteristics of biblical and theological studies in the twentieth century, especially in New Testament studies, is the rediscovery of eschatology. Connected to a redemptive-historical reading of Scripture as one unfolding story, it became a compelling framework for mission. An eschatological foundation for mission was developed in the early 1950s.

The problem faced by the missionary tradition was that the liberal tradition collapsed eschatology into the Western progress story; thus, mission simply contributes to the ongoing cultural, political, social, and technological progress of the West. The evangelical tradition reduced eschatology to an otherworldly, personal immortality; thus, mission is simply evangelism with no concern for this world. The New Testament rejects both understandings. God's kingdom is about the power of God breaking into history to restore

8. Johannes Blauw, *The Missionary Nature of the Church: A Survey of the Biblical Theology of Mission* (London: Lutterworth Press, 1962).

the whole creation. It is restorative and comprehensive. But it is not yet fully here. There remains a battle with the powers of evil for the creation—a battle that will continue to the End. The church tastes of the power of the kingdom and therefore is a sign that points to the kingdom in its life, deeds, and words. Wilhelm Andersen notes that "at Willingen, in contrast to earlier world missionary conferences, the close connection between missions and eschatology was clearly emphasized, and with a considerable measure of general agreement."[9]

At the beginning of the twentieth century, New Testament scholars began to focus on the centrality of eschatology to the entire life and ministry of Jesus, as well as to the early church and to the whole New Testament. After a half century of debate, the period "during and just after World War II saw the emergence of a 'consensus' position: the kingdom for Jesus was both present and future."[10] This already-not-yet era of the kingdom was crucial for mission and played an important role at Willingen. Mission gives meaning to this era of redemptive history. "And this gospel of the kingdom will be preached in the whole world as a testimony to all nations, and then the end will come" (Matt. 24:14).

Eschatology was important for mission for three reasons. First, the kingdom is God's power at work in the world to heal and renew. The church must embody that healing power, both as a community and as an instrument in society. Since the renewing work of the kingdom is comprehensive, so is the church's mission. Second, since the kingdom is God's restoration present in history, an otherworldly future in heaven is rejected; but since the kingdom is not yet fully here, an optimistic confidence in progress to usher in the kingdom is rejected. And third, the time between the resurrection and the second coming is precisely a time of mission. The final judgment is delayed to allow the gathering of all nations into the kingdom. This defines this redemptive-historical era. Newbigin puts this strongly:

> The meaning of this "overlap of the ages" in which we live, the time between the coming of Christ and His coming again, is that it is the time given for the witness of the apostolic Church to the ends of the earth. The end of all things, which has been revealed in Christ, is—so to say—held back until witness has

---

9. Wilhelm Andersen, *Toward a Theology of Missions: A Study of the Encounter between the Missionary Enterprise and the Church and Its Theology* (London: SCM, 1955), 56. Cf. Hans Jochen Margull, *Hope in Action: The Church's Task in the World* (Philadelphia: Muhlenberg, 1962), 13–26.

10. Eldon Jay Epp, "Mediating Approaches to the Kingdom: Werner Georg Kümmel and George Eldon Ladd," in *The Kingdom of God in 20th-Century Interpretation*, ed. Wendell Willis (Peabody, MA: Hendrickson, 1987), 36–37.

been borne to the whole world concerning the judgment and salvation revealed in Christ. The implication of a true eschatological perspective will be missionary obedience, and the eschatology which does not issue in such obedience is a false eschatology.[11]

Christ

The powerful influence of eschatology had a formative impact on other scriptural themes as well, which would further shape missionary ecclesiology. The most obvious is *Christology*. What was clear was that the kingdom of God was the central theme in the Gospels, even in the whole New Testament. The kingdom defined the ministry of Jesus: in his life he made known the kingdom; in his death he accomplished the victory of the kingdom; in his resurrection he inaugurated the kingdom; in his gift of the Spirit, he poured out the power of the kingdom.

Much classic Christology starts by defining the relationship between the divine and human natures of Jesus. The human ministry of Jesus is neglected, and the cross and resurrection are disconnected from the coming kingdom. With the growing focus on the kingdom, the earthly ministry of Jesus in making known the kingdom in words and deeds received increasing attention. Thus the content of Jesus's kingdom mission shapes the mission of the church: "As the Father has sent me, I am sending you" (John 20:21). This focus on the earthly life of Jesus can be taken up, as it was later in the century and has been in our day, in such a way as to diminish the divinity and the universal significance of Christ, including in his death and resurrection. However, it need not be taken up this way. For most at Willingen, the emphasis on Christ's earthly ministry did not take away from his divinity or from his cosmic authority as Lord or from the universal significance of his death and resurrection, wherein he accomplishes and inaugurates a worldwide kingdom. Yet at the same time it motivated a ministry of justice and compassion, as well as evangelism—word and deed in Christ's way.

Salvation

Eschatology also affected the understanding of *salvation*, and this also played a role in shaping a missional church. The way one understands salvation will deeply shape one's view of mission. The formative influence of eschatology on salvation was twofold: salvation is comprehensive in its scope and

11. Lesslie Newbigin, *The Household of God: Lectures on the Nature of the Church* (New York: Friendship Press, 1954), 153–54.

restorative in its essence and is not simply individual and otherworldly; and salvation is present but will not come fully until the future. For the first part of the twentieth century, salvation was understood either in individual or in immanent-social terms: either as salvation of the individual in an otherworldly future or as the salvation of society realizable by the efforts of humanity. In 1950 these two visions of eschatology and salvation were still dominant. The first means that mission is about our efforts today to usher in salvation and is often characteristic of the more liberal tradition. The second means that mission is only about evangelism for an otherworldly future and is often characteristic of evangelicals.

The emphasis of the Jewish context of the kingdom makes clear that salvation is the restoration of the whole creation as the climax of cosmic history. In Jesus, this has broken into history but will not be realized until he returns. The coming of the kingdom is the restoration of God's rule over all human life, all nations, and all creation. On the one hand, the mission of the church to announce and embody salvation is to be equally comprehensive. On the other hand, since we can get only a foretaste now of what will come fully when Christ returns, the church's mission will be only a sign.

Spirit

Theological reflection on the *Spirit* in light of the eschatological context of Scripture was also significant for missionary ecclesiology. Traditionally in theology, the Spirit is understood in terms of distributing salvation to individuals or working in the institutional church. However, the advent of eschatology began to reshape pneumatology, in both biblical and theological studies, and to put the work of the Spirit in a new light.[12] The starting point for understanding the Spirit is the *eschatological context*. "The Spirit brings the reality of the new world to come into the midst of the old world that is. . . . [The Spirit is] the recognizable presence of a future that has been promised but is not yet in sight."[13] The Spirit is the firstfruits and earnest of the comprehensive salvation of the kingdom[14]—a first real portion that ensures the rest in the future.

Next, the Spirit must be understood in a *christological context*. The last days have dawned and are present by the power of the Spirit in Jesus. Jesus

---

12. See Oscar Cullmann, "Eschatology and Missions in the New Testament," in *The Theology of the Christian Mission*, ed. Gerald H. Anderson (London: SCM, 1961), 45–46.

13. Lesslie Newbigin, *The Open Secret: An Introduction to the Theology of Mission*, rev. ed. (Grand Rapids: Eerdmans, 1995), 63.

14. *Missions under the Cross*, 189.

reveals and accomplishes salvation of the last days in the power of the Spirit and then sends the Spirit. There follows a *missional context*: Christ pours out the Spirit, and the movement in the biblical story is from the one (Jesus) to the many (nations) and from the center (Jerusalem) to the ends of the earth, incorporating the nations into the salvation of the last days until the consummation. Eschatology, Jesus, the Spirit, and mission are tightly woven together in the New Testament. But finally, we need the *ecclesiological context*: the Spirit is poured out on the church. The church is first of all the *place* of the Spirit's mission to bring salvation to God's people and then an *instrument* of the Spirit's mission to bring the kingdom into the world.

Church

The impact of eschatology on *ecclesiology* is also important for mission. The joint statement of the Willingen participants confesses that Christ "created in Himself one new humanity."[15] Behind these words is a developing ecclesiology increasingly formed by the narrative and eschatology of Scripture. The church is the new humanity that has already begun to taste the eschatological salvation of the new creation. The church is not simply another religious community that exists as a voluntary society in the private realm. It is nothing less than the new humanity that has been formed to become what the Adamic humanity failed to be. As such, the church comes to expression in the totality of its life, and not only as it gathers for worship and fellowship. The church cannot be reduced to its gathered and institutional expression. This emphasis on the church as the new humanity is made also by its relationship to the kingdom: the church is a sign, foretaste, and instrument of the end-time kingdom.

This expression of the church as the new humankind developed over against long-established patterns of ecclesial definition that reduce the church to a community gathered or organized as an institution. Contrariwise, when the members of the church are scattered about in their various vocations, they remain the church. This is expressed in another 1950s ecumenical gathering: "the laity are not mere fragments of the church who are scattered about in the world and who come together again for worship, instruction, and specifically Christian fellowship on Sundays. They are the church's representatives, no matter where they are."[16] This is an ecclesiological statement. Before these words, we read that the scattered work of believers in the world

15. *Missions under the Cross*, 189.
16. *The Evanston Report: The Second Assembly of the World Council of Churches 1954* (New York: Harper and Brothers, 1955), 161.

"springs from the rediscovery of the true nature of the Church as the People of God."[17]

This kind of ecclesiology gives expression to the biblical notion that God is gathering a people whose entire lives are a picture of the new humanity that will inhabit the new creation. This ecclesiological insight opens the way for a much broader view of mission as the distinctive and restored humanity in all of life in every cultural context for the sake of the world.

This is the important point: the *missio Dei* simply could not have developed in the way it did without the coalescence of these biblical and theological developments.[18] Much talk of God's mission simply is not informed by these theological developments that shaped it. A theology of mission desperately needs a missionary theology. God's mission emerged as a unifying framework that corralled all these insights and fashioned them into a coherent theology of mission.

Summary of Willingen

At Willingen, we find the shattering of all the colonial and Christendom assumptions that captured mission in the earlier part of the century. Expressing the nature of the church in terms of participation in God's mission freed it from its nonmissionary nature. Moreover, it liberated mission from geographical limitations. The church is sent to every inhabited area of the world; mission is in the church's immediate neighborhood as well as to the ends of the earth; and no line can be drawn between the Christian West and the non-Christian South or East.

Lesslie Newbigin and the Developments of a Missionary Church

At Willingen, Newbigin played an important role brokering a compromise between competing views as he authored the final statement.[19] In so doing,

---

17. *Evanston Report*, 161.

18. We have found in our speaking that resistance to a missionary ecclesiology is often rooted in other theological commitments of which those who are most hesitant are often unaware. This also demonstrates the importance of missional theology, including systematic theology, shaped by a narrative and missional reading of Scripture.

19. Perhaps Flett overstates the case: "The final report [of Willingen] appears to have been *Newbigin's own invention*"! John G. Flett, *The Witness of God: The Trinity, Missio Dei, Karl Barth and the Nature of Christian Community* (Grand Rapids: Eerdmans, 2010), 154 (emphasis added).

he formulated a theological framework that would provide the context for the discussion of mission in the decades that followed. His role continued in the aftermath of Willingen as he authored two significant books—*The Household of God* and *One Body, One Gospel, One World*.[20] On the one hand, these books express an ecumenical consensus concerning the missionary nature of the church. The great twentieth-century missiologist David Bosch comments that the latter book "summarized a consensus that had now been reached": (1) the church is mission, (2) the home base is everywhere, and (3) mission in partnership.[21] On the other hand, these books make a creative contribution to the ongoing discussion of missionary church. Newbigin relates that his motivation for writing *The Household of God* was that the "Ecumenical Movement was not being undergirded by an adequate doctrine of the Church."[22] Newbigin's book sets out to provide just that.

In the closing chapters of *The Household of God*, Newbigin formulates an ecclesiology that he believes will move beyond the existing ecclesiological tensions in the ecumenical tradition by arguing that the church can be understood only in terms of its eschatological and missionary nature. It is a strong and expanded expression of the missionary ecclesiology evident at Willingen. If there is any development beyond Willingen, it is in Newbigin's stronger treatment of the Spirit and the Spirit's relation to eschatology and mission. His fervent commitment to a missionary church is seen in these words: "The very general belief of Christians in most Churches that the Church can exist without being a mission involves a radical contradiction of the truth of the Church's being, and . . . no recovery of the wholeness of the Church's nature is possible without a recovery of its radical missionary nature."[23]

After Willingen and Beyond

The contours of a missionary ecclesiology were firmly in place by 1952. Remarkable advances were made in recovering a biblical understanding of the missionary church in the early twentieth century. Yet in the period that followed Willingen, the conversation shifted in an entirely different direction for almost half a century, at least in the ecumenical movement. And it seems

20. Newbigin, *Household of God*, originally published in 1953; *One Body, One Gospel, One World: The Christian Mission Today* (London: International Missionary Council, 1958).

21. David J. Bosch, *Transforming Mission: Paradigm Shifts in Theology of Mission* (Maryknoll, NY: Orbis Books, 1991), 370.

22. Lesslie Newbigin, *Unfinished Agenda: An Updated Autobiography*, exp. and rev. ed. (Edinburgh: Saint Andrew Press, 1993), 128.

23. Newbigin, *Household of God*, 170.

that a missionary ecclesiology never really took hold deeply in the evangelical tradition. The individualism, the otherworldly salvation, and the reactionary response to the ecumenical movement inoculated many against any movement toward a missionary church.

A forty-year interlude would arrest the development of a missionary ecclesiology. Powerful secular winds began to blow the movement toward a missionary church in a new direction. The journey toward a missionary ecclesiology would resume in earnest at the end of the twentieth century with the tireless work of folks such as Lesslie Newbigin, David Bosch, and Wilbert Shenk, who would call us back to the missionary nature of the church that had been discovered.

Since Johannes Hoekendijk was probably the most prominent advocate of this new direction after Willingen, we might call this period the "Hoekendijkian interlude." On the one hand, we believe that this interlude took the church in a wrong direction. On the other hand, much good would come of it: it would deepen and modify many aspects of the understanding of a missionary church. To understand ecclesiological discussion today, it is important to turn to this shift that took place in the 1960s.

4

Competing Visions for a Missionary Church

In the previous chapters we traced the emergence of a missionary church in the first half of the twentieth century. At Willingen, the redemptive-historical and eschatological framework of the *missio Dei* allowed the contours of a full-blown missionary ecclesiology to emerge. The church's missionary nature is the result of participation in the mission of the triune God as narrated in Scripture. However, at Willingen there were two competing and quite divergent understandings of the *missio Dei* present. The received statement seemed to paper over significant differences. Yet it was the classical and orthodox understanding that found expression in the final documents. A more radical understanding, which sidelined the church, would take missionary ecclesiology in an entirely different direction in the following decades. This new direction departed sharply from the developments of the previous period.

Lesslie Newbigin judged this new direction to be a costly mistake. Nevertheless, his own understanding of mission was expanded and refined. He returned to Britain in the mid-1970s and shortly thereafter commenced his call for a missionary encounter with Western culture. At the heart of this project was a summons to recover the missionary nature of the church in the context of Western culture. The missionary ecclesiology evident in his writings during this time, read widely in North America, reflected the developments of the first half of the twentieth century. There were now new emphases and nuanced modifications as a result of the shift in mission theology. Nevertheless, Newbigin's missionary ecclesiology was substantially that of the classical paradigm that had developed between 1938 and 1952. This ecclesiology has continued to have wide appeal since the 1980s and was a formative influence on the publication of *Missional Church* in 1998. So, if we are to understand the current missionary church discussion in North America, we must understand the two directions of the missionary church conversation.

The Need for New Structures

There were two reasons a consistent missionary ecclesiology did not emerge following the important advances of Tambaram. First, there was no theological framework to draw together the various components. This had now been provided at Willingen in the narrative of God's mission. The Bible tells a story of God's mission centered in Christ, and the church's missionary nature is understood by discerning the central role that the church is called to play in that story, especially as it continues the mission of Jesus.

The second reason was that the structures of missionary societies, of denominational and ecumenical bodies of churches, and—perhaps most importantly—of local congregations and leadership still manifested Christendom patterns. The new vision of God's mission stressed the missionary nature of the church, and this inevitably raised questions about the incompatibility of current structural forms of church life with the church's missionary nature. Thus the next step was to reshape those institutional structures.

The challenge to overhaul obsolete Christendom structures gained momentum throughout the late 1950s. More people became "convinced that one of the main hindrances in the pursuit of the evangelistic calling of the Church lies in the traditional structure of the local congregation."[1] Newbigin often echoed this concern: "Does the very structure of our congregations contradict the missionary calling of the church?"[2] The New Delhi assembly authorized a study project on the missionary structure of the congregation to find patterns, structures, and forms of ministry consistent with the missionary nature of the church.

The report of this project appeared in 1967 and was titled *The Church for Others and the Church for the World: A Quest for Structures for the Missionary Congregation*. But alas: as David Bosch laments, the report "had

1. *The New Delhi Report: The Third Assembly of the World Council of Churches, 1961*, ed. W. A. Visser 't Hooft (New York: Association Press, 1962), 189.
2. Lesslie Newbigin, "Developments during 1962: An Editorial Survey," *International Review of Mission* 52 (1963): 9.

precious little to say about the 'missionary structure of the congregation.'"[3]
Between Willingen and the release of the report fifteen years later, the mission
of the church was swept into the tides of secularism, and in the process the
congregation had been pushed to the margins of the *missio Dei*. A new vision
of mission now prevailed in ecumenical circles, with Johannes Hoekendijk as
its primary champion and powerful spokesman.

A New Paradigm for Mission

This new view of mission was already present at Willingen. However, it did not
win the day. As Hoekendijk and others expressed it, the reigning ecumenical
view of mission was too Christocentric and needed to be trinitarian. It was
also too church-centric and needed to find its center in the world instead. It
was too concerned with salvation history and needed to shift to the revolutionary developments in world history.

The contrast can be highlighted in this way: The traditional paradigm of
mission that developed from Tambaram to Willingen found its primary focus
in the ecclesial community that had its origin in the universal work of Jesus
Christ with the vocation to continue his mission in the world in the power of
the Spirit. The new paradigm featured a shift in focus from God's redemptive work through Christ in the church to his providential work by the Spirit
in the world. The traditional paradigm is Christocentric and ecclesiocentric;
the new paradigm is pneumocentric and cosmocentric.

In the new paradigm, the laity becomes the primary agent of mission as
they participate with the Spirit in what he is doing in the world. The congregation is reduced to an instrumental role in God's mission as it restructures
itself to enable the laity to carry out their callings in political, social, and
economic activity to relieve victims of hunger, political oppression, and racial
discrimination. The church is no longer a place that experiences a foretaste of
God's redemptive work. The communal witness of the congregation, evangelism and conversion, worship and church planting are all minimized, if not
entirely eclipsed. Worship, nurture, fellowship, and discipleship constitute a
barrier to involvement in the world.

The goal of mission is the humanization or the *shalom* of society. This
takes place through the efforts of individual Christians in cooperation with
social institutions aimed at the transformation of oppressive political, social,

3. David J. Bosch, *Transforming Mission: Paradigm Shifts in Theology of Mission* (Maryknoll, NY: Orbis Books, 1991), 382.

and economic structures. The church attends to where the Spirit is at work—during the 1960s it observed the Spirit's work, for example, in the civil rights movements that empowered African Americans, in the humanization of industrial relations, in urban renewal, in justice for women, and so on—and joins him in his mission. Thus the church takes its cue from "the signs of the times," what God is doing in the world, rather than from what God has done in Jesus Christ. The church structures of the traditional paradigm have become rigid and introverted and need to be completely overhauled so that they may become more flexible to equip members for direct action in society. We might diagram the differing views this way:

Traditional missionary church paradigm
[God ➞ *CHRIST* ➞ Spirit] ➞ Church ➞ World

Emerging secular paradigm
[God ➞ Christ ➞ *SPIRIT*] ➞ World ➞ Church

Evidence of this shift appeared at a student conference in 1960. Newbigin, along with other leading advocates of the traditional paradigm of mission, were unable to connect with the students. Hoekendijk, however, was received with great enthusiasm.[4] By the fourth assembly of the World Council of Churches (WCC), held in Uppsala, Sweden, in 1968, the pneumocentric vision had become the "received view" in ecumenical circles.[5] A secular spirit overpowered and reshaped what it meant to be a missionary church. This approach remains quite influential, especially in more liberal churches, and has morphed as it has moved from its original, secular setting into a new, pluralistic context. Surprisingly, it has even been expressed more recently by some evangelicals.

But this shift didn't go uncontested at Uppsala. In that assembly it was sharply criticized by evangelical delegates. And this introduced, quite understandably, probably the most acrimonious time between the ecumenical and evangelical traditions.[6] As Newbigin sat in that assembly, on the one hand, he resisted the "deafening barrage" and "high-pressure propaganda" of the

4. Rodger Bassham, *Mission Theology: 1948–1975: Years of Worldwide Creative Tension—Ecumenical, Evangelical, and Roman Catholic* (Pasadena, CA: William Carey Library, 1979), 47. Cf. Newbigin's account of this conference, *Unfinished Agenda: An Updated Autobiography*, exp. and rev. ed. (Edinburgh: Saint Andrew Press, 1993), 164–65.
5. Bosch, *Transforming Mission*, 383.
6. David Bosch describes the relationship between the evangelical and ecumenical traditions from 1966 to 1973 as a "period of confrontation." "'Ecumenicals' and 'Evangelicals': A Growing Relationship?," *Ecumenical Review* 40, nos. 3–4 (July–October 1988): 462.

church-growth advocates, who seemed unable to see the insights of this new vision. They appeared to reduce mission to evangelism. But, on the other hand, he also felt the "shattering experience" of seeing the ecumenical assembly reduce "mission to nothing but a desperate struggle to solve insoluble problems." He says that the "saddest thing was that we were not able to seriously listen to one another."[7]

The New Mission Paradigm and Newbigin

While he was more appreciative of the important insights of the emerging secular vision than the church-growth advocates were, Newbigin was nonetheless very critical of the vision as a whole and emerged as a vigorous and vocal opponent. He remained committed to the traditional understanding of mission. Yet he saw many important emphases in the new vision that would renew and expand his own view. It is good, before expounding his critique, to note what those insights are and why this emerging vision of mission is so seductively attractive, not just then but today, and not just among more liberal traditions but among some evangelicals today.

Appreciation for the New Paradigm of Mission

The new paradigm feeds off a mounting frustration with the introversion of the church and a preoccupation with the church's own institutional life amidst terrible injustice and suffering in the world. The past missionary conferences, its proponents believed, had focused too exclusively on the church and had not paid sufficient attention to the broader horizon of mission—the kingdom in the world. This reinforced an ecclesiocentrism that was preoccupied with the inner life of the institutional church. Hoekendijk's book *The Church Inside Out* oozes with a passion to see a church *for the world*. In it, Hoekendijk vigorously resists an ingrown and self-absorbed church. So, in this new paradigm, the church is radically oriented outward. It is not hard to see the pull of this prophetic critique. Bosch insightfully observes that the criticisms of the church in this new paradigm of mission "are pertinent only insofar as they express a theological ideal raised to the level of prophetic judgment."[8]

This certainly aligns with Newbigin's concerns, and yet this paradigm shift was theologically problematic from its outset. Nevertheless, the orientation to the world was a welcome emphasis. But what of the new paradigm's further

---

7. Newbigin, *Unfinished Agenda*, 219.
8. Bosch, *Transforming Mission*, 385.

components—a shift from church to world, a move away from Christocentrism, an uncritical identification of revolutionary movements with God's
providential work in the Spirit, a reduction of the church's mission to participation in those movements, a minimization of evangelism and the church's
gathered life, a call for changing structures to equip the laity?

A turning point for Newbigin was an overnight flight from Bombay to
Rome, when he pored through the entire New Testament, noting every reference to "the world." He says that the "result of this was to set my mind
moving in a new direction in which it was to travel for the next ten years.
My thoughts for the past decade had been centered in the Church. This fresh
exposure to the word of God set me thinking about the work of God in the
world outside the church." He says, moreover, "this was the beginning of a
shift in perspective which enabled me to understand the concern of people
like Hoekendijk and Paul Lehman which I had failed to understand at Willingen."[9] This new direction of thinking led Newbigin to affirm certain insights
of the new cosmocentric vision of mission.

Newbigin did not essentially or radically revise his theology of mission or
his understanding of the church. Moreover, later he came to believe he had
been a little too enamored with this new vision, and he pulled back. Nevertheless, he eventually incorporated a number of insights into his already-
existing theological and ecclesiological framework. He expanded and deepened, modified and refined his understanding of the mission of the church.
Yet his theological direction remained intact. Newbigin affirmed at least five
components of the new paradigm.

Deepened Understanding of the Trinity

First, Newbigin welcomed a deepened understanding of the mission of
the *triune* God. In the early 1960s he confesses that the missiology of his
One Body, One Gospel, One World "was too exclusively church-centred in
its understanding of mission. Only a fully trinitarian doctrine would be adequate, setting the work of Christ in the Church in the context of the over-
ruling providence of the Father in all the life of the world and the sovereign
freedom of the Spirit who is the Lord and not the auxiliary of the Church."[10]

We need to note carefully what Newbigin is affirming here. He does not
acquiesce to the criticisms that Christocentrism is not trinitarian or that an
ecclesiocentrism needs to be replaced by the world as the center of mission.
These he rigorously resists. His words "setting the work of Christ in the

9. Newbigin, *Unfinished Agenda*, 144.
10. Newbigin, *Unfinished Agenda*, 187.

Church" are the operative ones. But now he believes that certain dimensions of the Father's and the Spirit's work have not been related sufficiently to the church's mission. These new emphases are found worked out most fully in his book *The Open Secret*, in which he sets out the mission of the triune God.[11]

In terms of the work of the Father, the Father's providential work in world history and his redemptive work in salvation history, as the setting of the coming of the kingdom in Jesus, had not received enough attention. In terms of the work of the Holy Spirit, Newbigin believes the sovereign freedom of the Spirit's work had not been sufficiently emphasized: "The active agent of mission is a power that rules, guides, goes before the church: the free, sovereign, living power of the Spirit of God."[12] Newbigin is concerned that without this emphasis, the church becomes the primary subject of mission while the Spirit is merely a supplementary empowering presence. When the church is the primary agent, mission becomes a matter of strength and organization, of strategy and execution. It is a matter of "mobilizing and allocating resources."[13] It is like a "military operation" or a "sales campaign."[14] This is a managerial ecclesiology[15] preoccupied with the proper organizational structures and programs and with the most effective strategies and methods, all aimed at numerical success. By contrast, mission is "not part of any missionary 'strategy' devised by the church. It was the free and sovereign deed of God, who goes before the church. . . . The mission is not ours but God's."[16]

The Social Calling of the Church

A second component of the new paradigm that Newbigin affirmed was the emphasis on the *social, political, and economic calling* of the church in society. To be sure, this had always been part of his vision for mission. Nevertheless, he placed a new urgency and priority on this dimension of the church's mission as glaring injustices became increasingly visible and intolerable in this revolutionary period. And this new urgency and priority appear in Newbigin's later writings. Newbigin comments that as he returned from his position as an ecumenical bureaucrat to the bishopric in Madras, India, in

11. Lesslie Newbigin, *The Open Secret: An Introduction to the Theology of Mission*, rev. ed. (Grand Rapids: Eerdmans, 1995), 19–65. The first edition was published in 1978.
12. Newbigin, *Open Secret*, 56.
13. Newbigin, *Open Secret*, 64.
14. Newbigin, *Open Secret*, 62.
15. Samuel Escobar speaks of a "managerial missiology." See Escobar, "A Movement Divided: Three Approaches to World Evangelization Stand in Tension with One Another," *Transformation: An International Journal of Holistic Mission Studies* 8, no. 4 (October 1991): 9.
16. Newbigin, *Open Secret*, 64.

1965, in the wake of these changes, he was much more committed to involvement in public affairs. In fact, he says his own point of view had changed. His years in the World Council of Churches had accustomed him to think about public issues and the witness of the church in the political and social sphere. He now rejected an "ecclesiastical domesticity" and says, further, "Looking back in 1965 upon my earlier ministries in Kanchi and Madurai I felt that I had been too narrowly ecclesiastical in my concerns." He resolved to challenge the strong church in Madras to take up the calling to pursue justice in public life.[17] The urgency and importance continue in Newbigin's writing, sometimes to the point of prophetic denunciation of churches that neglect it.

The Mission of the Laity

Third, Newbigin was wholeheartedly on board with the renewed stress on the mission of the *laity* in their various callings in culture. A sacred-secular dichotomy had nurtured a clericalism that left the people of God bereft of any sense of their missional calling in their daily vocations. The new emphasis on joining the work of the Spirit in mission in the various spheres of society restored the dignity of the calling of the laity. Hendrik Kraemer observed in 1961, "Never in church history . . . has the role and responsibility of the laity in church and world been a matter of so basic, systematic, comprehensive and intensive discussion in the total oikoumene as today." Indeed, as Elizabeth Adler and Jonah Katoneene comment, the "rediscovery of the laity was probably the most important aspect of the renewal of the church in the 1950s and 1960s."[18]

A "theology of the laity" had been developing throughout the early twentieth century, especially under the leadership of J. H. Oldham and Kraemer.[19] In April 1951, Kraemer paid a visit to India and challenged Newbigin that "the Church in India was not equipped and was not equipping itself for its real theological and missionary tasks." He listed a number of areas in which the church needed to grow, but commented that its most important omission was "equipping its lay membership for its secular witness."[20] Kraemer's visit influenced Newbigin, and he addressed the issue immediately thereafter, both in practice and in writing.[21] This concern for the mission of the laity gained

17. Newbigin, *Unfinished Agenda*, 203.
18. Quoted in Elizabeth Adler and Jonah Katoneene, "Laity," in *Dictionary of the Ecumenical Movement*, ed. Nicholas Lossky et al. (Geneva: World Council of Churches, 2002), 658.
19. For details, see Adler and Katoneene, "Laity," 658–64.
20. Newbigin, *Unfinished Agenda*, 119. Cf. Hendrik Kraemer, "On Tour throughout South-East Asia," *Ecumenical Review* 4, no. 2 (January 1952): 124–25, 127–28.
21. Lesslie Newbigin, "Our Task Today" (unpublished charge given to the fourth meeting of the diocesan council, Tirumangalam, India, December 18–20, 1951); Newbigin, "The

momentum throughout the 1950s with the new winds blowing, and solidified Newbigin's conviction that this was the "place where the primary witness to the sovereignty of Christ must be given."[22]

As Newbigin was being installed in his bishopric in Madras, he delivered a public address on the lordship of Christ over public life. He challenged the church to embrace its calling in culture. Since Christ "is Lord of all, absolutely and without qualification," then "the entire membership of the Church in their secular occupations are called to be signs of this lordship in every area of public life." The church is the "Church *for* the nation—not withdrawing into the sheltered existence of a minority community, but playing its full part in every aspect of national life . . . because all these things belong to Christ and because the Church has been set in the nation as a sign and instrument of Christ's plan for its perfecting."[23] This stress on the mission of the laity in society and culture remained a significant and central plank in Newbigin's missionary ecclesiology throughout his life.

The Local Congregation

Fourth, there was a renewed focus on the *local congregation* as the primary expression of the church's life. The urgent social and political needs of the 1960s focused attention on the needs of people in a certain place. The church was not just this ideal new humanity spread across the world but also comprised particular communities living amidst the needs and peoples of a certain location. Attention turned to the local congregation.

In the New Testament, the word *ekklēsia* refers both to the entire people of God that belong to Christ and to the local congregation. Theological reflection on the missionary church had neglected the latter. At Willingen, there was renewed emphasis on the local congregation, but it did not receive sustained attention until a decade later. Following the lead of Willingen, the New Delhi report states that "every Christian congregation is part of that mission, with a responsibility to bear witness to Christ in its own neighbourhood and to share in the bearing of that witness to the ends of the earth."[24] This signaled a renewed interest in the local congregation that developed rapidly in the following decades. Yet Newbigin could write in the late 1960s, "Talk about the Church as a missionary community has become rather common. But most

---

Christian Layman in the World and in the Church," *National Christian Council Review* 72 (1952): 185–89.

22. Lesslie Newbigin, "The Work of the Holy Spirit in the Life of the Asian Churches," in *A Decisive Hour for the Christian World Mission*, ed. Norman Goodall et al. (London: SCM, 1960), 28.

23. Newbigin, *Unfinished Agenda*, 203.

24. *New Delhi Report*, 249.

of it has left untouched the centre of the Church's life. It is only within very recent years that the light of the missionary doctrine of the Church has been turned steadily on the local congregation."[25]

Newbigin embraced the challenge and focused on the shape of the missionary congregation in its local place. He reflected theologically on what it meant for a church to be *for* its place, on how it could be deeply involved in the concerns of its own neighborhood, and on how it could organize itself both to live amid its neighbors and to equip the laity for the sake of its place.

Congregational and Leadership Structures

And so the fifth component he affirmed was the need for *congregational structures and forms of leadership* that both lived for the neighborhood and nurtured the mission of the laity. Every "Christian congregation and every church needs both a 'missionary spirit' . . . and a 'missionary structure.'"[26] The missionary spirit that developed in the early part of the twentieth century was not sufficient; it needed missionary structures to faithfully channel that spirit. There was intense frustration with the rigidity of the church's institutional structures—a "morphological fundamentalism," as it was called in the 1967 report.[27] The ingrown nature of the church had given rise to certain kinds of congregational structures and forms of ministry. These antiquated forms were designed only to maintain the institutional life of the church and thus were often an obstruction to mission in the world. And there was institutional inertia, a resolute resistance to change. The church had become inflexible, unable to change its institutional life to match its missional identity. Thus these structures of the congregation needed to be overhauled to enable the church to embrace its orientation to the world.

The questions that were posed were, "What must the structure of a congregation be like so as not to hinder the proclamation of the gospel?" and "How may the congregation be structured as to enable it to participate more truly in God's mission to the whole world?"[28] Many suggestions were made,[29] including support for zonal structures that would form ecclesial communities

25. Lesslie Newbigin, *Honest Religion for Secular Man* (London: SCM, 1966), 105.

26. Jan A. B. Jongeneel, *Philosophy, Science, and Theology of Mission in the 19th and 20th Centuries, Part II* (Frankfurt: Peter Lang, 1997), 173.

27. *The Church for Others and the Church for the World: A Quest for Structures for the Missionary Congregations; Final Report of the Western European Working Group and the North American Working Group of the Department of Studies in Evangelism* (Geneva: World Council of Churches, 1967), 19.

28. Jongeneel, *Philosophy, Science, and Theology*, 173.

29. For a list, see Jongeneel, *Philosophy, Science, and Theology*, 173.

in the midst of various spheres of modern social life (such as the factory or law office), and "go-structures" versus "come-structures."[30] But the secular tide blew the discussion off course, and the "anti-ecclesiological thrust"[31] of the new paradigm meant that questions were never really addressed sufficiently.

Newbigin believed that the call for new congregational structures was urgent. In 1957 he wrote, "We are saying that we have recovered a radically missionary theology of the Church. But the actual structure of our Churches (younger as well as older) does not reflect that theology. On the contrary it continues placidly to reflect the static 'Christendom' theology of the eighteenth century."[32] The forms of the church—organizational, leadership, liturgical, educational, theological—had developed during a time when the church had become "the religious department of European society rather than the task force selected and appointed for world mission."[33] Thus he believed "bold experiments" in "forms of ministry" and in "forms of congregational life"[34] were urgent, and hoped that study on the missionary structure of the congregation leading up to the 1967 report *The Church for Others and the Church for the World* would provide "new models of ministry and congregational life directed more to mission than to mere maintenance."[35] Newbigin considered the failure of this study program to be one of the major disappointments of his life. So he affirmed the quest for new structures but rejected the ecclesiology behind the quest: "Since the study of the missionary structure of the congregation has been prolific of polysyllabic slogans, I will venture to plead for a judicious combination of morphological radicalism with evangelical fundamentalism."[36]

Critique of the New Paradigm of Mission

An outward face, a deepened trinitarian understanding of mission, a radical commitment to the social calling of the church, the central importance

30. See Newbigin, *Honest Religion*, 111–17. Here Newbigin urges "daring experiments" and attempts to flesh this out very creatively. Cf. Newbigin, "Work of the Holy Spirit," 32, for a brief discussion of "bold experiments" in the structures of congregational life. "Come and go structures" are distinguished by whether the church equips members to go into the world or expects unbelievers to come to them.

31. Jongeneel, *Philosophy, Science, and Theology*, 90.

32. Newbigin, *Unfinished Agenda*, 148.

33. Newbigin, *Honest Religion*, 103.

34. Newbigin, "Work of the Holy Spirit," 30, 32.

35. Newbigin, *Unfinished Agenda*, 194.

36. Lesslie Newbigin, "The Call to Missions—the Call to Unity," in *The Church Crossing Frontiers*, ed. Peter Beyerhaus and Carl Hallencreutz (Lund, Sweden: Gleerup, 1969), 264.

of the calling of the laity, the local congregation, the need for new structures to equip the church for its calling—Newbigin enthusiastically embraced all these things. And all found a permanent place in his missionary ecclesiology. Nevertheless, despite all his sympathy for these new trends, he was also sharply critical of the new paradigm. Indeed, this was by far his overriding response. We note four of those criticisms.

A Trinity with a Diminished Christology

First, while the new paradigm claimed to be trinitarian over against Christocentric, Newbigin vigorously denies that such an opposition can be made. "A Trinitarian perspective can only be an enlargement and development of a Christocentric one," he argues, "and not an alternative set over against it, for the doctrine of the Trinity is the theological articulation of what it means to say that Jesus is the unique Word of God incarnate in world history."[37]

In fact, both views profess to be trinitarian. What was new was a fresh emphasis on the work of the Spirit, especially beyond the borders of the church. While that insight recovered something of Scripture's teaching, its overemphasis diminished the centrality of Christ in Scripture. In addition, the Spirit was disconnected from the work of Christ and from the mission of the church—a position that cannot be squared with Scripture. Disconnected from the work of Christ, the Spirit can become anything.

The traditional paradigm was far more trinitarian to begin with and could become even more so with the prompting of this new challenge. The real thrust of the new approach to mission was not a more faithful trinitarian framework that in turn led to political and social engagement. Rather, it was the other way around: an activist concern to engage the political and social issues of the day led to a rearticulation of the Trinity to provide the theological justification for radical involvement.

A Church Reduced to Its Instrumental Role

Second, Hoekendijk reduces the church to its *instrumental* role in God's mission. He defines the church in terms of its vocation in the public life of culture; it is only a means of God's mission in the world, not the end or locus of God's mission. Hoekendijk puts it this way: "The *nature* of the church can be sufficiently defined by its *function*."[38] Newbigin registers strong protest.

37. Lesslie Newbigin, "Ecumenical Amnesia," *International Bulletin of Missionary Research* 18, no. 1 (1994): 2.
38. Johannes Christiaan Hoekendijk, "The Church in Missionary Thinking," *International Review of Mission* 41, 163 (July 1952): 334 (emphasis in the original).

The church "is not just a means to an end—the church is not just an organization for carrying out programs of service. . . . Nor, on the other hand, is it an end in itself, an organization existing for the benefit of its members." This second mistake is common, and many Christians "regard the church as a private society or club which exists to cater to the needs of its members." But this is a "monstrous caricature of the church."[39] And it is precisely this "monstrous caricature" that feeds Hoekendijk's righteous indignation and passionate reaction. It leads him to describe the church only in terms of its instrumental means to seek the justice of the kingdom.

Yet, Newbigin insists, this is a caricature as well. The church is an end of God's mission in the sense that it is a foretaste of the salvation accomplished in Christ and given to us by the Spirit. That is precisely what makes it also a means. Thus the church is both the place and the instrument, the locus and the agent, the end and the means of God's mission: God works *in* and *through* the church. It is only because the church is a real foretaste that it can be a witness to and an instrument of the kingdom. "The life in Christ is not merely the instrument of the apostolic mission, it is also its end and purpose. The Church can be instrumental to the divine purpose of salvation only because she is more than instrumental—because she is in fact herself the Body of Christ." So Newbigin, while affirming Hoekendijk's contention that the essential nature of the church is mission, believes that that mission must be "churchly" in the sense of a community that embodies what it announces and works for: "Just as we must insist that a Church which has ceased to be a mission has lost the essential character of a Church, so we must also say that a mission which is not at the same time truly a Church is not a true expression of the divine apostolate. *An unchurchly mission is as much a monstrosity as an unmissionary Church.*"[40]

Thus the church not only works for the kingdom in the world but is itself a provisional embodiment of the kingdom now. "There can be for me no escape from the conviction that the essential contribution of the Church to peace and justice in the world is a fellowship which actually realizes (even if only in foretaste) that peace and justice which Christ has won for all peoples in his atoning death and resurrection."[41] Newbigin's stress on the nature of the church as a sign, foretaste, and instrument of the kingdom has rightly played an important role in the ongoing conversation on the missional nature of the church.

39. Lesslie Newbigin, *Journey into Joy* (Grand Rapids: Eerdmans, 1972), 110.
40. Lesslie Newbigin, *The Household of God: Lectures on the Nature of the Church* (New York: Friendship Press, 1954), 169 (emphasis added).
41. Newbigin, *Unfinished Agenda*, 240.

A Defective View of Mission

A third area in which Newbigin critiques the new paradigm is its understanding of mission. Newbigin stresses essential aspects of the church's mission that have been eclipsed: evangelism, church planting, and missions. He laments the missionary spirit of the day: "The world, not the Church, was the place where God was at work. It was far more important to get people involved in action for justice and development than to have them converted, baptized and brought into the church."[42] Newbigin observes with sadness that "very many of the participants [of the New Delhi assembly in 1961] visiting India for the first time were moved by the sight of so many without bread, not many were apparently moved by the sight of so many without the gospel. . . . Half of this world is hungry, and we are learning to share our bread. . . . We have now also to learn . . . how to share that living bread with all who will receive him."[43] Newbigin "denounced sharply" those who affirmed social justice and technological development but rejected evangelistic activity to convert people to the Christian faith.[44] During this difficult secular period, he wrote six convictions to keep himself on track. The first was that "it matters supremely to bring more people to know Jesus as Saviour."[45]

But his critique was not only in terms of reduction and eclipse—calling attention to what had been left out. The very social calling of the church itself is distorted in the new paradigm. It is no longer an enacted prayer for the coming kingdom or a visible sign of good news. It is a losing struggle to solve the insoluble problems of the world. It is accommodated to the humanistic progress myth of the day and its optimism that social, political, and economic problems can be solved by science, technology, and social organization.

Newbigin forged his understanding of the nature of social concern in contrast to the reductionism of this period: our deeds cannot build the kingdom but only witness to its presence and power; our social action is as an enacted prayer for the kingdom; the pursuit of justice and mercy arises from love for our neighbor; we do not separate our deeds from the name of Jesus but pray that our deeds might bring the conversion of those who see them.

42. Newbigin, *Unfinished Agenda*, 187.
43. Lesslie Newbigin, "Report of the Division of World Mission and Evangelism to the Central Committee," *Ecumenical Review* 15 (1962): 90, 94.
44. Lesslie Newbigin, "From the Editor," *International Review of Mission* 54, no. 216 (1965): 418.
45. Newbigin, *Unfinished Agenda*, 186.

The Eclipse of the Communal Life of the Church

A fourth and final issue hotly contested by Newbigin is the diminished importance of the gathered life of the church for worship, fellowship, prayer, and nourishment of new life in Christ. These dimensions of the communal life of the church had been lost in social activism. Newbigin sympathizes with the concern that had disconnected the communal life of the church from culture: worship and the internal life of the church may become otherworldly and escapist, a safe haven from costly discipleship and identification with the world's misery. But the alternative is not a faithful option. A church that immerses itself in the world's sorrow and pain but leaves a life of worship behind has simply become part of the world's misery with nothing to give the world.[46]

And so it was precisely at this time, remarkably, that Newbigin increased his affirmation of the importance of the church gathered for worship, Scripture, sacraments, fellowship, and prayer. The difficult mission of being "a committed people as the sign and agent and foretaste of what God intends" can happen only if the people's "life is constantly renewed through contact with God himself."[47] Indeed, "all true vitality in the work of missions depends in the last analysis upon the secret springs of supernatural life which they know who give time to communion with God. All true witness . . . has its source in a life of adoration and intercession."[48] The more costly the solidarity with the world's pain, the deeper will be the need for worship, Scripture, sacraments, fellowship, and prayer.

Newbigin and Raiser: The Different Paradigms Live On

While the precise approach of Hoekendijk and the 1960s version of mission have diminished with the passing of the secular decades, the spirit of this vision lives on. For our purposes, it is unnecessary to trace the story from the 1960s to today. However, a literary skirmish between Newbigin and Konrad Raiser, general secretary of the WCC from 1992 to 2004, highlights the continuing influence of this approach.

The initial skirmish between these two men took place in 1994 on the pages of the *International Bulletin of Missionary Research*. Newbigin fired the first volley across the bow with a lengthy review and strong critique of

46. Lesslie Newbigin, *Christ Our Eternal Contemporary* (Madras: Christian Literature Society of India, 1968), 79.
47. Newbigin, *Journey into Joy*, 112–13.
48. Newbigin, "Developments during 1962," 14.

Raiser's book *Ecumenism in Transition*.[49] Raiser's response was brief, but it did not engage the issues on a deep level.[50] Newbigin's response to Raiser in the same issue of the bulletin was likewise brief and more subdued.[51] One year later, Raiser delivered a public lecture at the bicentenary celebration of the London Mission Council, titled "Toward an Ecumenical Vision for the 21st Century."[52] Newbigin attended that lecture and was incited to draft a nine-page unpublished response to what he heard.[53] Both of these encounters are brief, the complexities of the issues are not given full justice, and many questions remain unanswered. However, these brief scuffles make clear the central issues of conflict between two very different visions of the missionary church.

In *Ecumenism in Transition*, Raiser articulates a decisive shift taking place in the ecumenical movement. He identifies the classical ecumenical paradigm, which he labels "Christocentric universalism."[54] Raiser explicates the Christocentric universalist paradigm in terms of four elements: First, the "all-determining central element in the paradigm is a deliberate *Christocentrism*" that highlights the divinity and lordship of Christ. A second element . is a "concentration on the church" that accentuates the unique identity and task of the church. The third element is the universal perspective. The Christ-event has universal significance, and therefore the church's mission also has universal validity. The final element is the paradigm's emphasis on salvation history and eschatology as the central category of thought. The dynamic framework of universal history provides the structure that encompasses and links the Christocentrism, the focus on the church, and the universalism of this paradigm.

Raiser believes that this classical paradigm is now facing challenges that question its future viability: religious pluralism, various forms of oppression and injustice, and the ecological threat.[55] He wants to catch the wave of the new paradigm that has been developing since the 1960s and ride it into the future.[56]

49. Newbigin, "Ecumenical Amnesia," 2–5; Konrad Raiser, *Ecumenism in Transition: A Paradigm Shift in the Ecumenical Movement?* (Geneva: World Council of Churches, 1991).
50. Konrad Raiser, "Is Ecumenical Apologetics Sufficient? A Response to Lesslie Newbigin's 'Ecumenical Amnesia,'" *International Bulletin of Missionary Research*, 18, no. 2 (1994): 50–51.
51. Lesslie Newbigin, "Reply to Konrad Raiser," *International Bulletin of Missionary Research* 18, no. 2 (1994): 51–52.
52. Konrad Raiser, "Toward an Ecumenical Vision for the 21st Century" (unpublished public lecture, 1995).
53. Lesslie Newbigin, "Reflections on the LMS/CWM Bicentennial: July 1995" (unpublished response to Konrad Raiser's keynote address, 1995).
54. Raiser, *Ecumenism in Transition*, 36–51.
55. Raiser, *Ecumenism in Transition*, 54–78.
56. Raiser, *Ecumenism in Transition*, 79–120.

He offers four contrasting elements to the classical paradigm. Fearing the Christomonistic and triumphalist tendencies of Christocentrism, Raiser stresses a trinitarianism that gives full scope to the working of the Spirit. In contrast to the ecclesiocentrism of traditional ecumenical theology, he calls for an understanding in which "the institutional distinctions between church and world and church and society fall into the background."[57] He fears that present ecclesiologies tend to lead to a haughty Christian exclusivism that lacks solidarity with the world. He fears that the universal emphasis leads to a triumphalist mission, which is unable to meet the challenges of pluralism, oppression, and ecological disaster. And so he proposes a humble service orientation centered in dialogue that contributes to a household of life. Finally, Raiser wants to replace the category of universal salvation history as the encompassing framework with a notion of the *oikoumenē*. The social, political, economic, and ecological crises all call for the guiding image of the *oikoumenē* as a household of life, which stresses concrete human stewardship in solidarity with all life forms.

Newbigin recognizes important insights in Raiser's views: trinitarian thought must be foundational; a focus on the importance of the church must not eclipse solidarity with the world; we must be concerned for *oikoumenē*, the fragile interdependence of the whole inhabited earth; the church's mission is to be one of humble service and not a crusading triumphalism; and the burning issues of religious pluralism, economic justice, and ecological stewardship must receive priority. However, he strongly critiques Raiser at several points.

Raiser's *Christology* is inadequate. The universal validity and finality of the atoning work of Jesus Christ and his cosmic lordship are eclipsed by a reductionist emphasis on the life of Jesus. According to Raiser, Jesus's life shows his loving and liberating care for all people, and the cross is the price he pays for devotion to God and to the marginalized. For Newbigin, this falls far short of the New Testament, which witnesses to the universal significance of Christ as the fullest revelation of God and his purpose for the world. And reducing the cross to the price paid for a mission that counters the powerful is true but utterly inadequate. The cross is nothing less than cosmic in its significance—the place where the victory of God's reign won over all that opposed it.

Raiser's *ecclesiology* is also inadequate. He has lost the distinctiveness of the church's life because the necessary distinction between the church and the unbelieving world is obscured. The Spirit is a deposit and the firstfruits, and this gives to the church its distinctive eschatological life and witness.

57. Raiser, *Ecumenism in Transition*, 73.

The church must be both separate from and in solidarity with the world. But Raiser has also lost the universal significance of the church and its mission. The church is a sign and foretaste of God's kingdom and is set apart as the new humanity who will one day inherit the new creation. All who wish to participate in God's coming kingdom must be baptized into this community.

Finally, Raiser's *view of mission* is inadequate. He reduces the church's role to what it can contribute toward peace, justice, and the integrity of creation. His rightful concern for the burning issues of pluralism, oppression, injustice, and ecological destruction leads him to neglect the missionary and evangelistic calling of the church. He also doesn't understand that by giving up the universal significance and centrality of Christ, he has abandoned God's solution to those problems.

In Raiser's response, he maintains that Newbigin's "entire critical reflection is based on the conviction of the non-negotiable truth of the earlier paradigm."[58] Newbigin protests that he does not regard the classical paradigm as unalterable.[59] In fact, a major shift had taken place in his own thinking during the 1960s in which he learned from the insights of that time and modified the classical paradigm.

And so the vision of the 1960s lives on, not just into the 1990s, as exemplified by Raiser, but up until today. What makes it so attractive is that it is a prophetic rebuke to an inward-looking, self-preoccupied, institutionally centered, and structurally rigid church. "In light of the terrible conditions under which millions of starving, oppressed, and exploited people were living," this vision of mission championed by Hoekendijk and Raiser reveals "a holy impatience with any complacency on the part of the church."[60] No doubt this is why some evangelical folk in the missional and emergent conversations today who are likewise tired of an introverted and inflexible church are, sadly, uncritically embracing this vision even while championing Newbigin.

58. Raiser, "Is Ecumenical Apologetics Sufficient?," 50.
59. Newbigin, "Reply to Konrad Raiser," 51.
60. Bosch, *Transforming Mission*, 385.

5

A Missionary Church
in Western Culture

Newbigin and a Missionary Encounter with the West

The somewhat modified classical understanding of the church's participation in the mission of God remained the conviction of Lesslie Newbigin throughout his life. When his writings on the issue of mission in Western culture became prominent in the 1980s, it is *this* missionary ecclesiology that was dispersed throughout North America and beyond. Many who do not know the history that formed Newbigin were first confronted by a missionary understanding of the church in these works. The meteoric rise of "missional" as it describes church is a result of his persistent call during his retirement years for a missionary encounter with Western culture.

The term *missionary encounter* was the fruit of Newbigin's forty years as a missionary in India. When missionaries go to a foreign country they must, first, learn to live as participants in the culture, adopting its forms and institutions. To communicate the gospel, they must use the language of that culture. But the problem is that all cultures are shaped by a religious vision of life that is contrary to the gospel; it forms every part of the culture, including language. To adopt the forms and language of a culture threatens to reshape the gospel. But the gospel is equally a comprehensive religious vision. So the missionary problem is how to communicate the gospel—one way of looking at the whole world in light of Jesus Christ—in forms that look at the whole world in a different light. How does one convey the gospel in the forms of a different religious vision without allowing the gospel to be accommodated to that vision? Only if the gospel is communicated in a way that challenges the idolatry of the culture can there be a conversion from cultural idolatry to Jesus Christ.

On his return to Britain in 1974 with new eyes formed by four decades in a Hindu culture, Newbigin discovered a church that had accommodated itself to its culture and thereby surrendered its missionary identity and calling. The church was timid about the truth of the gospel, and the primary root of this lack of confidence was the enthronement of the modern scientific worldview. The "biblical message has been so thoroughly adapted to fit into our modern Western culture that we are unable to hear the radical challenge, the call for radical conversion which it presents in our culture."[1] The Western church had accommodated itself to the idolatrous Western worldview and was an "advanced case of syncretism."[2] And Newbigin wondered, "Can the West be converted?"[3]

Newbigin argued that this task was the most urgent item on the agenda of missiology: "It would seem, therefore, that there is no higher priority for the research work of missiologists than to ask the question of what would be involved in a genuinely missionary encounter between the gospel and this modern Western culture."[4] He devoted the remainder of his life to fostering a missionary encounter between the gospel and modern Western culture. Arguably his most important books of this time dealing with a missionary encounter with the West are *The Other Side of 1984* (1983), *Foolishness to the Greeks* (1986), and *The Gospel in a Pluralist Society* (1989).[5]

The Urgency of a Missionary Encounter with the West

Why did Newbigin believe this task was so urgent? Western culture is the *most powerful* global force at work in the world today. Because of the process of globalization, Western culture now "has more worldwide influence than any other culture, including that of Islam."[6] It is the *most pervasive*

---

1. Lesslie Newbigin, "The Bible and Our Contemporary Mission," *Clergy Review* 69, no. 1 (1984): 11.
2. Lesslie Newbigin, *The Other Side of 1984: Questions for the Churches* (Geneva: World Council of Churches, 1983), 23.
3. Lesslie Newbigin, "Can the West Be Converted?," *International Bulletin of Missionary Research* 11, no. 1 (January 1987): 2–7.
4. Lesslie Newbigin, *Foolishness to the Greeks: The Gospel and Western Culture* (Grand Rapids: Eerdmans, 1986), 3.
5. Lesslie Newbigin, *The Gospel in a Pluralist Society* (Grand Rapids: Eerdmans, 1989).
6. Lesslie Newbigin, "Culture of Modernity," in *Dictionary of Mission: Theology, History, Perspectives*, ed. Karl Müller et al. (Maryknoll, NY: Orbis Books, 1997), 98–99.

cultural force in today's world, spreading to all the urban areas of the world. Western culture is the *most dangerous* foe the church has faced in its long history. "The church is awakening slowly to the fact that modernity is the most powerful enemy it has faced in its two thousand years of history."[7] Wherever Western culture goes, "it becomes the controlling doctrine for public life and drives religion into a smaller and smaller enclave."[8] It is also "precisely this powerful culture which is *most resistant* to the Gospel."[9] We have imagined that we live in a secular society, deceived by the myth of neutrality, but it "is a pagan society, and its paganism having been born out of the rejection of Christianity is far more resistant to the gospel than the pre-Christian paganism with which cross-cultural missions have been familiar. Here, surely, is the most challenging missionary frontier of our time."[10] The long association of Western culture with the Christian faith appears to have made it increasingly immune to the critique of the gospel. And finally, the church in the West had been living so long in a state of syncretism with this culture that it is hard to imagine any alternative. For centuries, instead of challenging Western culture's idolatry, it has been content to live in a "cozy domestication with the 'modern' worldview."[11]

And so Newbigin does not primarily address his challenge to the unbelieving world but to the church, so it might again gain confidence in its own gospel—"everything depends on a recovery of confidence in the gospel."[12] There are at least three tasks that will equip the church in the West for a missionary encounter: a cultural task, a theological task, and an ecclesiological task.

The Cultural Task: Exposing the Religious Credo

The first task is *cultural*. If the gospel and church are to be liberated from their syncretism for a missionary encounter, the religious beliefs at the center of Western culture need to be unmasked. In the same way that good missionaries labor to understand the religious beliefs at the core of the culture to which they are sent, so must the Western church understand the religious

---

7. Lesslie Newbigin, *Living Hope in a Changing World* (London: Alpha International Holy Trinity Brompton, 2003), 83.

8. Lesslie Newbigin, "Gospel and Culture—but Which Culture?," *Missionalia* 17, no. 3 (1989): 213.

9. Lesslie Newbigin, *Mission and the Crisis of Western Culture* (Edinburgh: Handsel, 1989), 1 (emphasis added).

10. Newbigin, *Foolishness to the Greeks*, 20.

11. Lesslie Newbigin, "Pluralism in the Church," *ReNews (Presbyterians for Renewal)* 4, no. 2 (May 1993): 1.

12. Lesslie Newbigin, *A Word in Season: Perspectives on Christian World Missions* (Grand Rapids: Eerdmans, 1994), 187.

beliefs at the core of its culture. "Incomparably the most urgent missionary task for the next few decades is the mission to 'modernity.' . . . It calls for the use of sharp intellectual tools, to probe behind the unquestioned assumptions of modernity and uncover the hidden credo which supports them."[13]

A credo is a set of religious beliefs. They function as a directing power at the root of culture that integrates and shapes all other areas. They are a "set of beliefs, experiences, and practices that seek to grasp and express the ultimate nature of things, that which gives shape and meaning to human life, that which claims final loyalty."[14] The problem in the West is that there is a dangerous myth that we live in a neutral culture that pretends to have no creed and thus conceals its own religious nature. Yet these religious beliefs, which enslave Western culture and hobble the church to encounter its own culture with the gospel, lie hidden below the surface level of culture like tectonic plates, unseen, yet shaping all that is above. It requires sharp tools to dig below the surface level of our lived culture to uncover this hidden credo so the church may see it.

Newbigin employs two digging tools to expose the religious creed: narrating the religious story of Western culture and unmasking the illusion of autonomous reason that has imprisoned the gospel in a private realm. The problem the church faces, if it is to encounter its culture with the gospel, is that it has been deceived by the myth of a neutral culture. The first task is to tell the religious story of the West to expose the myth of neutrality. The problem is that the Western church is like a fish in water and doesn't recognize the pollution in which it swims. The telling of the story of the West can give the church critical distance so it can see the pollution.

The metanarrative of Western humanism is not neutral: it offers a comprehensive vision of life that demands ultimate allegiance. Seminal to the Western master-narrative is the notion of progress, which interprets the purpose of universal history. We hear how humanity might be saved, and there is an eschatological vision of the end of history. The Western story is progress toward a paradise of freedom, prosperity, and peace created by humanity.

Western culture is humanistic in the deeply religious sense of having confidence that human beings can save themselves. Humanity builds this paradise and humans save themselves by science, technology, economics, and politics. Universal reason is emancipated from dogma and disciplined by the scientific method to conquer all the evils that enslave men and women. Science is translated into technology to subdue nature and into economic

13. Newbigin, "Gospel and Culture," 214.
14. Newbigin, *Foolishness to the Greeks*, 3.

and political or social organization to control human culture. All of this will achieve a new world. This vision of universal history came to maturity in the eighteenth-century Enlightenment. There was a "collective conversion" of Europe from Christendom to this new religious vision.[15] The progress toward this humanist paradise achieved in the nineteenth century seemed to confirm this faith.

But the events in the twentieth century in Europe led to a growing loss of confidence in the Enlightenment-progress faith, as it "failed disastrously to deliver what was promised."[16] And so a new spirit began to pervade the West: there was a collapse of modernity into postmodernity. We didn't believe these big stories anymore. Having no story to judge the truth has led to relativism, pluralism, and the reduction of truth claims to power.[17] However, the bigger threat is that the public life of Western culture still embodies the modern vision of life. But now it takes on a new global and economic form. Modernism remains the major challenge the world faces.[18]

This new form of modernity is economic. It has its roots in the eighteenth century: it is in economics that "the Enlightenment was to have perhaps its most far-reaching consequences."[19] The "new economics" of the Enlightenment would "create unlimited material growth" and "higher levels of fulfilment and happiness" through the creation of an economic society. This economic idolatry reshapes cultural life and spreads through technology, business, and education to become a global culture. Globalization is modernization on a global scale. To understand it, says Newbigin, we must dig down to a "deeper level" than political and economic systems, to "the level of fundamental beliefs, of ultimate commitments, in fact of idolatries."[20]

Economic modernity has produced today the "meaningless hedonism of a consumer society."[21] This religious vision is creating a growing divide between

15. Newbigin, *Foolishness to the Greeks*, 23.

16. Lesslie Newbigin, *Truth and Authority in Modernity* (Valley Forge, PA: Trinity Press International, 1996), 73–74.

17. Lesslie Newbigin, *Proper Confidence: Faith, Doubt, and Certainty in Christian Discipleship* (Grand Rapids: Eerdmans, 1995), 27; Newbigin, "Religious Pluralism: A Missiological Approach," *Studia Missionalia* 42 (1993): 231–34; Newbigin, *Truth and Authority in Modernity*, 7–9, 82.

18. Lesslie Newbigin, "Modernity in Context," in *Modern, Postmodern and Christian*, ed. John Reid, Lesslie Newbigin, and David Pullinger, Lausanne Occasional Paper No. 27 (Carberry, Scotland: Handsel, 1996), 8.

19. Newbigin, *Other Side of 1984*, 11.

20. Lesslie Newbigin, "The Gospel as Public Truth: Swanwick Opening Statement" (unpublished address, 1992), 6.

21. Lesslie Newbigin, "It Seems to Me," *Transmission* (Spring 1997): 4; cf. Newbigin, *Foolishness to the Greeks*, 30–31.

rich and poor and destroying the environment. Global economic modernity and consumerism: these are the central idolatrous threats to the church today.

Newbigin sees himself as a missionary who is attempting to expose the roots of a culture that is enervating the church's witness. To the degree that the church is captive to these idols, it cannot offer a gospel that challenges them. He exposes the religious vision that is crippling the church, calling the church to again embody and tell the gospel as the true story.

The second digging tool exposes the idol of autonomous reason. In the modern vision, reason plays a messianic role to build the new paradise. Reason must be liberated from its bondage to religious dogma by the scientific method if it is to be able to reshape the world through technology and the rational organization of society. Thus reason must be autonomous, free of religious commitments. In this way reason is exalted as the final arbiter of truth. This leads to a deep-rooted dualism at the foundation of our culture. Only truth claims validated by reason may play a role in shaping the public square. All others, including the gospel, must be relegated to the private realm of values and opinion, mere tastes that have no claim to universal validity. This is the problem facing the church: it has acquiesced to this religious vision and allowed the gospel to become privatized.

The idol of autonomous reason is masked by a false claim to objectivity. The claim is that reason, disciplined by the scientific method, can rise above our subjectivity, including religious commitments, to gain objective knowledge. Yet this is simply not how scientific knowledge works. Autonomous reason is an illusion; even scientific reason works in the context of the authority of some socially embodied tradition with its beliefs and assumptions. The gospel has been wrongly imprisoned within the bounds of reason for two centuries. This must be reversed: reason must be liberated to rightly function within the bounds of the gospel. The church must recover a standpoint where reason makes sense of the world in light of the ultimate truth of the gospel.

The Theological Task: Recovering the Gospel as Public and Narrative Truth

In a missionary encounter, the church must take its stand within the biblical story and understand its culture in light of this story. The problem that Newbigin found as he returned to Western culture was that exactly the reverse was the case: the church took its stand within its culture and tailored the authority of Scripture to fit modernist assumptions. The Bible has been part of the culture for so long that it has accommodated itself to the fundamental beliefs of the culture and appears unable to challenge them. If there is to be a missionary encounter with Western culture, there is an "urgent need for the development of a coherent and intellectually tenable doctrine of Scriptural authority."[22]

Newbigin believed that the Christian faith is a particular way of understanding universal history and the whole world, which finds in the life, death, and resurrection of Christ the decisive clue for that story. The Bible is a cosmic story that unfolds God's purpose in history to restore and recover his whole creation and the entirety of human life from sin and its effects. God's purpose is ultimately revealed and accomplished in Jesus Christ and implemented by the Spirit in and through the church. This is the true story of the world, and it is a different story from all other cultural stories.

If we are to recover this understanding of the Bible for a missionary encounter with the West, there is a threefold task. First, the Bible has been relegated to the private realm and so must be recovered *as truth*. As long as scientific reason is considered to be ultimate truth, the gospel is reduced to a mere religious taste that one prefers. It must be recovered as true.

Thus the Bible has lost its comprehensive authority, and so the gospel and biblical story must be recovered *as comprehensive public truth*. The Bible not only speaks about so-called spiritual things. It tells the true story of the whole world and of the human situation. It is public truth (true for all), and it is comprehensive truth (its truth extends to all human life).

Finally, the Bible has been reduced to either a record of religious experiences or a collection of theological propositions and must be recovered *as narrative truth*. The triumph of the Enlightenment religious vision split the church into liberal and fundamentalist camps. Liberals simply embraced the religious creed of modernity and reduced the Bible to a mere "collection of records and religious experience . . . having . . . no unique authority which sets it apart from all other books."[23] This brought forth the rightful reaction of conservative Christians, who want to preserve the Bible's divine authority. They did so, however, with the very Enlightenment tools that produced the liberal tradition; they remained within the vision of humanism. The conservative churches reshape the truth of Scripture by reducing it to an account of timeless dogmas about God, nature, and humankind. Both camps undermine the given narrative unity, instead producing their own construct: a historical-critical construct or a systematic-theological one.

22. Lesslie Newbigin, "New Birth into a Living Hope" (unpublished address, 1995), 7.
23. Lesslie Newbigin, "The Bible: Good News for Secularised People," Newbigin Archives, University of Birmingham (keynote address, Europe and Middle East Regional Conference, Eisenach, Germany, April 1991), 6; cf. Newbigin, *Truth to Tell: The Gospel as Public Truth* (Grand Rapids: Eerdmans, 1991), 43–44.

The reason the recovery of the Bible as the one true story of the world is so important for a missionary encounter is that "if this biblical story is not the one that controls our thinking then inevitably we shall be swept into the story that the world tells about itself. We shall become increasingly indistinguishable from the pagan world of which we are a part."[24]

The Ecclesiological Task: A Missionary Church beyond Privatization and Christendom

Newbigin puts the question to the church: If there is to be a missionary encounter with culture, "What must we be?"[25] The first thing the church must recover is its *missionary nature*. The church of Christendom has schooled the church to be primarily concerned about its own institutional life. It has become an inward-looking body that enjoys the benefits of salvation without recognizing the call to be a channel of that salvation to the world. In God's mission, God works his salvation first *in* a people and then *through* that people for the sake of the world. God first *blesses* his people so that they might *be a blessing*. The church of Christendom enjoyed the first step without taking up the responsibility of the second.

Second, the church must reject the privatized role it has been assigned in modernity. Like the gospel, the church is relegated to a private realm of values. However, the church is not a private religious community but is the new humankind, called to embody the comprehensive sovereignty of the creator God in all of life. Sadly, the church has often capitulated to the notion that it is a voluntary religious body that takes its place in culture. It reduces the gospel of the kingdom to the individual and reduces salvation to an otherworldly future. The good news is that God is restoring a people to be the new humanity that Adamic humanity failed to be. Its gathered and institutional life is to nurture the church in its new creation life in Christ so Christians might be the new humanity restored to God's original creational intention in their whole lives.

Third, the church must recover a vision of what it means to be a distinctive people. A people who live in terms of a missionary encounter will both live in solidarity with their contemporaries and live separate as a distinctive people. They will live by a different story and offer an alternative to human life—one rooted in the gospel. If the church is to live out the gospel as public truth, it must do so in its life together as it embodies "a new social order."[26]

---

24. Lesslie Newbigin, "Biblical Authority," Newbigin Archives, University of Birmingham (unpublished article, 1997), 2.
25. Newbigin, *Foolishness to the Greeks*, 124–50. Cf. Newbigin, *Other Side of 1984*, 55–62; Newbigin, *Gospel in a Pluralist Society*, 222–32.
26. Newbigin, *Truth to Tell*, 85.

But it also must do so in its scattered life in the public square. All believers must learn to understand how the gospel enables them to live out their vocations under the lordship of Christ.

A Missionary Church in Western Culture

Newbigin was not the only person who called for a missionary encounter with Western culture and for a missionary ecclesiology as an essential component. Two other significant missiologists are worthy of mention: David Bosch and Wilbert Shenk.[27] These men likewise stressed that central to a missionary encounter with Western culture was the need to recover a missionary ecclesiology. These men joined Newbigin as progenitors of the missionary church in North America.

Bosch's watershed book *Transforming Mission* was highly significant. Much can be found in its pages about the historical development of the *missio Dei* and the missionary nature of the church. Indeed, these are the first two elements of Bosch's ecumenical paradigm of mission.[28] No doubt this landmark book has played an important role in introducing a missionary ecclesiology. However, surprisingly Bosch did not share Newbigin's (and Shenk's) sense of urgency about the importance of a missiology of Western culture. Even when his massive work *Transforming Mission* had just appeared, he himself recognized already that "he had not yet truly engaged the challenge of modern culture to the gospel. And he sensed this to be a priority concern for our day."[29] He "felt a moral obligation to turn his attention to this theme" and so wrote an essay for a conference in early 1992. It appeared as a short book subtitled *Toward a Missiology of Western Culture*, published posthumously in 1995.[30]

As the first item on the agenda of a missiology of Western culture, Bosch addresses the importance of a missionary theology and ecclesiology. He affirms that "mission refers to a permanent and intrinsic dimension of the church's

27. There are other authors worthy of mention: Charles Van Engen, *God's Missionary People: Rethinking the Purpose of Local Church* (Grand Rapids: Baker, 1991); Stanley Hauerwas and William Willimon, *Resident Aliens: A Provocative Christian Assessment of Culture and Ministry for People Who Know That Something Is Wrong* (Nashville: Abingdon, 1989).

28. David J. Bosch, *Transforming Mission: Paradigm Shifts in Theology of Mission* (Maryknoll, NY: Orbis Books, 1991), 368–93.

29. Wilbert R. Shenk, foreword to *Believing in the Future: Toward a Missiology of Western Culture*, by David J. Bosch (Valley Forge, PA: Trinity Press International, 1995), ix.

30. Bosch's *Transforming Mission* appeared in 1991. He wrote *Believing in the Future* on a missiology of Western culture for a meeting in January 1992. He was tragically killed in a car accident in April 1992.

life." But in the West, in contrast to the church in the Southern Hemisphere, and because of the symbiosis between church and society, the church has lost its missionary identity. It has become a "cultic community" that is primarily concerned with "individual salvation" and "pastoral care." Mission, then, is not part of the "essence of the church" but "remains a contingent activity." Bosch refers to Vatican II's statement that the church "is missionary by its very nature," to Barth's contention that the "church's mission is not secondary to its being" but that the "church exists in being sent and in building itself up for its mission," and finally to Brunner's famous adage that the "church exists by mission, just as fire exists by burning." Then he says, "Unless the church of the West begins to understand this, . . . we will not achieve more than merely patch up the church."[31]

Shenk has written prolifically on the issue of the church's mission in Western culture. He has also directed study groups that grappled with different aspects of this mission and has initiated a project with Trinity Press International to publish a series of books that address the issue. In all this, Shenk is passionate about the need to recover the missionary nature of the church. We can focus on his important book *Write the Vision* to hear the heartbeat of his missionary ecclesiology.[32] In this short book, the goal of a missionary ecclesiology is at the heart of his call for a renewal of the church in Western culture. He is rightly concerned that the church has been part of Western culture for a millennium and a half, and thus has taken its identity from its sociohistorical context rather than from God's covenant call on its life. In so doing, it has lost its distinctive missionary vocation.

The "church lives from the consciousness of its fundamental identity." This identity and consciousness should consist of "two missional aspects: the inward and the outward." The "inward mission consciousness" of the church is a deep awareness that its "fundamental purpose is mission." To gain this awareness it must recover three things: First, it must recover the Great Commission as a *"foundational ecclesiological statement"* that joins the church with its apostolic nature. Second, it must recover the normative twofold model of mission in Acts, consisting of the organic and sending mode, in which the organic mode—the mode that depicts the church as living out its missionary identity at home as a witness to God's kingdom—is "at the heart of the disciple community's life."[33] Third, it must recover an understanding of the church within the context of the kingdom of God to which it witnesses.

31. Bosch, *Believing in the Future*, 28–32.
32. Wilbert Shenk, *Write the Vision: The Church Renewed* (Valley Forge, PA: Trinity Press International, 1995).
33. Shenk, *Write the Vision*, 86–92.

There must also be an "outward mission consciousness" in which the church "adopts a missionary perspective toward their culture" that "requires assuming a countercultural stance" and a "self-conscious standing against the mainstream."[34] This last point is important: there are two sides to a missionary church—the inward and the outward. The inward side means that a missionary church must understand its identity in terms of being a distinctive people for the sake of the world and must organize its life accordingly. The outward side means that a missionary church must understand the idolatry of its culture and must stand against it in a countercultural posture.

Following Newbigin, Bosch, and Shenk in the quest for a missionary encounter with Western culture is the Gospel and Our Culture Network (GOCN). Formed in the 1990s to perpetuate Newbigin's vision in North America, this movement too wants to recover a missionary church. The GOCN is a movement made up of theological educators, pastors, denominational administrators, and congregational leaders from a variety of confessional traditions (but primarily mainline churches) devoted to the task of fostering a missionary encounter with North American culture. The movement is generated by both cultural and ecclesiastical changes. Culturally, rapid changes are taking place in North America as it shifts from a modern to a postmodern society. Ecclesiastically, the church finds itself in a new situation, dislocated from its former place of importance. Against this background, members of the GOCN ask the following question: What does it mean for a church increasingly on the margins of North American culture to encounter its culture in a missionary way?

The work of the GOCN is three-pronged. The first prong is social and cultural analysis: What are the foundations and societal practices of North American culture? The second is biblical and theological reflection: What is the gospel to which the church is called to bear witness? The third is ecclesiological and missional clarity: What kind of church is needed to present a faithful and relevant witness of the gospel to North American culture?

The missionary ecclesiology that developed from 1938 to 1952 and was then blown off course in the secular decades was reintroduced into the North American scene by Newbigin, Bosch, and Shenk and was then taken up and popularized by the labors of the GOCN. It was the writing of a book on missional church by some leaders of the GOCN that brought the missional church discussion into the mainstream of North American church life.

Two leaders call for our attention in this book: Darrell Guder and George Hunsberger. These are the two men who best understood Newbigin and the

34. Shenk, *Write the Vision*, 93–95.

background of twentieth-century missionary history. It was especially through their labors in the GOCN that Newbigin was reintroduced into the North American context.

The Publication of *Missional Church*

The discussion of a missionary church (now re-termed *missional* church) was resumed in earnest with the publication of the book *Missional Church*.[35] Following the publication of this book, the notion of a "missional church" captured the imagination of Christians in many traditions. The market has been inundated by a steady flow of books on the topic since that time.

There are two narratives of which the authors see themselves a part. The first is the one we have been telling: the missionary ecclesiology that developed in the early twentieth century, culminating in Willingen and expressed by Newbigin, but which had been blown off course by the secular winds of the 1960s. *Missional Church* returned to this early missionary ecclesiology and to the task that had been abandoned: discovering structures for the missionary congregation. However, this marked not simply a return to Willingen but a contextual updating of missional church for the North American setting in the late twentieth century.

A second historical narrative important for understanding the GOCN is the rise and fall of Christendom. Here the authors grasped another important element in Newbigin's missionary ecclesiology but appropriated it differently. This ultimately led to different emphases. Below we briefly sketch the narrative the authors worked with and quickly note the differences between Newbigin and *Missional Church*.

Contemporary thinking about the church and its current structures has been shaped by Christendom. The church of Christendom was molded by changes that took place in the fourth century when Constantine became a Christian and legalized the Christian faith, and when Theodosius made Christianity the religion of the Roman Empire. The church moved from a marginal position to a dominant one in society; it changed from being socially, politically, and intellectually peripheral to being in a position of power and superiority, from being economically weak and poor to being in a position of immense wealth, from being an oppressed minority to being the oppressive majority, from being a *religio illicita* to becoming the only religion of the empire, and from being a group of resident aliens in a pagan environment to being

---

35. Darrell L. Guder, ed., *Missional Church: A Vision for the Sending of the Church in North America* (Grand Rapids: Eerdmans, 1998).

an established church in a professedly Christian state. This could not help but have a dramatic impact on the church's structures and self-understanding. Under the Christendom *symphonia* of church and state, the church lost its sense of being a distinct community that embodied an alternative story. The prophetic-critical dimension of the church's relation to its culture diminished. The church became part of the constellation of powers within the Christian state, taking its place alongside the political, economic, military, social, and intellectual powers.

Shenk tells the same story. Christendom has been the prevailing model of church since the fourth century. When Christianity became the religion of the state, "it took its place alongside of the other powers controlling society but was thus itself redefined by its new role." As a result of its new role as one more power in this religio-political synthesis, the established church "surrendered the vital critical relationship to its culture that is indispensable to a sense of mission." Thus the "Christendom model of church may be characterized as *a church without mission.*"[36]

The writers of *Missional Church* argue along similar lines. The term *Christendom* refers to "an official ecclesiastical status through legal establishment" that has been characteristic of European churches for centuries. But today various historical factors have converged to break down this historical Christendom, and now the church no longer holds an established place. However, many assumptions about the church and mission that were forged during the era of historical Christendom continue to shape the church's life in the present. The Christendom that is present in North America is not "official" but "functional." It is synonymous with a "Christian culture" or a "churched culture," where the church exists in a culture that has the deep imprint of the Christian faith.[37]

The problem with the post-Christendom church is that it continues to maintain many of the characteristics and attitudes of the Christendom church but at the same time has lost its place of power within culture. *Missional Church* can be understood as an attempt to reenvision ecclesiology in the context of this new post-Christendom situation. And this "Christendom narrative" of *Missional Church* has played an important role in the development of missionary church discussion in the twenty-first century.

The centering metaphor for *Missional Church* is that of an alternative or contrast community. The authors see at least three problems that eclipse the missional nature of the church in North America. First, there is an individualistic notion of mission that diminishes both the importance of the ecclesial

36. Shenk, *Write the Vision*, 33–35 (emphasis in the original).
37. Guder, *Missional Church*, 48.

community and its mission as a people called out and sent to bear witness to the good news. Second, the North American church is in an advanced state of syncretism, dreadfully accommodated to the powers of Western culture. This requires a renewed emphasis on the countercultural side of the gospel. Third, the authors attribute the sad state of the church to its Christendom heritage, wherein a "functional Christendom" still prevails.

Over against these three problems, the book offers a threefold antidote. Against individualism, there is a stress on the communal dimensions of the missionary witness of the church. Against the accommodation of the faith to the cultural powers, the prophetic-critical side of the church's relation to culture is emphasized. Finally, an anti-Christendom thrust seeks to recover the church as a distinctive community that lives in a different story than that of the surrounding culture.

These emphases are timely even now, almost two decades later. Newbigin would have affirmed each of these points. This is not surprising, of course, since *Missional Church* is self-consciously intended to carry forward Newbigin's legacy.

Yet it seems that a neo-Anabaptist orientation to the book omits other aspects of a missional ecclesiology that were also present in Newbigin. In fact, the four theologians invited to discuss the book with the team of authors were all committed to an Anabaptist ecclesiology.[38] We deeply appreciate the role of the Anabaptist voice in recovering a missionary ecclesiology, especially that of theologically robust writers such as Wilbert Shenk. However, in light of this theological orientation, especially in the critical chapter on the relationship of the church to culture,[39] important aspects of Newbigin's missionary ecclesiology were eclipsed. This would have implications for the conversations about a missionary church in the following decades.

We can make this clear by reference to David Bosch's taxonomy of Christian positions on the church and its relationship to its cultural and political context.[40] Bosch distinguishes five traditions: Constantinian, Pietist, Reformist, Liberationist, and Anabaptist.[41] According to Bosch, the Anabaptist model emphasizes that "the primary task of the church is simply to *be* the church,

---

38. Guder, *Missional Church*, 8.
39. "Missional Witness: The Church as Apostle to the World," chap. 5 in Guder, *Missional Church*.
40. The dominance of a more popular neo-Anabaptist influence on the missional church movement may also be attributed to Bosch, who himself "changed his mind" and moved toward this tradition. See David J. Bosch, "How My Mind Has Changed: Mission and the Alternative Community," in *Journal of Theology for Southern Africa* 41 (December 1982): 6–10.
41. David J. Bosch, "God's Reign and the Rulers of This World: Missiological Reflections on Church-State Relationships," in *The Good News of the Kingdom: Mission Theology in the*

the *true* community of committed believers which, by its very existence and example, becomes a challenge to society and state." It exists "as a kind of antibody in society, in that it lives a life of radical discipleship as an 'alternative community.'"[42] This is, indeed, the thrust of *Missional Church*.

This is fully in line with Newbigin, as far as it goes. But it leaves important areas of his missionary ecclesiology untouched. This can be seen by reconsidering the three emphases above. Newbigin indeed affirmed the communal dimension of the missionary witness of the church. However, he also maintained throughout his life that the "primary witness to the sovereignty of Christ must be given, and can only be given, in the ordinary secular work of lay men and women in business, in politics, in professional work, as farmer, factory worker, and so on."[43] This is the case because the "enormous preponderance of the Church's witness is the witness of its thousands of members who work in the field, home, office, mill or law court."[44] The church spends the majority of its life in its scattered existence. How does it live as the new humanity in the public square?

Newbigin did accentuate the critical side of the church's relationship to culture. So much so, in fact, that the Roman Catholic scholar Stephen Bevans interprets Newbigin's model of contextualization as "countercultural" and the Dutch neo-Calvinist philosopher Sander Griffioen accuses Newbigin of minimizing the positive side of cultural development.[45] Yet Newbigin also believed that, as part of its mission to the world, the church should live at home in culture and participate in the unfolding of culture as believers live in public life under the lordship of Christ.[46] The people of God must participate in the development of culture while standing against its idolatrous direction.

Third Millennium, ed. Charles Van Engen, Dean S. Gilliland, and Paul Pierson (Maryknoll, NY: Orbis Books, 1993), 89–95.

42. Bosch, "God's Reign," 92.

43. Lesslie Newbigin, "The Work of the Holy Spirit in the Life of the Asian Churches," in *A Decisive Hour for the Christian World Mission*, ed. Norman Goodall et al. (London: SCM, 1960), 28.

44. Lesslie Newbigin, "Our Task Today" (unpublished charge given to the fourth meeting of the diocesan council, Tirumangalam, India, December 18–20, 1951), 6.

45. Stephen Bevans, *Models of Contextual Theology*, rev. and exp. ed. (Maryknoll, NY: Orbis Books, 2002), 117–38; Sander Griffioen, "Newbigin's Philosophy of Culture," *Trinity Journal for Theology and Ministry: The Gospel in the Public Square; Essays by and in Honor of Lesslie Newbigin*, 4, no. 2 (2010): 99–111. It is significant that it is these two traditions— Roman Catholicism and Dutch neo-Calvinism—that have rich doctrines of creation, including the creation mandate.

46. See Michael W. Goheen, "Is Lesslie Newbigin's Model of Contextualization Anticultural?," *Mission Studies* 19, no. 2 (October 2002): 136–58.

Newbigin was a fierce critic of the distortions of Christendom and their negative impact on the church. At the same time, he also recognized the positive contribution that Christendom had made to Western culture. Christendom was the "first great attempt to translate the universal claim of Christ into political terms."[47] In the process, "the gospel was wrought into the very stuff of [Western Europe's] social and personal life,"[48] and we "still live largely on the spiritual capital it generated."[49] The problem with Christendom is not that the church took cultural power—that was right and proper. The problem occurs when it loses its critical-prophetical stance to its idolatry. Christendom is a different missionary setting from the ancient church. Both have possibilities and dangers. The problem in Christendom is that the church failed to challenge the idolatries of its culture when it had power.

The different emphases of *Missional Church* in relation to Newbigin's post-Willingen missionary ecclesiology had a certain influence in setting the course for the missionary church discussion. There are important omissions in *Missional Church*, perhaps partly because it had to accommodate different theological standpoints as a multiauthored work. Nevertheless, it is a book rich with theological and ecclesial insight in its exposition of the concept of the missionary church. The book picked up Newbigin's rich missionary ecclesiology and returned the North American church to this conversation.

The Missional Church Conversation Today

Subsequent to the publication of *Missional Church*, the GOCN sponsored conferences and continued to publish books to diffuse its missional church vision.[50] A number of its early leaders continued to publish on the subject; of these, Guder and Hunsberger most consistently represented the Newbigin legacy.[51] The GOCN with its conferences and publications wanted to start a

47. Lesslie Newbigin, *Sign of the Kingdom* (Grand Rapids: Eerdmans, 1980), 47.
48. Lesslie Newbigin, *The Household of God: Lectures on the Nature of the Church* (New York: Friendship Press, 1953), 1.
49. Lesslie Newbigin, *Priorities for a New Decade* (Birmingham, UK: National Student Christian Press and Resource Centre, 1980), 6.
50. George R. Hunsberger, ed., *The Church between Gospel and Culture: The Emerging Mission in North America* (Grand Rapids: Eerdmans, 1996); Craig Van Gelder, ed., *Confident Witness—Changing World: Rediscovering the Gospel in North America* (Grand Rapids: Eerdmans, 1999); James V. Brownson et al., eds., *Stormfront: The Good News of God* (Grand Rapids: Eerdmans, 2003); Lois Y. Barrett, ed., *Treasure in Clay Jars: Patterns in Missional Faithfulness* (Grand Rapids: Eerdmans, 2004).
51. Darrell L. Guder, *The Continuing Conversion of the Church* (Grand Rapids: Eerdmans, 2000); Guder, *Called to Witness: Doing Missional Theology* (Grand Rapids: Eerdmans, 2015);

conversation about Newbigin's missionary ecclesiology. This goal has been admirably successful. The next step to missionary congregations had been hindered by the secular decades. The GOCN's hope was to get the train of a missional church back on the track in the North American setting, moving toward missionary structures.

The language of missional church pervades most discussions of ecclesiology today in North America. There has been a flood of literature using various adjectives to describe church, all of which are attempting to work out what it means to be a faithful missionary church today. Normally the acknowledged source and authority of much of this ecclesiology is Newbigin. In what follows in this book, we intend to survey some of this literature in light of Newbigin's missionary ecclesiology.

The remainder of this book unfolds by setting the missional, emergent, and center church conversations in dialogue with Newbigin's missionary ecclesiology, both by highlighting the positive developments and by retrieving Newbigin's voice as it critiques and enriches the discussion today.

This is primarily a work of historical theology. We do not believe that Newbigin's missionary ecclesiology is normative, nor do we believe he has spoken the final word. That place must be reserved for Scripture. However, Newbigin's voice is exceedingly important. His experience is unparalleled, his theological mind unusually sharp and deeply formed by the gospel. We believe that some of the important emphases in Newbigin's missionary ecclesiology do not feature prominently in today's discussion. Perhaps, among other reasons, it is because he was such a prolific author and only his more recent books are well known. Moreover, his most important books are difficult and do not yield their deep wisdom to single readings. Or maybe the early twentieth-century discussion on mission and church that set the context for Newbigin's work is not familiar. In any case, we hope to set today's ecclesiological discussion in dialogue with the man whom many would acknowledge as *the* significant figure in the development of a missionary ecclesiology.

Theologian Hendrikus Berkhof says that the church cannot be rightly understood apart from its missionary or apostolary nature—its orientation to the world. He says that the "necessity of re-studying ecclesiology, in fact all of theology, from the standpoint of the relationship to the world has (only) slowly begun to take hold, mainly through the unceasing harping on it by nontheologian H. Kraemer."[52] He wrote this in the early 1970s. Today we can

---

George R. Hunsberger, *The Story That Chooses Us: A Tapestry of Missional Vision* (Grand Rapids: Eerdmans, 2015).

52. Hendrikus Berkhof, *Christian Faith: An Introduction to the Study of the Faith*, trans. Sierd Woudstra (Grand Rapids: Eerdmans, 1979), 411.

update that comment in two ways: it has taken hold with a vengeance, and a more influential figure than even Kraemer is his disciple Lesslie Newbigin. Our hope is that the rich resources Newbigin left for the task of pursuing a missionary ecclesiology will not be lost among the many voices clamoring for the missionary renewal of the church in the twenty-first century.

PART 2

The Missional Church Conversation

6

Theological Foundations

The book *Missional Church*[1] introduced decades of rich theological reflection on the missionary church to a new generation of leaders in North America. The book was a product of the Gospel and Our Culture Network, which formed to pursue in the North American context questions raised by Lesslie Newbigin concerning the missionary nature of the church in the West.

The starting point for the book *Missional Church* was a "missiological consensus" that had long been forming during the twentieth century. Newbigin was a major participant in this long historical conversation, and on his return to Britain from India he worked out that missiological consensus in the context of Western culture. It was this consensus, with a focus on Western culture, that was mediated by Newbigin to the authors of *Missional Church*. Their purpose was to carry forward Newbigin's agenda into North America.

There are three major points of consensus. The first is the mission of the triune God. Mission in the preceding three centuries had been defined as an activity of the church that consisted of taking the gospel from Western nations to the rest of the world. In the new consensus, the starting point for mission is no longer the church but God's purpose to restore and heal the creation. God is a "missionary God"[2] whose redemptive work in the biblical story is defined by sending: the Father sends the Son, and the Father and the Son send the Spirit.

1. Darrell L. Guder, ed., *Missional Church: A Vision for the Sending of the Church in North America* (Grand Rapids: Eerdmans, 1998).
2. Newbigin does not use this terminology.

The second point of consensus is the missionary nature of the church. The church is taken up in the sending work on God's behalf and is defined as a sent people. "As the Father has sent me, I am sending you" (John 20:21). The church is an instrument of God's mission that is blessed to be a blessing to the nations. Thus the mission of the church derives from the nature and sending work of God.

The third point of consensus is that this understanding of mission—the *missio Dei* and the missionary nature of the church—must be worked out in the context of Western culture. The churches in Western culture are hobbled by the legacy of Christendom, which reduces mission to another activity of the church: specifically evangelism as member recruitment, church planting in home mission, and cross-cultural missionary work. The church in North America must be freed from this Christendom legacy and must learn to be a missionary people amid its own culture.

The goal in publishing *Missional Church* was to ignite a conversation in North America that would wrestle with how this "missiological consensus" might work itself out in North America. The authors succeeded, and in the past twenty-five years a profuse literature has grown on the topic. In this group of three chapters, we will summarize some of the major themes in this conversation and probe how this discussion carried forth the historical trajectory of the "missiological consensus" that Newbigin forged.

Our approach will not be to offer an extended analysis of the missional church conversation (MCC). This would be impossible given the diversity and breadth of this conversation and the limited space of three short chapters. Rather, we have a threefold goal: first, to identify general trends and themes in the MCC; second, to connect these themes historically to Newbigin and the twentieth-century conversation and see how they have developed; and, finally, to probe where Newbigin's missionary ecclesiology might critique and enrich the current conversation. We write for pastors and practitioners who need to understand the important issues regarding what it means to be a missionary congregation.

In these three chapters, we take the three points of the missiological consensus as our structure: the theological basis for the missionary church, the missionary congregation, and Western culture as a mission field.

A Theological Basis for the Missionary Church Today

For all who have read even portions of the material on mission by missiologists and theologians in the middle decades of the twentieth century, it is evident that the conversation at that time was generally more focused on theological foundations than is the current MCC. That is not to say that there is little theological reflection today—there is—but it is to say that the conversation today has shifted more to working out the implications of this theology of the missionary church for the local congregation.

Perhaps this is because of where *Missional Church* picked up the historical conversation. During the period of the 1930s–1950s, there was a search for a theological framework to pull together the missiological, biblical, and theological insights of the twentieth century into a new paradigm of mission. With that task complete and a consensus established, it was clear to many at the time that the next task was to work this out in the local congregation. The conversation beginning in the 1960s shifted to the local congregation and structures that would enable it to carry out its task. But this next step was never realized because a new secular paradigm of mission emerged that marginalized the local congregation.

The intention of the authors of *Missional Church*, or at least of some among them, was to pick up the conversation where it had left off and recontextualize it in the North American setting. It may be that in the current MCC there is an assumption that this theological consensus is sufficient and now the task is to get on with the work of figuring out what it looks like concretely in the local congregation. Perhaps, for others, it may be the result of North American pragmatism. For some, the move to implement the insights of *Missional Church* in the local congregation is born out of a desire for ready-made formulas and models that bring rapid success—understood in terms of growth and multiplication in the face of increasing decline.

Whatever the reasons, what we find generally in the missional church literature is the assumption of the theological and missiological starting points that were hammered out in the twentieth century, were summarized in Newbigin's writings, and were expressed in *Missional Church*. On the one hand, this is a positive development insofar as important theological insights are now diffused into the mainstream of this conversation, and we now see the fruit as these are implemented in the local congregation. On the other hand, sometimes the general lack of familiarity with *both* the rich twentieth-century conversations that give substance to the consensus *and* Newbigin's work has left this conversation lacking the theological and missiological depth that is important for a missionary church.

In the rest of this section of the book, we sketch the theological foundations on which the missional church movement has built its discussion. We bring Newbigin's voice into this conversation as it critiques, affirms, and enriches.

The Mission of the Triune God

The theological conviction that the church's mission must be understood in terms of participating in the mission of the triune God is now widespread across confessional and cultural boundaries. And it is no different in the MCC. This serves as a theological starting point. It is as the church participates in God's mission that it can truly become a church that is missionary by its very nature. This conviction continues to guide the discussion.

But, of course, God's mission can be a wax nose—shaped to one's preference. It can be understood in various ways—and this, in turn, will define the missionary nature of the church differently. We are interested in how the MCC has generally understood it and how this measures up to Newbigin. We will address this issue in terms of two fundamental aspects of Newbigin's understanding: his *narrative* and *Christocentric* approach to the triune mission of God.

Narrative Approach to the Triune Mission of God

We wonder whether the way David Bosch articulated the *missio Dei* has become more definitive in the MCC than Newbigin's articulation. Bosch's brief discussion speaks of God's mission in terms of a brief formula: the Father sends the Son, the Father and Son send the Spirit, and the Father and Son send the church into the world in the power of the Spirit.[3] Darrell Guder quotes Bosch's brief summary in the first chapter of *Missional Church*. But he does so only after noting that God's mission unfolds in the biblical story. While his summary of the narrative is brief, the order is significant: the formula of sending is a succinct, descriptive summary of the biblical story that employs the metaphor of "sending." The sending formula functions as a "portable narrative"[4] that bundles together many elements from the scriptural story without having to refer to the entirety of the matter. In much of the missional church literature, the sending formula articulated by Bosch is assumed but the *storied shape* that fills it with meaning is not given the same prominence.

The primary category Newbigin employs when speaking of God's mission, consistently and repeatedly, is the notion of story. Indeed, it is "virtually impossible to read anything ever written by Lesslie Newbigin without gaining

3. David J. Bosch, *Transforming Mission: Paradigm Shifts in Theology of Mission* (Maryknoll, NY: Orbis Books, 1991), 399, 547.
4. N. T. Wright, "Reading Paul, Thinking Scripture," in *Scripture's Doctrine and Theology's Bible*, ed. M. Bockmuehl and A. J. Torrance (Grand Rapids: Baker Academic, 2008), 59–71.

a sense of his feel for history, his awareness of being part of a story, indeed of being caught up in *the* story of the unfolding drama of the purposes of God."[5]

The work of Konrad Raiser, former director of the World Council of Churches, can show how important "story" is for understanding God's mission, not just in Newbigin but also in the original formulation of Willingen. Raiser labels as "Christocentric universalism" the paradigm that characterizes the critical time when the *missio Dei* paradigm was forming.[6] He rightly identifies Newbigin as a leading spokesperson. The focus of this paradigm is the universal significance of Christ—his message is true for all peoples. Therefore, the church's mission to embody and announce this message also has universal import. Since the message is true, all people must hear the good news. What is important here is that Raiser rightly recognizes the indispensability of the biblical story to this whole paradigm.

The significance of Christ's work for all people followed by the universal claim the church makes for its gospel and its mission is established in terms of redemptive history and eschatology as the "central category of thought."[7] It is this story that binds together Christ, the church, and their universality. Raiser puts it this way: "The dynamic conception of universal history as realizing God's plan of salvation is thus the decisive link in the chain holding the basic elements of the paradigm together."[8] It is this fundamental understanding of the Christian faith that shapes Newbigin's understanding of the *missio Dei*. The Bible is the true story of the world and the Father sending the Son and both sending the Spirit, and the church is part of this story and can't be rightly understood without it.

Likewise, in his important book *The Mission of God,*[9] written to summarize Willingen, Georg Vicedom says we must speak of the mission of the triune God only in terms of the redemptive-historical nature of Scripture. He writes that "the entire *Heilsgeschichte* [salvation history] exhibits itself as a history of *missio Dei.*" When discussing God's mission, "we must remain within the framework of genuine theology, which, of course, can never be a thought-system about God, but which should always and only describe the activity of God in history."[10] Thus the *missio Dei* must be expressed in terms

5. Nicholas J. Wood, *Faiths and Faithfulness: Pluralism, Dialogue, and Mission in the Work of Kenneth Cragg and Lesslie Newbigin* (Milton Keynes, UK: Paternoster, 2009), 147.

6. Konrad Raiser, *Ecumenism in Transition: A Paradigm Shift in the Ecumenical Movement* (Geneva: World Council of Churches, 1991), 36.

7. Raiser, *Ecumenism in Transition*, 45.

8. Raiser, *Ecumenism in Transition*, 45.

9. Georg F. Vicedom, *The Mission of God: An Introduction to a Theology of Mission*, trans. Gilbert A. Thiele and Dennis Hilgendorf (St. Louis: Concordia, 1965).

10. Vicedom, *Mission of God*, 9.

of the story of God's mighty acts in history for the restoration of his world. The trinitarian formula of sending is a theological suitcase that bundles together God's mighty acts in history and carries the story.

Newbigin's understanding of the core of the Christian faith is fundamentally narrative: the Bible tells the story of cosmic history, beginning in creation and ending with new creation. The Father is working out his purpose in history to restore creation, beginning with Israel. Christ comes as the fulfillment of this story and stands at its center to reveal and accomplish God's purpose.[11] The Spirit implements God's purpose in and through the church. This is the *missio Dei*.

We see this clearly in *The Gospel in a Pluralist Society*, where Newbigin begins with the biblical story, moves to Christ, and then moves on to the church's mission. We find this movement in the order of four chapters: "The Bible as Universal History," "Christ, the Clue to History," "The Logic of Mission," and "Mission: Word, Deed, and New Being." The Bible is a story of God's purpose whose overall structure gives us the origin, meaning, and end of cosmic history. In the life, death, and resurrection of Jesus, God reveals and accomplishes the ultimate goal of his purpose, which gives meaning to universal history. From the work of Christ necessarily flows the mission of the church, making known the End in life, word, and deed in the power of the Spirit. Newbigin speaks of the historical logic: mission must follow Christ. "So the logic of mission is this: the true meaning of the human story has been disclosed. Because it is the truth, it must be shared universally."[12] In this context Newbigin speaks twice of the "trinitarian model" of God's mission.[13] The mission of the triune God is one theological way of expressing the story of God's redeeming work that includes his people. When Newbigin says that "the church's mission is rooted in the triune nature of God himself," he is referring first and foremost to the narrative of God's redemptive work in Scripture.[14]

As the fundamental category of story has drifted from its central place in shaping the *missio Dei*, there have been many alternative proposals to ground the missionary nature of the church in the triune nature of God.[15] Many of

11. Lesslie Newbigin, *Proper Confidence: Faith, Doubt, and Certainty in Christian Discipleship* (Grand Rapids: Eerdmans, 1995), 88; cf. Newbigin, "Biblical Authority," Newbigin Archives, University of Birmingham (unpublished article, 1997), 2.

12. Lesslie Newbigin, *The Gospel in a Pluralist Society* (Grand Rapids: Eerdmans, 1989), 125.

13. Newbigin, *Gospel in a Pluralist Society*, 118–19, 135.

14. Lesslie Newbigin, *The Open Secret: An Introduction to the Theology of Mission*, rev. ed. (Grand Rapids: Eerdmans, 1995), 65.

15. See, e.g., Ross Hastings, *Missional God, Missional Church: Hope for Re-evangelizing the West* (Downers Grove, IL: InterVarsity, 2012); Craig Van Gelder and Dwight J. Zscheile, *The Missional Church in Perspective: Mapping Trends and Shaping the Conversation* (Grand

these gravitate toward the social nature of the Trinity. But this is to construct a different theological foundation for the missionary church and to take it in a different direction. Newbigin would no doubt agree with Anthony Thiselton, who says that the "narrative approach" to the Trinity is basic and that other models of the triune nature of God expressed in the terms *immanent*, *economic*, and *social* "constitute second-stage developments in understanding the Holy Trinity."[16]

We do not doubt that work in systematic theology on the Trinity may articulate, deepen, and enrich our understanding and may contribute to the MCC.[17] We do admit a certain unease here, because reflection on the social Trinity can quickly become disconnected from Scripture and soar into speculation to support a variety of already-existing theological and ecclesiological assumptions. In any case, the narrative approach to the Trinity is basic. The work of the triune God that unfolds historically in the biblical narrative must inform all further theological reflection on the missionary church. Apart from the story of Scripture, theological reflection on the Trinity becomes speculative and abstract and is vulnerable to being filled with content other than Scripture. Even the "trinitarian sending formula" can be filled either with the content and unity of the biblical story or with something else. Moreover, the narrative approach to the Trinity keeps the work of the Spirit tethered tightly to its Christocentric mooring, shutting down speculation about the Spirit's work in the world that ignores the historical trajectory of the story. This is why it is so important for the formation process in the local congregation to nourish God's people in the story of Scripture.

Christocentric Approach to the Triune Mission of God

The historical logic of mission is that the true meaning of cosmic history and purpose of human life has been disclosed in the life, death, resurrection, and exaltation of Jesus, and since it is universally true for all it must be made known to all. This is the starting point to understand the church's mission as part of the mission of the triune God. It is centered in Jesus Christ, who has fully revealed and accomplished God's purpose. And so he sends us: "As

---

Rapids: Baker Academic, 2011), 1–124; Van Gelder and Zscheile, *Participating in God's Mission: A Theological Missiology for the Church in America* (Grand Rapids: Eerdmans, 2018), chap. 9.

16. Anthony Thiselton, *Systematic Theology* (Grand Rapids: Eerdmans, 2015), 39.

17. There are a few places in Newbigin's work where elements of the social nature of the Trinity are present along with its implication for the church: e.g., *The Household of God: Lectures on the Nature of the Church* (New York: Friendship Press, 1954), 130; *The Welfare State: A Christian Perspective* (Oxford: Oxford Institute for Church and Society, 1985), 11. But the narrative approach is pervasive and basic.

the Father has sent me, I am sending you" (John 20:21). This expresses the vision of God's mission for many in the twentieth century and certainly for Newbigin. The text in John was one of his favorites.

This text has also captured writers in the MCC and ushered in a christological starting point for God's mission.[18] It has become the basis for an incarnational approach to mission. The focus is on the earthly ministry of Jesus as a model and pattern for our own mission. We are sent to follow Jesus in the way he carried out his kingdom mission in his life. That which characterized his mission is to characterize ours.

This has led writers to develop missional living and practices that align closely with the life of Jesus. This is especially evident in the desire to identify with the marginalized, the outsider, and the poor. This is a welcome emphasis in the missional church literature and is surely a biblical emphasis that reflects Newbigin's "mission in Christ's way" and repeated use of John 20:21. An incarnational approach to mission and church has borne much good fruit for the missionary congregation in its local place. But the question is whether this christological focus is too narrow.

Bosch points out the way that mission is shaped differently when building on various aspects of Christ's work.[19] For example, liberation theology has focused on the incarnation and solidarity with the poor; much of the Western Protestant church on the cross, stressing forgiveness and reconciliation in mission; the Eastern church on the resurrection, stressing new creation; the Calvinist tradition on the ascension and bringing the whole world under the lordship of Christ; Pentecostals and charismatics on the sending of the Spirit and his work in mission; and many evangelical groups on the second coming of Jesus and the urgency of mission. It seems inevitable that we assume some christological starting point, and it appears to be difficult to begin with a biblically integrated one.

The incarnational approach to the mission of God focuses on the life ministry of Jesus. This may be prompted by the fact that in the evangelical tradition the life of Jesus, what N. T. Wright calls the "missing middle,"[20] has been severely neglected. This is in keeping with Bosch's comment that Protestant churches have an underdeveloped understanding of the incarnation and that this has adversely affected their view of mission.[21] Moreover, an

18. See, e.g., Alan Hirsch, *The Forgotten Ways: Reactivating the Missional Church* (Grand Rapids: Brazos, 2006), 129–32.
19. Bosch, *Transforming Mission*, 524–30.
20. N. T. Wright, *How God Became King: The Forgotten Story of the Gospels* (San Francisco: HarperOne, 2012), 3–24.
21. Bosch, *Transforming Mission*, 524.

incarnational starting point enables these authors to stress the importance of solidarity with the local community—something that is desperately needed in the Western church. These are all important reasons for starting with the incarnation as one expounds the mission of God.

Newbigin speaks of mission in Christ's way[22] and regularly turns to John 20:21. Newbigin will speak of the "total fact of Christ" or the "total event of Christ" or the "Christ-event" to describe the way God has revealed and accomplished his purpose in the *entirety* of Jesus's person and work.[23] The whole of his life and ministry is one integrated event of salvation in which each individual historical moment—incarnation, life, death, resurrection, ascension, Pentecost, return—has its necessary and meaningful place. It is precisely in the total fact of Christ and in each historical moment that the kingdom comes.

If we were to trace Newbigin's development, we would see him accentuate different aspects of Christ's work at different times for contextual reasons. As the MCC does, he often grounds mission in the various aspects of the historical life of Jesus. Most often he stresses the cross and resurrection as the hinge of universal history in his christological starting point for the church's mission. In any case, we should aim for what he attempted: a full-orbed and integrated biblical Christology that offers a rich foundation for the mission of the church. Our starting point in Jesus will shape our view of mission. And we need a comprehensive and integral Christology at the heart of our understanding of God's mission.[24]

The Missionary Nature of the Church

The Reunion of Church and Mission

Newbigin laments the separation of mission and church—"which God has joined together"—as "one of the great calamities of missionary history," and therefore urges "the healing of this division [as] one of the great tasks of our time."[25] In the nineteenth and early twentieth centuries, mission had

22. Lesslie Newbigin, *Mission in Christ's Way* (Geneva: World Council of Churches, 1987).

23. Lesslie Newbigin, *A Faith for This One World* (London: SCM, 1961), 59, 62; Newbigin, "Biblical Authority," 2.

24. A good example of this kind of full Christology in a work that attends to incarnation as the basis for mission is Darrell L. Guder, *The Continuing Conversion of the Church* (Grand Rapids: Eerdmans, 2000), 28–48, 191–92.

25. Lesslie Newbigin, *One Body, One Gospel, One World: The Christian Mission Today* (London: International Missionary Council, 1958), 26.

been reduced to cross-cultural activity carried out by Western missionary societies in the non-Western parts of the world. The church supported that missionary activity with funds and personnel, and perhaps also by circulating prayer letters, praying, hosting missionaries on furlough, and trying to remain excited by their stories and slides. But the real role of the church was reduced to the pastoral nurture of believers. This distorted both mission and the church. The only way to recover a missionary church is to heal the division of mission and church and to see that mission belongs to the very nature of the church. We traced this healing historically through the twentieth century. This theological insight has become a standard part of the MCC. The very term *missional church*, with *missional* as an adjective to define the nature of the church, gives expression to the healing of this division.

The union of mission and church has nurtured rich fruit in the MCC. There is a heightened awareness that the church does not exist for itself but for the sake of its neighborhood and for the world. This has led to an incarnational witness that is much more deeply involved in meeting the needs of the neighborhood. Selfish introversion and preoccupation with the maintenance of the church is deplored. There are many important conversations that have emerged concerning what kind of congregational and leadership structures would facilitate the vocation of the church in the world. There is fruitful reflection on how to engage our neighbors with the gospel in a more organic and contextual evangelism. There is renewed dialogue about practices and rhythms that would equip and enable God's people to be involved with their unbelieving neighbors. We nurture a consciousness that we are all "missionaries" on our own "mission field." All this, which we will discuss later, is the good fruit of the union of church and mission.

With the reunion of church and mission, the questions that arose historically and remain today are concerned with the nature of mission and of the church. When we say *missionary church*, what does the adjective mean and what does the noun describe?

What Is Mission?

What does *mission* mean when it defines the nature of the church? In the MCC, much emphasis is put on the word *sent*—mission means that the church is a sent body. This is often set over against the attractional church of Christendom that multiplies programs and invites people into its institutional life. *Mission* describes the church as a centrifugal body rather than a centripetal one. All of this is helpful. But the question is, sent to . . . what?

Word and Deed

Much missional church literature has emphasized a loving and incarnational presence that leads to evangelism and meeting needs in deeds of mercy.[26] This is noteworthy, because the MCC that we are discussing has been part of the evangelical tradition. Typically, evangelicals have pitted word against deed, evangelism against works of justice and mercy. It is evangelistic words that proclaim the gospel that constitutes mission. Most of the MCC rejects this false dichotomy.

This is based on the recovery of two strains of biblical teaching. Many—but not all—in the MCC have recovered a more biblical view of salvation. Salvation is understood more holistically in terms of the restoration of the whole of human life. It is no longer considered to be an escape from the world to heaven but the restoration of the world. Salvation is not reduced to the "soul" but encompasses the whole of bodily life.

This stands in contrast to the way salvation has traditionally been understood in the evangelical church. It was drastically reduced to the future of the individual (soul?) in an otherworldly heaven. Often the benefits of the gospel are limited to forgiveness of sins and justification by faith, which gets us into heaven. The goal is not the healing of this creation but getting right with God and escaping from the world to where he is. And this impairs mission: mission becomes an evangelistic strategy that saves individuals for heaven. However, if God's salvation reaches the whole person, then deeds of mercy must demonstrate that salvation in places where sin's effects have brought misery. There can be no dichotomy.

The second strand of biblical teaching that heals this fissure is the recovery of the life ministry of Jesus. Sadly, the importance of the life of Jesus has been marginalized in much evangelical theology of the past. Christology has often been reduced to the cross—and even further, to what the cross accomplishes for the individual. Or it has been reduced to Christ's divine-human nature. The recovery of the neglected life of Jesus as he makes known the kingdom allows the MCC to set aside the false dichotomy of word and deed. If we follow in the way of Jesus, his mission was one of both word and deed. His deeds authenticated his words, and his words explained his deeds. The two went together to make known the good news of the kingdom. An incarnational approach does not rend asunder what Jesus has put together.[27]

26. See, e.g., Michael Frost and Alan Hirsch, *The Shaping of Things to Come: Innovation and Mission for the 21st-Century Church* (Peabody, MA: Hendrickson, 2003); Hugh Halter and Matt Smay, *The Tangible Kingdom: Creating Incarnational Community* (San Francisco: Jossey-Bass, 2008).

27. Hirsch, *Forgotten Ways*; Michael Frost, *Incarnate: The Body of Christ in an Age of Disengagement* (Downers Grove, IL: InterVarsity, 2014); Hugh Halter, *Flesh: Bringing the Incarnation Down to Earth* (Colorado Springs: David C. Cook, 2014).

To be sure, the polarity between word and deed has been healing since the time of the Lausanne Movement in the 1970s, but this process is far from complete. Indeed, the dichotomy remains strong in evangelical churches. Mission continues to be ravaged by a false polarity between evangelistic words and deeds of mercy and justice. Such a dichotomy cannot stand when we take seriously a biblical view of salvation and the kingdom mission of Jesus. The MCC contributes to the healing of this false duality.

So Much More Than Word and Deed

Newbigin roundly rejected any division between word and deed. In fact, he saved some of his strongest condemnation for those who perpetuated it. He believed that this dichotomy was "profoundly weakening the Church's witness."[28] But his understanding of mission made, so to speak, three further "moves" toward a deeper, broader, and more integrated view of mission. The question here is whether and to what degree the MCC has followed him down this path.

The first move is *to root both word and deed in the deeper reality of new being.*[29] For Newbigin, the primary mission of the people of God throughout the entire biblical story is to live as the new humanity amidst the nations where humanity has been defaced by idolatry. With the coming of Jesus and the Spirit there is a new reality, a new power to restore the people of God to their true and full humanity. Words and deeds flow from this deeper reality. To heal the dispute between word and deed, both evangelicals and ecumenicals need to recover the prior reality of a new power brought by Christ and the Spirit to bring a foretaste of the kingdom. By this renewing power, the community will challenge by life, word, and deed the ruling idolatrous powers of the culture. Thus there will be a missionary encounter between this comprehensive renewing power and the idolatrous power at work in culture.

The second move is *to recognize that this new being is characteristic of the church as both a gathered and a scattered community.* It is the "total life of the community" that includes the way the church as the new humanity both together and as a scattered community throughout the week acts "responsibly as believers in the course of their secular duties as citizens."[30] The church is the new humanity that has been restored to its creational role, which Adamic humanity forfeited. Thus the whole of their cultural life as the image

---

28. Newbigin, *Gospel in a Pluralist Society*, 136.
29. Newbigin, *Gospel in a Pluralist Society*, 128–40.
30. Newbigin, *Gospel in a Pluralist Society*, 137–39.

of God—which is all of it!—is being restored. Mission is living out that new humanity together and amid the public life of culture. There is a dimension of mission in every part of life, for all of it bears witness to the healing of human life. This has huge implications for the discipleship ministry of the local congregation. Rarely is the stress put on forming men and women for the places where they spend most of their time!

The third move is to see the church's mission as *to make known the good news that Jesus is restoring humanity to the ends of the earth*. Mission is the witness of a local congregation in its place in the whole of its gathered and scattered life, in its deeds of justice and mercy, and in its words that proclaim the gospel. However, each local congregation must take responsibility for the task of making sure there are communities like this in every part of the world. Everyone must be able to see and hear the good news that radiates from these communities. And if there is no community, then one must be planted. So people must continue to be sent, both locally and globally.

Two Important Distinctions

Newbigin made this holistic and robust understanding of mission known with two important distinctions formulated during the 1960s, when *mission* was broadening out to describe the whole of the church's life. On the one hand, he affirmed as biblical the growing breadth of mission that defined the whole gathered and scattered life of the church as mission. On the other hand, he was concerned that the word could describe everything and therefore nothing, and that the intentional activities of outreach, whether at home or abroad, that had traditionally been characterized as *mission* would be lost.

He made two distinctions to affirm both a broadening of mission and the intentional activities. The first is between missionary *dimension* and missionary *intention*. Since the church is the new humankind summoned to bear witness to the gospel and the renewing work of God in all of life, the whole life of the church has a missionary dimension. Marriage and family, work and worship, political involvement and use of technology, economic life and education, sports and art—there is a missionary dimension in all of these aspects of life as we witness to the lordship of Christ. But while the whole life of the church has a missionary *dimension*, not all of it has mission as its primary *intention*.[31] There are intentional activities to invite people to follow Jesus, such as evangelism and church planting, both cross-culturally and at home, that are essential to the mission of the church.

31. Newbigin, *One Body, One Gospel, One World*, 21.

He made a further distinction between *mission* and *missions*. The cross-cultural missionary movement of the previous centuries was threatened by a broader view that stressed mission in one's own context. It was also threatened by a bad conscience because of the association of cross-cultural missions with oppressive colonialism. Newbigin responded by identifying the specifically missionary task of the church in places where there was no witness. While *mission* is the whole vocation of the church for which God has sent the church into the world, *missions* (with an *s*) establishes a witnessing presence in places and for peoples of the world where there is none, with the goal of planting missionary congregations to continue the witness. Each local congregation has a responsibility, not only to its own neighborhood but also to be involved in the global missionary task of the church taking the gospel to the ends of the earth. While missions needs to shed its colonial cloak and be rethought, the task remains.

One evident casualty in the MCC is missions. Missions was not highlighted in *Missional Church*, since that book focused on the North American context. Yet it was a significant omission: the ensuing conversation has neglected missions, and—even worse—sometimes *missional* has been set over against *missions*.[32]

The question is whether the MCC reflects Newbigin's theologically rich view of mission. His writings repeatedly elaborate at least five aspects of witness: (1) new being and communal life; (2) vocation of believers in public life; (3) deeds of justice, peace, and mercy; (4) evangelism; and (5) missions.[33] The primary mission of the church is its new being—to be and live out the distinctive life of the new humanity in a world that serves other gods. This distinctive life shaped by the gospel will be embodied in the communal as well as in the scattered life of the church, particularly in the vocations of believers in the public life of culture. From this new being flow deeds of justice, mercy, and peace that witness to the coming kingdom and evangelistic words that explain the new being and invite others to follow Christ and come join the new humanity. And finally, communities that witness to the coming kingdom in life, deeds, and words must be established in every part of the world so that all may see, hear, and believe.

Perhaps a touchstone for whether our vision is undergirded by a robust theological foundation of the missionary church may be the degree to which it can find an organic place for each of these aspects of mission in its missional ecclesiology.

32. Michael W. Goheen, *The Church and Its Vocation: Lesslie Newbigin's Missionary Ecclesiology* (Grand Rapids: Baker Academic, 2018), 97–101.
33. See Goheen, *Church and Its Vocation*, 78–101.

What Is the Church?

Newbigin asks, "Is it not an illusion that constantly fogs our thinking about the Church that we think of it as something which exists manifestly on Sunday, is in a kind of state of suspended animation from Monday to Saturday?" He goes on to express his ecclesiological conviction: "The truth of course is that the Church exists in its prime reality from Monday to Saturday, in all its members, dispersed throughout the fields and homes and offices and factories, bearing the royal priesthood of Christ into every corner of His world. On the Lord's day it is withdrawn into itself to renew its being in the Lord Himself."[34] When he asks whether it is an illusion to think of the church as existing only on Sunday, he expresses something that is, sadly, quite characteristic of much evangelical Christianity. The church is a private religious institution gathered on Sunday for worship, instruction, fellowship, and prayer. *Church* defines a voluntary organization that carries out "religious" activities for the benefit of its members. Of course, this is a caricature of the church in Scripture. Yet—sadly—this very caricature defines and shapes much of the work of pastors and leaders.

While the language of gathered and scattered is not widely employed,[35] there is in the MCC an understanding of the church that rejects a reduction of the church to an institution or a gathered community. The church is the church *both* as it is involved in the life of its neighborhood *and* as it gathers for fellowship, worship, teaching, and prayer. For many in the MCC, church is no longer bound by the limits of an institution, a gathered community, or its rites and practices.

This leads missional church writers to urge churches to live in growing solidarity with their communities. Moreover, they rightly recognize the danger that often threatens the life of believers of becoming entangled in the ever-expanding programs and ministries of the institutional church, which is detrimental to mission because it dominates the time of believers. They urge a "re-entry" of the church into the life of its community. They invite the church to rethink budgets, congregational structures, and leadership structures that do not cater to the needs of church members but are oriented outward to the community. They encourage churches to nurture creative reflection on various practices and rhythms that bring the people of God into intimate relational

---

34. Lesslie Newbigin, "Bible Studies: Four Talks on 1 Peter," in *We Were Brought Together*, ed. David M. Taylor (Sydney: Australian Council for the World Council of Churches, 1960), 96–97.

35. An exception is Hugh Halter and Matt Smay, *And: The Gathered and Scattered Church* (Grand Rapids: Zondervan, 2010), although their concern and usage are different.

contact with unbelievers.[36] They explore ways that churches can make the needs of the neighborhood as important as the needs of church members. Thinking of the church as a scattered community has led to an image of the church living among its neighbors in solidarity, love, and hospitality—living for the sake of the world.[37] All of this can only be affirmed as it works out the missionary nature of the church.

There are questions that arise when this vision of the missional church is set in light of Newbigin's missionary ecclesiology. The first question is whether sufficient emphasis has been given to both separation from and solidarity with the world. It seems to be very difficult to hold together these two dimensions of the missionary calling of the church. As we look at the traditional evangelical church, the separation of the church from the world has been accentuated, so that there is little solidarity with the pain and misery of the world. It has been rightly said that the church is to be in the world but not of it; instead, it is of the world but not in it! This troubles missional church advocates. In response to a lack of "being in the world," many in the MCC stress the importance of solidarity and downplay the distinctive identity of the church.

Newbigin speaks of a posture toward the world in which the church is both *for* the world and *against* the world. There is a twofold danger of sacralization and secularization by which the church may refuse to embrace its missionary nature. Down either path lie disobedience and betrayal. The first is sacralization, wherein the church defines its life within the boundaries of the institutional church. It focuses on its rites, language, and institutional forms. It is preoccupied with its inner life. Along this path, the church becomes introverted and self-absorbed, with little concern to reach its neighborhood and the world. The communal and institutional life of the church absorbs the time, energy, and money of believers—including burned-out pastors! There is little contact, let alone solidarity, of the church with its unbelieving neighbors. This has been the path of the traditional church.

In reaction, the missional church writers stress the importance of solidarity with their neighbors and the needs of their communities. And this has often been a healthy corrective. However, here lurks the danger of secularization, a threat of which some authors are aware but not all. Here the desire to break down the distinctiveness of the church as the new humanity and to live deeply into the cultural community makes the church vulnerable to the idolatry of the world. The people of God become so immersed in the world that they are

36. See, e.g., Michael Frost, *Exiles: Living Missionally in a Post-Christian Culture* (Grand Rapids: Baker Books, 2006); Frost, *Surprise the World: The Five Habits of Highly Missional People* (Colorado Springs: NavPress, 2016).
37. See, e.g., Halter and Smay, *Tangible Kingdom.*

in danger of being assimilated into its spiritual currents. The problem comes when solidarity trumps antithesis. In both paths the church avoids the clash, the offense, and the suffering of a missionary encounter.

The starting point for a faithful witness, says Newbigin, is the cross and resurrection of Jesus, which offer a pattern for the life of the missionary church. The church must be in solidarity with the world and separate from the world in the same way that Christ is. "The Cross is in one sense an act of total identification with the world. But in another sense it is an act of radical separation. It is both of these at the same time."[38] Both solidarity and separation, close identification and distinctive difference belong "to the essence of the Church's life in the world."[39] Many—not all—within the MCC risk playing down the church's distinctive identity as the new humanity in order to live in solidarity with their neighbors.

There are two other questions that this raises, which will be treated in more detail in the next chapter. Has the stress on the scattered life of the church to meet the needs of its neighborhood minimized the importance of the communal, institutional, and gathered life of the church? And has the scattered life of the church been limited to involvement in its own neighborhood and missed more significant ways the scattered church bears witness, such as through the vocations and callings of believers in public life?

Underlying all these questions concerning the gathered and scattered life of the church is the uneasy feeling that perhaps the astonishing scriptural vision of the church as the new humanity has not taken deep root among some within the MCC. The powerful humanist story continues to batter against such a notion and drives us to reduce our identity to a private "spiritual" community that has no right to the public square. We may love our community in merciful deeds and tell them about Jesus, but that is as far as it goes. Newbigin laments that we have often not understood ourselves as "humanity reborn" or "humanity remade in Christ," which "the Church in principle is."[40] A good doctrine of creation as the backdrop of the biblical story reminds us that the goal of the biblical story from Abraham to today is to restore humanity to its Adamic integrity as image-bearers of God and as culture-makers. The church is the firstfruits of God's saving purpose, *already* a provisional expression of the new humanity, accompanied by the mandate to speak good news and invite all into it.

38. Lesslie Newbigin, *The Good Shepherd: Meditations on Christian Ministry in Today's World* (Grand Rapids: Eerdmans, 1977), 98.

39. Lesslie Newbigin, "The Bible Study Lectures," in *Digest of the Proceedings of the Ninth Meeting of the Consultation on Church Union (COCU)*, ed. Paul A. Crow Jr. (Princeton: Consultation on Church Union, 1970), 202.

40. Newbigin, *Faith for This One World*, 65, 82.

7

The Missionary Congregation

I n this chapter we shift the language from *church* to *congregation*. This gives expression to the conviction that the primary place the church expresses its missionary identity is in the context of the local congregation. The word *ekklēsia* in Scripture is used to describe both local congregations and the entire people of God that belong to Jesus Christ. When we speak of the church as *missionary*, we are describing not simply the universal church but local expressions of the new humanity. This conviction was expressed clearly at Willingen and continued to grow in subsequent decades. It characterized Newbigin's ecclesiological reflection, especially from the 1960s on. The missional church conversation (MCC) understands this dimension of the missionary church well and makes helpful contributions to what a missionary congregation should be. We begin with a summary of those fruitful developments in the MCC and then ask some critical questions.

Fruitful Developments

The most constructive and beneficial area within the MCC is not found in the theological basis for the missionary church but in a discussion of its concrete implications for the local congregation. There are a host of enriching insights that take us deeper into what a missionary church might look like.

Incarnational Presence in the Neighborhood

At Willingen, fresh attention was focused on what it meant for the church to be a missionary people as a local congregation in its own neighborhood. This captured Newbigin and remained a central focus of his theological reflection on the missionary church. He refers to the local congregation as a hermeneutic of the gospel and stresses that it must "be a community that does not live for itself but is deeply involved in the concerns of its neighborhood. It will be the church for the specific place where it lives, not the church for those who wish to be members of it—or, rather, will be for them insofar as they are willing to be *for* the wider community."[1] Thus the church must be perceived in its own neighborhood as a place from which the good news overflows to the community in word and deed.

This last statement sounds good, but we hear leaders asking, "What does that look like concretely?" This turn to the local congregation as good news for its place has been taken up in the MCC with a wealth of insight for what it means to be the church for the world in a particular location. Much of the conversation on this forms around "incarnational" language. Taking a cue from the incarnation of Jesus, authors have worked out the implications of what it might mean to follow the model of Jesus's incarnation for the church's ministry.[2]

The focus on incarnation is set against the backdrop of a church that is turned inward on its own institutional life and is distant from its neighborhood. Regularly this is blamed on Christendom. Often the church is a building in a neighborhood where members gather for various practices and activities that are for their own benefit. Those who attend Sunday morning services may not live in or know the neighborhood. The surrounding neighbors may conclude that what happens in this church building is for the sake of its members and certainly not for the benefit of the community. Over against this, missional church authors argue that the church must incarnate itself in a neighborhood and be seen as good news for that place.

For example, Michael Frost and Alan Hirsch say, "For us, the Incarnation is an absolutely fundamental doctrine, not just as an irreducible part of the Christian confession, but also as a theological prism through which we view

---

1. Lesslie Newbigin, *The Gospel in a Pluralist Society* (Grand Rapids: Eerdmans, 1989), 229.

2. See, e.g., Michael Frost and Alan Hirsch, *The Shaping of Things to Come: Innovation and Mission for the 21st-Century Church* (Peabody, MA: Hendrickson, 2003); Alan Hirsch, *The Forgotten Ways: Reactivating the Missional Church* (Grand Rapids: Brazos, 2006); Michael Frost, *Incarnate: The Body of Christ in an Age of Disengagement* (Downers Grove, IL: InterVarsity, 2014); Hugh Halter, *Flesh: Bringing the Incarnation Down to Earth* (Colorado Springs: David C. Cook, 2014).

our entire missional task in the world."[3] They move from Christology, with a heavy emphasis on Christ's incarnation and ministry practices, to missiology. Mission is following Jesus's pattern and practices of incarnational presence in our cultural context. From missiology they move to ecclesiology: the nature, functions, and forms of the church in its practice and life.

Hirsch more specifically identifies four aspects of Jesus's incarnation that provide a pattern for our missional impulse: presence—spending time with and being directly present to people; proximity—being directly and actively involved in people's lives; powerlessness—taking the posture of servanthood and humility in our relationships; and proclamation—sharing the gospel story.[4]

Being incarnational means becoming part of and conforming the life of the congregation to the people group in which the church is placed. This means, for example, that the church's cultural expressions of worship, institutional structures, and leadership should be familiar and should resonate with those who live in the neighborhood. A church that is in the inner city where the poor, uneducated, and marginalized live will look very different from a church in the suburbs that is in the vicinity of a state university. Moreover, being incarnational will mean identifying with the people of the neighborhood. The people who attend the church, and especially its leaders, will actually live in the neighborhood. They will enter into the life of that place and seek to understand the world in which their neighbors live. They will inhabit the neighborhood, both with their bodily presence and with their imaginations. They will live among, listen to, and love unconditionally those in their local context. It will be in the neighborhood that they spend time and develop relationships, friendships, and networks. They will enter the pains and joys of the neighborhood. The church will be woven into the life of the neighborhood, and the members will really be members of that place. Hospitality will be an essential practice.

When this happens, the church is in a position to act and speak in a way that brings Jesus and the good news to the folk of a specific place in a way that is relevant. There is always the danger that relevance will mean syncretistic compromise. But a church that is culturally distant from the place where it is called to be and speak good news will not have a message for that place.

The MCC issues a powerful challenge in this area to churches that have become ingrown and exist only for the sake of their members. It offers wise counsel to existing churches for ways to incarnate the love of Christ in words and deeds that communicate good news. And, perhaps especially, although

---

3. Frost and Hirsch, *Shaping of Things to Come*, 35.
4. Hirsch, *Forgotten Ways*, 131–34.

this is not its main intent, it also offers an approach to church planting that bypasses the pragmatic, business-model strategies often offered today.

The problems that hinder congregations today from living out solidarity with their neighbors in the local community and communicating good news in life, word, and deed are outdated congregational structures, antiquated models of leadership, and secularized patterns of life. This incarnational approach to mission must be translated into the functions and forms of the church that enable and equip the church for its mission. The missional church literature has much wisdom to offer in these three areas.

Congregational Structures

Like many in the MCC, Newbigin also believes that congregational structures are a major barrier to the church living into its missionary identity. He expresses this conviction many times in strong language: "Does the very structure of our congregations contradict the missionary calling of the church?"[5] He writes often on the topic, offering theological criteria for structural renewal and concrete suggestions for what this might look like.[6]

One of his major disappointments was the failure of a major study project in the ecumenical tradition to give substantial direction to structural renewal. *Missional Church* believed itself to be returning to this tradition of a missionary church at the point when the theology of a missionary church, translated into new ecclesial structures, failed to materialize. The MCC has continued this historical trajectory and has moved significantly beyond the twentieth-century discussion, Newbigin, and *Missional Church*.

The two important characteristics of congregational structures that can equip and mobilize the church for its missional calling, according to Newbigin, are that they should be smaller and more flexible. There have been a multiplicity of suggestions and proposals offered to that end. There are many helpful insights if one is willing to wade through the proliferating literature.[7]

One of the most helpful is missional communities. These communities are clusters of small to midsize groups that share their lives with one another with missional intention. They take responsibility for living together missionally in a particular place and invite others into their community. They are often

5. Lesslie Newbigin, "Developments during 1962: An Editorial Survey," *International Review of Mission* 52 (1963): 9.
6. Michael W. Goheen, *The Church and Its Vocation: Lesslie Newbigin's Missionary Ecclesiology* (Grand Rapids: Baker Academic, 2018), 120–26.
7. Alan J. Roxburgh, *Structured for Mission: Renewing the Culture of the Church* (Downers Grove, IL: InterVarsity, 2015).

characterized by lay leadership and structurally connected to other missional communities.

There is wide diversity in possible expressions of missional communities, which enables them to be utilized in different kinds of settings: these groups may seek to establish a Christian communal presence in an unchurched subculture or people group; they may provide an organizing structure for larger network-based churches; they may be used as an evangelistic strategy for hard-to-reach people groups; they may be employed as an outreach strategy for larger churches; and they may be vehicles for spiritual formation or community transformation.[8]

Michael Breen stresses intensive discipleship of leaders who in turn disciple others, until over time this gives birth to movements of missional communities. The lack of intensive discipleship in the church makes this emphasis attractive for the missionary church.[9] Breen has also given attention to the size of missional communities and the way different kinds of spaces can function in the process of equipping and enabling God's people to take up their missional vocation. He speaks of five different sizes of groups: celebration gatherings (more than one hundred people), missional communities (twenty to fifty people), small groups or cells (three to twelve people), and accountability partners (two people). The valuable point is that different-sized groups can function in different ways in discipling God's people for their vocation. Here sociology can offer insight for the sake of theology.[10]

Tim Chester and Steve Timmis reflect extensively on missional communities and the local congregation. One helpful aspect of their thinking is that they work out how missional communities (or, as they call them, "gospel communities") look across the whole range of congregational life, including evangelism, social involvement, church planting, world mission, discipleship and training, pastoral care, theological training, and ministry for youth and children.[11] In a later book they focus attention on "everyday mission": what it means to be good neighbors, to do good in the local community, and to bear witness to Christ in the context of ordinary life. They reenvision church as

8. Reggie McNeal, *Missional Communities: The Rise of the Post-congregational Church* (San Francisco: Jossey-Bass, 2011), 37.

9. Mike Breen, *Building a Discipling Culture*, 2nd ed. (Pawleys Island, SC: 3DM, 2011); Breen, *Huddle Participants Guide* (Pawleys Island, SC: 3DM, 2012); Breen, *Huddle Leadership Guide*, 2nd ed. (Pawleys Island, SC: 3DM, 2012); Breen, *Multiplying Missional Leaders*, 2nd ed. (Pawleys Island, SC: 3DM, 2012); Breen, *Leading Kingdom Movements*, 2nd ed. (Pawleys Island, SC: 3DM, 2013).

10. Breen, *Leading Kingdom Movements*, 42.

11. Tim Chester and Steve Timmis, *Total Church: A Radical Reshaping around Gospel and Community* (Leicester, UK: Inter-Varsity, 2007).

a community of people who share everyday life together in a local place and commit to being on mission together. This "gospel community" is a "group of people with a shared life and a shared mission. They have a common identity with a commitment to pastoring one another with the gospel and working together to witness to Christ in their context."[12]

Newbigin had already suggested different kinds of small groups: neighborhood groups incarnate in neighborhoods, work groups that witness to Christ together in certain work settings, frontier groups made up of Christians in the same sector of public life, and action groups organized around a particular evangelistic or sociopolitical goal. The suggestions for smaller, flexible, and outward-oriented structures have followed most of these same paths but have become increasingly creative and have made use of sociological insight in helpful ways. Moreover, most of the proposals have helpfully woven issues of leadership into their discussions.

There is great enthusiasm for small groups in the MCC, but sometimes there is not the requisite awareness that they bring potential dangers. Indeed, some of these dangers are more than hypothetical. Newbigin's words of warning are salutary. He warns against the twin and opposite dangers of introversion or activism—the danger of losing the insights of the great traditions of the church and the danger that small groups will be disconnected from the universal body of Christ.[13] These dangers need much more exploration and attention.

Leadership

The twentieth-century discussion of the missionary church recognized that if the church is to be renewed in its vocation, it will need a new kind of leadership. Newbigin recognized this as well. In the second-to-last chapter of perhaps his most famous book, *The Gospel in a Pluralist Society*, titled "Ministerial Leadership for a Missionary Congregation," he asks how "congregations may be helped to become what they are called to be." The answer is *faithful leadership*. "What kind of ministerial leadership will nourish the Church in its faithfulness to the gospel in a pluralist society?"[14] he queries. *Missional Church* picked up this question in a chapter, and the discussion has continued unabated in the MCC. Like the discussion of congregational structures, the contribution of this conversation has produced growing insight for the missionary congregation.

---

12. Tim Chester and Steve Timmis, *Everyday Church: Gospel Communities on Mission* (Wheaton: Crossway, 2012), 104.
13. Goheen, *Church and Its Vocation*, 125–26.
14. Newbigin, *Gospel in a Pluralist Society*, 234.

Alan Roxburgh has given significant shape to the conversation about missional leadership.[15] He explains that it is important for leaders to be able to develop a missional imagination and ethos in a church and then understand the process of change to move churches toward that missional identity. He also stresses how important it is for leaders to understand cultural changes and what they mean for leadership practices, and he offers important critical engagement on how leadership models and imaginations have been shaped by modern culture. Ed Stetzer highlights the need for missional leadership to lead communities in cultural exegesis to understand their local communities.[16] These are important challenges that have not been recognized as important for pastoral leadership. Cultural studies have certainly not featured prominently in theological education, and leaders are thrown into congregations without the tools to analyze their cultural context. This makes them and the congregations they lead vulnerable to the powerful idolatrous winds blowing the church to and fro. Particularly at this time we are reminded of the church's captivity to ideologies of the Left and Right that destroy the church's witness. The inability of leaders to understand their culture and enable their congregations to follow their lead is more disastrous than is often realized.

Frost and Hirsch analyze Ephesians 4 and discern five leadership functions:

1. Apostolic: pioneers new missionary congregations and oversees their development
2. Prophetic: discerns the realities of the context and communicates them
3. Evangelistic: communicates the gospel in ways that draw forth faith and discipleship
4. Pastoral: leads, nurtures, protects, and cares for the church
5. Teaching: communicates God's Word so that his people may obey[17]

This is quite helpful in enabling us to see the various functions of leadership. It helps also to show that normally pastors cannot have all the gifts needed to lead a missional congregation. Moreover, it highlights functions and offices

---

15. Alan J. Roxburgh, *The Sky Is Falling: Leaders Lost in Transition* (Eagle, ID: ACI, 2005); Alan J. Roxburgh and Fred Romanuk, *The Missional Leader: Equipping Your Church to Reach a Changing World* (San Francisco: Jossey-Bass, 2006); Mark Lou Branson and Alan J. Roxburgh, *Leadership, God's Agency, and Disruptions: Confronting Modernity's Wager* (Eugene, OR: Cascade Books, 2020).

16. Ed Stetzer, *Planting Missional Churches: Planting a Church That's Biblically Sound and Reaching People in Culture* (Nashville: B&H Academic, 2006).

17. Frost and Hirsch, *Forgotten Ways*, 197–218.

that have been neglected in the development of the Christendom church. Leaders who are permanently settled to lead in one place continue to play a role in the leadership of the church but the mobile and nonlocalized ministries of apostles, prophets, and evangelists have been eclipsed by Christendom.[18] Newbigin laments the "practical elimination of the universal, travelling ministry of apostles, prophets, and evangelists," and Frost and Hirsch similarly want to recover these lost ministries.[19]

Reggie McNeal highlights the importance of shifting from programs to people. Too many pastors administer and coordinate numerous programs in the church. But it is the discipleship and development of people, and especially other leaders, that is needed for a church to flourish.[20]

Darrell Guder stresses other important dimensions of leadership: The church needs "word-equippers" since the Word of God is the power of God unto salvation and the light that will illuminate the path of the missional church. This traditional role of the leader must not be neglected. He also emphasizes the importance of mentoring other leaders and modeling for them a missional life. And he highlights the need for leaders to equip members of the local community for their vocations in public life.[21]

This latter point was one of the primary emphases of Newbigin in his extensive writing on congregational leadership. This has generally been neglected in the MCC, something that diverges from Newbigin's own strong convictions. This is an area that needs much more attention.[22] Two quotations of Newbigin reveal his passion and its importance:

Only half of the pastor's work is to gather the people together for worship. The other half is to send them back to their daily tasks equipped to be the salt of the earth and the light of the world. If we forget this second part, the other can be positively dangerous.[23]

18. Frost and Hirsch, *Forgotten Ways*, 165–81.

19. Lesslie Newbigin, "Ministry" (address given at a conference in Croyden, UK, 1982), 8. See also Lesslie Newbigin, "How Shall We Understand Sacraments and Ministry?" (unpublished paper, 1983), 9.

20. Reggie McNeal, *The Present Future: Six Tough Questions for the Church* (San Francisco: Jossey-Bass, 2003); McNeal, *Missional Renaissance: Changing the Scorecard for the Church* (San Francisco: Jossey-Bass, 2009).

21. Darrell L. Guder, *Called to Witness: Doing Missional Theology* (Grand Rapids: Eerdmans, 2015), 150–63.

22. Michael W. Goheen and Craig G. Bartholomew, *Living at the Crossroads: An Introduction to a Christian Worldview* (Grand Rapids: Baker Academic, 2008). Mike's experience while church planting and pastoring to help his people prepare for their vocations was the primary impetus for the book.

23. Lesslie Newbigin, *The Good Shepherd: Meditations on Christian Ministry in Today's World* (Grand Rapids: Eerdmans, 1977), 80.

At the most sophisticated level we have to think of our task in a city like Madras to train our lay members who are playing key roles in life of government, business, and the professions to become ministers of Christ in these secular situations. All of this is involved in our calling and ordination.[24]

Practices and Rhythms

A missional way of life must be nourished and fostered by spiritual practices and daily rhythms. The twentieth-century discussion of the missionary church foregrounded the need for various kinds of spiritual practices and rhythms that would nourish believers for their missional calling in the world. These various practices need to be observed at three levels—those of the congregation, the family, and the individual. Newbigin focused on the importance of Word, prayer, and sacrament for nourishing God's people for their missional calling. His primary concern was the life of the congregation, but he spoke also of his own spiritual practices in prayer.[25] He gravitated often to John 15 and the image of abiding in the vine so that the sap of Christ's life by the Spirit might flow to us. His urgent call to prayer needs to be heard again.

What the MCC has offered is a development of these spiritual practices and rhythms. While it sometimes draws on traditional spiritual practices from church history, one of its primary contributions is a recognition of how our patterns of life in a secular world have hindered a missional spirituality.

Nathan Finn and Keith Whitfield have explored the importance of spiritual practices for the missional church.[26] The authors define spiritual formation broadly as "the cultivation of grace-motivated spiritual practices and habits, drawn from the authoritative Scriptures and the best of the Christian tradition, that the Holy Spirit uses to foster spiritual maturity in the life of the believer for the glory of God, the health of the church, and the sake of the world."[27] Their book is primarily concerned with the latter part of the definition: How can spiritual practices orient, shape, direct, and empower our lives for our missional calling? It treats the Spirit's work through the scriptural story, congregational practices, embracing God's love, lament, and worship in relationship to global mission, cultural engagement, and justice.

24. Newbigin, *Good Shepherd*, 76.
25. One of the helpful things that Newbigin recounted to Mike Goheen about his prayer life was the way every week was structured in terms of Holy Week, with every Friday being Good Friday, with a focus on the cross, and every Sunday being Easter, with a focus on the resurrection.
26. Nathan A. Finn and Keith S. Whitfield, eds., *Spirituality for the Sent: Casting a New Vision for the Missional Church* (Downers Grove, IL: InterVarsity, 2017).
27. Nathan A. Finn and Keith S. Whitfield, "The Missional Church and Spiritual Formation," in Finn and Whitfield, *Spirituality for the Sent*, 29.

In *The Symphony of Mission*, Jim Mullins highlights the three spiritual practices that will sustain our missional calling: subversive sabbath, where we refocus on God, recognize our creatureliness, and remember neighbors; prayer in many places and with all our senses; and the hopeful groan of lament as we live in the already-not-yet.[28]

Others have helpfully highlighted various practices with the acronyms BLESS and BELLS. The Soma community of churches and the Surge Network of churches in Phoenix advocate BLESS rhythms for our missional calling. Over a certain period of time, they commit themselves to following these practices:

- Bless others, including nonbelievers, those different from us, and the poor, at least three times a week.
- Listen to God in his Word and Spirit and to others to understand their stories and our culture's story.
- Eat with others, including unbelievers, believers, and the poor.
- Speak to God (prayer) and speak to unbelievers the story and message of Jesus (witness).
- Sabbath in rest, play, praise, and celebration.

Michael Frost invites us to foster "five habits of highly missional people."[29] He articulates these practices with a BELLS acronym:

- Bless: With words of affirmation, acts of kindness, or gift-giving, *bless* three people each week, at least one of whom is not a member of your church.
- Eat: Develop the habit of hospitality by *eating* with three people each week, at least one of whom is not a member of your church, and with the goal of crossing socioeconomic boundaries.
- Listen: Spend at least one period of the week in silence and solitude in order to *listen* for the Spirit's voice, following his prompting as he brings sin or a need or an unbeliever to mind.
- Learn: Spend at least one period of the week "*learning* Christ" by reading the Gospels or good books on the ministry of Jesus.

28. Michael W. Goheen and Jim Mullins, *The Symphony of Mission: Playing Your Part in God's Work in the World* (Grand Rapids: Baker Academic, 2019), 183–95.

29. Michael Frost, *Surprise the World: The Five Habits of Highly Missional People* (Colorado Springs: NavPress, 2016), xi.

- Sent: Identify yourself as a *sent one* by seeking opportunities to practice justice, reconciliation, and healing, and journal throughout the week about all the ways you alert others to the kingdom of God.

Practicing these habits will enable us to be generous, hospitable, attentive to the Spirit, Christlike, and missionally oriented to the world. Frost offers the helpful suggestion that we form triads—groups of three people—who meet weekly to hold one another accountable to these habits and encourage one another in their practice.[30]

Critical Questions

The MCC has offered helpful insights that have enriched the notion of the missionary church. However, there are a number of concerns that need to be addressed and to which we now turn.

Anti-institutional Posture

There is anti-institutional tendency in certain wings of the MCC. The church as institution is perceived to be a significant problem and one of the primary reasons the church in the West is in decline. We meet this trend later in the emergent church section in an even more pronounced way. It seems to be a default position among many who want to see the church renewed.

This has been expressed in the MCC in terms of various contrasts between attractional and incarnational, between centripetal and centrifugal, and between institution and movement. The church as institution is a rigid and introverted church without mission and is to be rejected. Institution is connected to an attractional or centripetal model. Worship and programs are designed to attract and draw the unbeliever to the church on Sunday morning. Alternatively, the church in mission is a movement, fluid and moving out to the world in an incarnational presence. This is what the missional church should be if it is faithful. But can we discount the church as institution so easily? Does it have to be either-or?

There is rightful concern reflected in these contrasts. They recognize the introversion of the church, its structural inflexibility, its focus on self-preservation and institutional maintenance, and its concern primarily for the pastoral care of its own members. But they have accepted an either-or dichotomy and rejected the important role of the institution because of the presence of institutional*ism*.

30. Frost, *Surprise the World*, 99–104.

David Bosch rightly recognizes that it is a sociological—or better, creational—law that a movement will either become an institution or disintegrate. Institution and movement may never be set against each other. If a movement is to exercise a dynamic influence in history over a period of time, it must become an institution. The problem is institutional*ism*: the white-hot conviction of mission was cooled down and crystallized in solidified institutional structures and petrified dogmas.[31]

Guder speaks of the "inevitability of institution" and aims for "the conversion of the institutional church."[32] He says that it is an "unavoidable dimension of real historical existence that institutions are formed and continued" and warns against a "docetic, nonhistorical process." He rightly makes it clear that the "problem is not *that* the church is institutional but *how* it is institutional."[33] Institutions are needed not only to transmit the Christian faith across generations but also to provide structures for fellowship and faith-formative practices that are necessary given the social nature of the Christian faith.

Newbigin believes that the "sociologist and the theologian will be one in insisting that the idea of a structure-less Christianity is a pure illusion."[34] He makes the theological point that while reading Anglican theologian Michael Ramsey's book *The Gospel and the Catholic Church*, he recognized clearly that the institutional "structure of the church is itself an expression of the Gospel."[35] What Newbigin opposed was self-serving maintenance, antiquated forms, and structural rigidity—symptoms of institutionalism. This is the problem, and the task of the church is to bring the institutional forms of the church into line with its missionary calling. Indeed, its institutional form is essential to its missionary calling as it becomes an expression of the gospel and offers an alternative way of social life.

In much of the MCC the static and ingrown institutional forms of the past, shaped as they often were by the nonmissional theology of Christendom, have been equated with institutional structures. Of course, since institutions are creational, it will be necessary to organize and structure a community somehow—witness the work for new structures amid the MCC. However, if

31. David J. Bosch, *Transforming Mission: Paradigm Shifts in Theology of Mission* (Maryknoll, NY: Orbis Books, 1991), 51.

32. Darrell L. Guder, *The Continuing Conversion of the Church* (Grand Rapids: Eerdmans, 2000), 181–204.

33. Darrell L. Guder, *The Incarnation and the Church's Witness* (Harrisburg, PA: Trinity Press International, 1999), 25.

34. Lesslie Newbigin, "The Form and Structure of the Visible Unity of the Church," *National Christian Council Review* (1972): 6.

35. Lesslie Newbigin, review of *Canterbury Pilgrim*, by Arthur Michael Ramsey, and *Great Christian Centuries to Come*, ed. Christian Martin, *Ecumenical Review* 27 (1975): 172.

the gains of the MCC are to play a role in God's mission there will need to be a more explicit recognition of the importance of the institutional church along with the commitment to renew it according to the missionary vocation of the church.

Most importantly, the institutional structure of the church is essential to its missional calling. The church is a people who need to organize themselves precisely so that the new life of Christ flows to God's people. In one of his first discussions of "laymen in the world," Newbigin speaks of the gospel as the "only source of the Church's life" and says, "Do we understand, do our congregations understand, that when the Word is truly preached and the sacraments duly administered, Christ Himself is present in the midst in all His saving power? . . . God's saving power is mediated to us in the word and sacraments of the Gospel."[36] The organization of the church as an institution provides stable and ongoing structures precisely for the purpose of accomplishing this kind of encounter through regular faith-forming practices but also for the use of gifts in fellowship.[37] In the New Testament this is the way the new life of Christ comes to God's people.

Detachment from the History and Tradition of the Church

A second concern is that some of the conversation about missionary congregations is detached from the history and tradition of the church. Seventeen hundred years of Christendom are often dismissed as a mistake, and one is sometimes given the impression that the construction of congregational and leadership structures is an act of *creatio ex nihilo* and constitutes the hope for the future of the church. North American pastors love the novel, and so this astonishing dismissal of tradition hardly registers attention. However, this trend loses much of the wisdom of the history of the church.[38]

Newbigin feared that the move to smaller groups—something he enthusiastically advocated—could lead to the loss of great traditions of the church. Experimentation and novelty are vulnerable to the "real danger that we lose the great essentials which have been preserved and handed on through the

36. Lesslie Newbigin, "Our Task Today" (unpublished charge given to the fourth meeting of the diocesan council, Tirumangalam, India, December 18–20, 1951), 4.

37. Hendrikus Berkhof makes the point well in *Christian Faith: An Introduction to the Study of the Faith*, trans. Sierd Woudstra (Grand Rapids: Eerdmans, 1986), 349–96, 415–25.

38. Exceptions to this general pattern are, e.g., Graham Hill, *Salt, Light, and a City: Ecclesiology for the Global Missional Community*, 2nd ed. (Eugene, OR: Wipf & Stock, 2017); Craig Van Gelder, *The Essence of the Church: A Community Created by the Spirit* (Grand Rapids: Baker Books, 2000); Guder, *Continuing Conversion*.

ordered life and liturgy of the great churches."[39] The thirst for the new can blind one to the wisdom of the past. When discussing the need for new forms of leadership, Newbigin asks what we are to do with our inherited traditions. While "daring experiments" are needed that imagine structures beyond what have been inherited, one cannot simply break with these traditions. Tradition is rooted in the gospel and has made its course through history. We have been incorporated into this living tradition. How do we move from within it to bring these traditional structures into conformity with the missionary calling of the church? Newbigin employs an organic metaphor over against a mechanical one. When machines are no longer serviceable, they can be scrapped. But a living organism maintains a continuity of life that must constantly adapt to its new environment. What is needed is the reformation of existing structures rather than either revolutionary destruction or conservative preservation.

Something of the disconnect with church history can be seen when, in more than one book, key authors in the conversation make rather dramatic statements about the importance of their proposals. Their proposals are ground-breaking, paradigm-shifting, history-making, a shift of historic proportions, and that which can turn around a declining Western church. Besides evincing too much confidence in changing structures, this manifests a lack of respect for years of church history as well as for their small place in it. Even if their proposals are significant and helpful, these authors are working within a tradition and are not as paradigm-shifting and history-making as they think.

All forms and structures of the church are contextualized attempts at a certain moment in history to be faithful to the gospel. There are always two dangers. The conservative danger is that one contextual form in history is considered biblically normative and claims comprehensive universal validity. In this case, one simply holds on to past traditions at all costs. The progressive danger is to dismiss the past and look for relevant forms in the present. A good view of church history is to immerse ourselves in the church and try to understand why church leaders of the past contextualized the matter in the way they did for their missional calling, what we can learn from them, and what we should hold on to. But the task to rethink the forms of the church *now* belongs to a healthy and vibrant church. It is a fresh task in every generation. Nevertheless, there remains much wisdom from those who have struggled with the same issues in the past.

39. Lesslie Newbigin, "Cooperation and Unity," *International Review of Mission* 59, no. 233 (January 1970): 73.

Eclipse of Important Elements

There are aspects that are central to Newbigin's missionary ecclesiology that have been neglected, if not eclipsed, within the MCC. We will briefly highlight five of these: unity, foreign missions, vocation, families, and worship and the means of grace.

We can note the first two by observing the breadth of Newbigin's discussion of structures. Congregational and leadership structures feature prominently in the MCC and in Newbigin. But structures of unity and cross-cultural missions are also the subject of intense scrutiny in Newbigin but lacking in most of the MCC. For Newbigin, both the unity of the church and cross-cultural missions, which erects a witness to the gospel in places where there was none, are nonnegotiable elements of what it means to be a missionary congregation.

For Newbigin, the unity of the church is essential to its missionary nature. This is most evident in his book *The Household of God*, where, after analyzing Protestant, Catholic, and Pentecostal ecclesiologies, he concludes by saying that the insights of all of these can be found only when we realize that mission is essential to the church.[40] His closing pages unpack two concepts: "the dependence of mission on unity" and "the dependence of unity on mission."[41] The church is not a religious body, but the *one* new humankind that is a picture of God's will at the end of universal history to bring unity to all things in heaven and on earth under Christ (Eph. 1:10; 2:11–22). It is only as the world sees a united body that they will believe that the Father has sent Jesus. The disinterest in unity is characteristic of the fissiparous evangelical church but needs to be given a higher priority. We have observed in the cities where we have ministered the powerful witness that is offered by churches that seek to be one for the good of the city.[42]

The second theme is cross-cultural missions. For Newbigin, mission is to the ends of the earth, and there must be a witnessing community in every part of the world so that all people can see and hear the good news. Mission for each congregation is both local and global. And so each congregation, if it is missional, is not to reach just its own community but also to participate in God's mission to the ends of the earth. "A true congregation of God anywhere in the world is at the same time part of God's mission to the ends of the earth."[43] And so it is "the duty and privilege of every part of the church

40. Lesslie Newbigin, *The Household of God: Lectures on the Nature of the Church* (New York: Friendship, 1954), 153–70.
41. Newbigin, *Household of God*, 170–74.
42. Surge Network in Phoenix, Arizona (http://surgenetwork.com/) and TrueCity in Hamilton, Ontario (https://www.truecity.ca/).
43. Lesslie Newbigin, "Report of the Division of World Mission and Evangelism to the Central Committee," *Ecumenical Review* 15 (1962): 89.

everywhere to be involved not only in the missionary task at its own door, but also in some other part of the total world-wide task."[44] It is not just that missions has been a theme lacking in much discussion of and writing on the missionary church. It has become the case that there is a tension between advocates of missional church and advocates of global missions, and this tension has spread to other parts of the world.

Two further neglected areas can be introduced under the broader theme of discipleship. There are many in the missional church movement who recognize that the church desperately needs a deeper and more rigorous discipleship. But interestingly, two areas—one that was central to Newbigin and another that featured prominently at Tambaram and Willingen—play little role in these discussions on discipleship. The first is *vocation*. Perhaps here we can see the biggest difference between Newbigin and the majority of the MCC. Newbigin believed it is in the various callings in public life that "the primary witness to the sovereignty of Christ must be given."[45] This is the case because the "enormous preponderance of the Church's witness is the witness of the thousands of its members who work in field, home, office, mill, or law court."[46] This theme of vocational mission played a big role in shaping the way Newbigin understood the local congregation, its worship, its discipleship, its congregational structures, and its leadership. The theme's virtual disappearance from most missional church literature is baffling.[47]

The second area of discipleship is the *family*. If the church in North America is doing everything right in terms of its own communal life—missionary structures, leadership, worship, discipleship—but is not training parents to form the next generation in faithfulness to the gospel, it will continue on its path toward demise. This was the concern at Tambaram that was repeated at Willingen. Sadly, Newbigin did not pick up this theme. But the MCC needs to!

The last theme is worship and the traditional means of grace. Newbigin recognized the power of liturgy and worship to form a congregation in its missionary identity. And he especially attended to what we might call

44. Lesslie Newbigin, *One Body, One Gospel, One World: The Christian Mission Today* (London: International Missionary Council, 1958), 31.

45. Lesslie Newbigin, "The Work of the Holy Spirit in the Life of the Asian Churches," in *A Decisive Hour for the Christian World Mission*, ed. Norman Goodall et al. (London: SCM, 1960), 28.

46. Newbigin, "Our Task Today," 6.

47. There are exceptions, of course. See, e.g., Frost, *Incarnate*; McNeal, *Present Future*. And there are encouraging signs in groups such as Made to Flourish (https://www.madetoflourish.org/), Surge School, Phoenix (http://surgenetwork.com/surge-school), and the Center for Faith and Work (https://faithandwork.com/), which runs the Gotham Fellowship in New York City (https://faithandwork.com/gotham-fellowship/).

the traditional means of grace—preaching, the Lord's Supper, baptism, and prayer. Opening up this theme ties us to the previous section: the loss of tradition. The thinness of much evangelical worship is a serious issue. Newbigin was concerned for familiar and contextual worship. But he abhorred worship that had let go of tradition and had become sloppy. The significance of worship, updated, fresh, and relevant yet informed by the wisdom of centuries of tradition, cannot be ignored by the MCC. Sometimes our worship is undermining what we're preaching and teaching about being a missionary people.[48]

Structural Renewal or Managerial Ecclesiology

To bring this chapter to a close, we offer a warning. Pastors concerned about the decline of the church and hungry for numerical success look for quick-fix solutions. Techniques, strategies, and methods in the form of the newest congregational and leadership structures are proffered as the remedy. There is a readiness to experiment with different models that have been "successful" elsewhere. And the pursuit of numerical growth so often seems to be a primary concern, often speaking so loudly that it drowns out all else. It has produced a growth industry of books, conferences, websites, seminars, consultants, and celebrity speakers ready to meet the consumer demand in pragmatic and capitalist America. Confidence is placed in novel structures and new ways of being church as the solution to the demise of the church in North America. Alan Roxburgh has rightly pointed to technocratic rationalism as a cultural spirit that constantly shapes our imagination and leads us to look to technique, strategy, effort, and know-how to solve our problems. Our addiction to technique and human agency leads us to a posture of management and control.[49] We need a missionary encounter with this form of idolatry!

To the degree that this is true—we know it is not true for all, but it is widespread—we need to be reminded that *Missional Church* offered a *theological* analysis and approach to the church in crisis that was consciously breaking with a managerial ecclesiology. Yet, to the degree that the MCC has returned to pragmatic solutions abandoned two decades ago, it goes against what was originally envisioned:

> Consulting agencies and programs whose sole aim is to help changing churches have proliferated. One can find a workshop or seminar on virtually every aspect

---

48. See Marva Dawn, "Worship to Form a Missional Community," *Direction* 28, no. 2 (1999): 139–52; Kevin Adams, *The Gospel in a Handshake: Framing Worship for Mission* (Eugene, OR: Cascade Books, 2019).

49. Alan J. Roxburgh, *Joining God in the Great Unraveling: Where We Are and What I've Learned* (Eugene, OR: Cascade Books, 2021).

of churchly life. The typical religious bookstore in North America overflows with books on successful churches with "add-water-and-stir" instructions on how to follow their example, how-to manuals for every conceivable problem a struggling congregation might face, and analyses of the myriad crises with which the church is grappling. . . . The basic thesis of this book is that the answer to the crisis of the North American church will not be found at the level of method and problem solving [and, we add, structural change]. . . . The problem is much more deeply rooted. It has to do with who we are and what we are for. The real issues in the current crisis of the Christian church are spiritual and theological.[50]

We are reminded again of the words of our friend Zack Eswine, previously paraphrased in chapter 1. Americans want things large, fast, and famous, but the kingdom of God comes small, slowly, and in mostly unnoticed ways and people. We add: we also want it easy and by human effort, but the kingdom comes with difficulty and suffering, and by God's surprising work. The discerning pastor has much to learn from the writing in the MCC on how congregational structures can equip and aid the missionary vocation of the church—this is our primary point here. Nevertheless, the church is in trouble in North America, and structural change will not renew it. This kind of problem is met only as the Spirit works in prayer and fasting, the power of the gospel, and truly transformed lives.

---

50. Darrell L. Guder, ed., *Missional Church: A Vision for the Sending of the Church in North America* (Grand Rapids: Eerdmans, 1998), 2–3.

8

Western Culture as a "Mission Field"

Across-cultural missionary knows that it is essential to understand the culture in which one wants to bear witness to the gospel. And so a "missionary going to serve in another country is advised to make a thorough study of its culture,"[1] says Lesslie Newbigin, before launching into a careful profile of Western culture. Missionaries know well that the witness of the church in communicating the gospel in word and deed will be shaped by the culture. And since all cultures are formed by an idolatrous religious core, understanding culture is a matter of life and death for the faithful missionary. The missiological tradition of the twentieth century that reflected theologically on the missionary church understood this well, since the majority of the contributors had significant cross-cultural experience. And so it was inevitable that a theological understanding of the missionary church would include culture as a fundamental component.

This, of course, was true for Newbigin. Culture shapes an understanding of the gospel; culture shapes the church's life—for good and for bad. So it is necessary to engage in a missiological analysis to understand the deepest foundations of culture. What are the insights that deepen our understanding of the gospel? What are the idolatries that threaten to deform or even falsify it? It is true that "much of the missional literature today fails to adequately

1. Lesslie Newbigin, *Foolishness to the Greeks: The Gospel and Western Culture* (Grand Rapids: Eerdmans, 1986), 21.

engage the complex interactions between the gospel and *our* culture(s)."[2] Perhaps this is because most of us don't share the cross-cultural experience of Newbigin and many of the contributors to the formation of a missionary theology and ecclesiology in the early and mid-twentieth century. Or maybe it is because, as Newbigin goes on to say, trying to study one's own culture is like asking a fish for a definition of water.[3] Or possibly it is because the gospel has been part of Western culture for so long that it is hard to gain any other vantage point. Or it may be that we have been deceived, at least subconsciously, by the myth that Western culture is neutral.

The Gospel and Our Culture Network (GOCN) expressed the centrality of culture in terms of the gospel-church-culture triad.[4] And while this topic seems to have receded in the ensuing conversation, the issue has not completely disappeared. There is much talk about the impact of Christendom, the West as a new mission field, and contextualization. Moreover, there have been some quite insightful treatments of cultural trends and idolatries.[5] However, rarely does the discussion explore these issues with the kind of religious depth and macro breadth that characterized the work of Newbigin. And it is hard to find a comprehensive and integrated framework for understanding the relationship between gospel and culture. Those of us who don't have extensive cross-cultural experience would do well to listen to those who do, and Newbigin is one of the most articulate.

Christendom

Newbigin chronicled the various ways that Christendom had a deleterious effect on the church. Christendom is an arrangement in which the culture is considered to be Christian, and the church finds its place as one more institution that makes its limited contribution to the culture. Newbigin's criticism focused primarily on two things. First, the Christendom church has turned inward, defining itself primarily in terms of its institutional and gathered life, its pastoral and nurturing role. Second, since the culture is considered to be Christian, the prophetic and critical role of the church's mission in culture is

2. Craig Van Gelder and Dwight J. Zscheile, *The Missional Church in Perspective: Mapping Trends and Shaping the Conversation* (Grand Rapids: Baker Academic, 2011), 61.

3. Newbigin, *Foolishness to the Greeks*, 21.

4. George R. Hunsberger, *The Story That Chooses Us: A Tapestry of Missional Vision* (Grand Rapids: Eerdmans, 2015).

5. For a critique of the disembodied life of postmodern culture, see, e.g., Michael Frost, *Incarnate: The Body of Christ in an Age of Disengagement* (Downers Grove, IL: InterVarsity, 2014).

blunted. The book *Missional Church* picks up this critique of Christendom, and the MCC has continued resolutely along the same path.

In the MCC, there is a rightful concern that Christendom has led us into syncretism because we have lost the posture of a missionary encounter and a necessary prophetic stance. Inheriting the myth of a Christian culture makes the church vulnerable to idolatrous cultural winds. Further, there is a justly harsh critique of the cultural imperialism, violence, abuse of power, corruption, and misguided alliances with political power that have characterized this so-called Christian society and sullied the gospel. To be sure, some recognize the cultural good of Christendom, but such recognition is rare and bereft of its missional import. There is, moreover, the critique of a Christendom mentality that motivates the church to attempt to regain power. Christendom is in our rearview mirror. We need to embrace our new exilic setting in a "post-Christian" society and not strive for power to recapture the center. The rise of Christian nationalism in the United States shows that these fears are not without warrant. And there is a concern that the church has become introverted during the Christendom era. It has focused its energy on the preservation of the institution of the church and concentrated its ministry on the pastoral care of members. Our structures have been directed to this end and need to be renovated for our new missional setting. Finally, the Christendom church misinterprets mission. It has lost its sense of mission to its local place and of a missionary encounter with culture. To the Christendom church, mission is something beyond the borders of the Christian nations.

We raise two issues that emerge from these critiques. First, as we lament the familiar deformities of Christendom—its violence, cultural imperialism, and so on—we need to do so from a missionary stance. That is, the problem is the church's failure to adopt the posture of a missionary encounter with the Germanic, Roman, and Greek threads of pagan culture that were woven together into Christendom, importing many idolatrous elements into Christendom. Many features of the Germanic or "barbarian" peoples—such as violence and warfare—were integrated into the *corpus Christianum*. Moreover, the lack of a missionary encounter with the Greek and Roman cultural heritage also led to much of the evil that characterized this period. A missionary approach places the blame where it belongs—on the idolatry of pagan culture and the failure of the church to counter it with the gospel. This is how Newbigin calls us to evaluate church history: How did the gospel encounter different forms of culture and society?[6]

---

6. Lesslie Newbigin, *Honest Religion for Secular Man* (Philadelphia: Westminster, 1966), 102.

The second issue is the increasingly common practice of describing our new situation as "exilic."[7] Without doubt, this is an important scriptural image for today that can shape our missional identity. Yet Newbigin offers a helpful caution. Even while Peter speaks to the early church as an exilic community (1 Pet. 1:1; 2:11–12), we must be cautious in the way we appropriate this language today. Newbigin warns that there are "vast differences" between the era of the early church, when it was on the margins of society, and our era, when the church continues to wield a great deal of power, not as an institution but in its members scattered throughout the public life of culture. Today we have power and influence in public life, and we must learn to use it faithfully in accordance with the gospel.[8] Similarly, Richard Mouw warns that appropriating the exilic image could serve as theological justification for avoiding the difficulty of a missional involvement in the public life of culture.[9] In general, the MCC has not followed Newbigin's lead in placing primary emphasis on the vocation of believers in culture. An exilic image could further reinforce this significant omission, or it could rightly help us as we involve ourselves in the institutions of public life.[10]

Yet, even with these caveats, there is no doubt that the MCC's insightful critiques of the church shaped by Christendom are important for recovering a missionary church. However, it is concerning how some writers summarily dismiss seventeen hundred years of church history in a cavalier manner. Alan Hirsch writes off this period as "Christendom-schmissendom,"[11] and Hugh Halter and Matt Smay disdainfully set aside 85 percent of the church's existence as a "1,700-year wedgie"![12] With less contempt for history, Michael Frost and Hirsch speak of the "bankruptcy of Christendom"[13] and exhort

7. See, e.g., Michael Frost, *Exiles: Living Missionally in a Post-Christian Culture* (Peabody, MA: Hendrickson, 2006); Tim Chester and Steve Timmis, *Everyday Church: Gospel Communities on Mission* (Wheaton: Crossway, 2012).

8. Lesslie Newbigin, "Bible Studies: Four Talks on 1 Peter by Bishop Newbigin," in *We Were Brought Together*, ed. David M. Taylor (Sydney: Australian Council for World Council of Churches, 1960), 101–4.

9. Richard Mouw, "This World Is Not My Home: What Some Mainline Protestants Are Rediscovering about Living as Exiles in a Foreign Culture," *Christianity Today*, April 24, 2000, 86–90.

10. See Leonhard Goppelt, *A Commentary on 1 Peter* (Grand Rapids: Eerdmans, 1993); Goppelt, *Theology of the New Testament: The Variety and Unity of the Apostolic Witness to Christ* (Grand Rapids: Eerdmans, 1982), 2:161–78.

11. Alan Hirsch, *The Forgotten Ways: Reactivating Apostolic Movements* (Grand Rapids: Brazos, 2006), 50.

12. Hugh Halter and Matt Smay, *The Tangible Kingdom: Creating Incarnational Community* (San Francisco: Jossey-Bass, 2008), 49–57.

13. Michael Frost and Alan Hirsch, *The Shaping of Things to Come: Innovation and Mission for the 21st Century Church* (Peabody, MA: Hendrickson, 2003), 14.

us, "Christendom—get over it."[14] This dismissal of the past smacks of "chronological snobbery,"[15] except that the default is not simply contemporary innovation, but a return to the early church when all was well. To dismiss seventeen hundred years of church history is to lose many resources that could enable us to become a more faithful missionary church today.

This disdainful attitude concerns us because it simply bypasses most of church history and the wisdom God has given the church. Moreover, it disregards the beneficial impact of the gospel on Western culture through the Christendom arrangement and all the gifts God has given us. There is also a third reason: we know friends and colleagues who are serious theological students, pastors, or scholars who want nothing to do with the missional church movement precisely because of this contempt for church's history. They ask, "Can we really take seriously a theological movement that sets aside 85 percent of the church's history?" Newbigin's understanding of Christendom exhibits far more balance and appreciation, along with a nuanced analysis of the past. We can note this in two ways.

First, there are two sides to cultural engagement: positively, the church is part of the culture and therefore participates in its development, and negatively, there is an encounter with the idolatry that shapes culture. For Newbigin, in Christendom the church "allied with established power . . . [and] lost its critical relation to the ruling authorities."[16] While the Christendom church forgot the antithetical tension with culture, it took responsibility for the cultural development and the social life of the culture. In fact, a church shaped by the prophets and the Gospels could not but take responsibility when it was offered cultural power.[17] Thus Christendom was the "first great attempt to translate the universal claims of Christ into political terms."[18] The result was that "the Gospel was wrought into the very stuff of [Europe's] social and political life,"[19] and "we still live largely on the spiritual capital it generated."[20] Therefore, we can and must acknowledge our "incalculable

14. Frost and Hirsch, *Shaping of Things to Come*, 8.

15. C. S. Lewis uses this term: "'Why—damn it—it's *medieval*,' I exclaimed; for I still had all the chronological snobbery of my period and used the names of the earlier periods as terms of abuse." *Surprised by Joy: The Shape of My Early Life* (New York: Harcourt, Brace, and World, 1955), 206.

16. Lesslie Newbigin, *Sign of the Kingdom* (Grand Rapids: Eerdmans, 1980), 48.

17. Newbigin, *Foolishness to the Greeks*, 101. See the whole chapter, "What Is to Be Done? The Dialogue with Politics," for a profound wrestling with Christendom and modern culture.

18. Newbigin, *Sign of the Kingdom*, 47.

19. Lesslie Newbigin, *The Household of God: Lectures on the Nature of the Church* (New York: Friendship Press, 1953), 1.

20. Lesslie Newbigin, *Priorities of a New Decade* (Birmingham, UK: National Student Christian Press and Resource Centre, 1980), 6.

debt" to Christendom and be thankful for the gifts we have inherited—"its science, its political democracy, and its traditions of ethical behavior."[21]

Richard Tarnas, who repudiates the Christian faith, recognizes this incalculable debt that Western culture owes to Christianity from our Christendom past. In a list of benefits of the Christian faith on Western culture, he includes Christian ethical values, a high estimation of reason, a recognition of the intelligibility of the world, the vocation of humanity to exercise dominion, the importance of human freedom, humanity's intrinsic dignity and inalienable rights, the moral responsibility of the individual, the imperative to care for the helpless and less fortunate, the unity of the human race, and an orientation toward the future and belief in historical progress.[22] Surely, part of our witness today is to point to Christ as the source of many of the gifts we enjoy, even as those gifts have been twisted and are now beginning to ebb away. Only in Christ will these gifts not degenerate into dissolution. Dismissing Christendom cuts off gratitude and an opportunity for witness.

Second, we might describe the life of the church in terms of two poles: its inner life of worship and nurture and its outer life of mission in the world. The missionary vision of the church in Christendom was diminished and the assumption of a "Christian culture" curtailed an awareness of a missionary encounter. This led to a disconnect between the inner institutional life of the church and its outer calling in culture. The Christendom church became a church that "thinks primarily of its duty to care for its own members, and its duty to those outside drops into second place."[23] This negatively impacted the church's life, its theology, and its theological education. However, that doesn't mean there isn't much to learn from the communal and institutional life of the church. One cannot leave behind the church's tradition.

A good example of taking hold of the insight of an older tradition for a new era is when Newbigin takes on the task of redefining the sacraments and patterns of leadership in missional terms.[24] He does not start from scratch but digs deep into the history of the church and engages the tradition to recover many rich insights of the theological tradition on the sacraments. He critiques their Christendom setting and relocates them in the context of the missionary understanding of the church. This is his modus operandi his entire life.

21. Newbigin, *Foolishness to the Greeks*, 125.

22. Richard Tarnas, *The Passion of the Western Mind: Understanding the Ideas That Have Shaped Our World View* (New York: Ballantine Books, 1991), 231.

23. Newbigin, *Sign of the Kingdom*, 48.

24. Lesslie Newbigin, "How Shall We Understand Sacraments and Ministry?" (unpublished paper, 1983).

This again highlights the importance of a missionary approach to church history. Newbigin suggests we read the church's history in terms of "successive encounters of the Gospel with different forms of human culture and society."[25] All encounters of the gospel in new missionary settings will evince both faithfulness and the marks of the then-contemporary cultural idolatry. The deformities of the Christendom church are on full display in the MCC, but its insights not so much.

Contextualization

The word *contextualization* is common enough in the MCC. This in itself is significant—demonstrating that this conversation has grasped the significant insight gained from cross-cultural missions that the gospel and its embodiment will necessarily take cultural form. This is an important insight, and no doubt we owe it to the missionary origins of the conversation. The impact of a Greek notion of truth in Western culture still makes it difficult for large swathes of the evangelical church in North America to understand just how central culture is to the Christian faith. Many have little awareness of their own culture—like fish in water!—or how deeply it shapes their lives. There is also suspicion that this discussion smacks of relativism. Moreover, Western culture is believed to be Christian or neutral. But many in the MCC have grasped and employed the insights of the missionary movement on culture and contextualization—and this is important!

There are two primary places where the language of contextualization is employed. First, they describe the importance of a sociological analysis to know our North American context. One of the goals of the GOCN was to bring the theology of a missionary church to bear in the North American setting. Craig Van Gelder and Dwight Zscheile believe that this remains an unfinished agenda. They offer their vision for a missionary church in the United States in *Participating in God's Mission*,[26] where they call attention to the appropriateness and urgency of developing a theological missiology for and a missiological approach to the church in the United States. They then spend five chapters telling the story of the United States from that standpoint, ending with a sociological interpretation of the American cultural environment and a discussion of how the church should organize itself in terms of the local congregation and leadership if it is to be faithful in this cultural

25. Newbigin, *Honest Religion*, 102.
26. Craig Van Gelder and Dwight J. Zscheile, *Participating in God's Mission: A Theological Missiology for the Church in America* (Grand Rapids: Eerdmans, 2018).

environment. This is certainly the approach we must take: understand the story and offer a missiological analysis of our cultural context before speaking of what it means to be a missionary congregation.

Second, the word *contextualization* is used in the context of incarnational mission to describe the importance of knowing the patterns and rhythms of the local community in which the church is set. It is connected to the incarnational impulse of mission that identifies with the neighborhood. The better we know our community, the better we are equipped to put a familiar and friendly face on the gospel. We are able to bring the gospel to bear on the felt needs of people.

Ed Stetzer and David Putnam use the imagery of "breaking the cultural codes of their communities." They say that many churches experience explosive growth because they have learned to connect with their communities. If we are to reach secular people in the increasingly post-Christian mission field of the West, we must understand the cultural landscape. We must learn from missionary history, since missionaries have understood the importance of culture for centuries. "They know that they must have a profound understanding of their host culture before planning a strategy to reach the unique people group that exists in that cultural context. This is why they first study the culture to find strategies that will work among the people who live in that cultural setting."[27] Since North America is now a mission field, we must now learn from mission history and implement what missionaries have learned about contextualization. We must break the cultural code of the West.

While Newbigin would feel rather uncomfortable with the frequent language of "success," "strategy," and "growth" throughout Stetzer and Putnam's book, the authors are correct in wanting to draw on mission history to learn what cross-cultural missionaries have learned from a deep immersion in a foreign culture. Their book is an attempt to work this out in a variety of areas—evangelism, spiritual formation, leadership, congregational life, ecumenical relations—as the local congregation inhabits and incarnates itself in its local setting. There is much insight to be gained as one reflects on "breaking the code" of the culture of the neighborhood.

There are two challenges that Newbigin's voice brings to this conversation. The first is that the missiological analysis is not *deep enough*. We mean this not in terms of analytical depth but in terms of religious depth. This can be illustrated by an aspect of Newbigin's thought that has not been appropriated. Sometimes he has been accused of speaking in general terms about the story

---

27. Ed Stetzer and David Putnam, *Breaking the Missional Code: Your Church Can Become a Missionary in Your Community* (Nashville: Broadman & Holman, 2006), 2.

(singular) of Western culture rather than about the many stories. Newbigin was quite aware of the plurality of stories in the West and quite capable of nuanced and sophisticated analysis. But what is sometimes not seen is that a missiological analysis must in some ways go deeper than sociological analyses. That is, what a missiological analysis is after is understanding the deepest religious beliefs of a culture, those beliefs that no one questions. A missiological analysis is after the religious tectonic plates that lie deep below the surface of culture, that are assumed by all the various stories in a culture. What are the beliefs that all agree on, that enable the culture to function?

Newbigin uses his experience as a missionary to make this point. He says that when he went to India, he slowly began to realize how important it was that the doctrines of *karma* and *samsara* had hardly been challenged in all the great revolutions from the Buddha to Gandhi. That is, these beliefs underlie all Hindu society, including its Buddhist reformation. India is the epitome of a pluralist society, and yet beneath it all were religious beliefs held in common. This is what Newbigin is after in his missiological analysis of Western culture. This is why he calls for the use of "sharp intellectual tools" to dig beneath and probe behind the "unquestioned assumptions of modernity and uncover the hidden credo that supports them."[28]

This is not in any way to discount the importance of understanding both the North American and the local contexts. That is essential. We ourselves have seen the differences between the United States and Canada, between Eastern and Western Canada, between different localities in the Phoenix and Vancouver areas, and so on. But it is important to recognize that beneath these various local and national expressions are the deeper religious beliefs of Western culture that no one questions.

A second contribution of Newbigin's voice is his concern that these views of contextualization are not *broad enough*. Contextualization is a clash of stories that takes place in all of life. Living under the lordship of Christ involves marriage and family, economics and politics, technology and art, business and education, entertainment and media, creation care and work, play and worship—all of life. The mission of God's people is to be the new humanity living under the lordship of Christ in all these areas. We must understand the deepest religious vision of our culture precisely because it affects all these areas of life in an idolatrous way. The calling of the church is to live out the life of the new humanity or kingdom of God rooted in Christ and by the power of the Spirit.

28. Lesslie Newbigin, "Gospel and Culture—but Which Culture?," *Missionalia* 17 (November 1989): 24.

Contextualization is the resolution of a missionary encounter, not simply between two different worldviews, although it is certainly that. It is an encounter between two spiritual powers struggling for all of human life—the power of the gospel and the demonic principalities and powers operating in human institutions. It is this deeper and broader vision of contextualization that must be grasped if we are to be faithful in a world torn apart by all kinds of idols.

We end with one more area that we feel a certain unease about: the use of contextualization to speak of success, growth, strategy, method, and so on. Newbigin is concerned that such language transports us "with alarming ease into the world of the military campaign or the commercial sales drive."[29] The language can be used in a biblical way and so does not necessarily mean a capitulation to pragmatism or a managerial ecclesiology. However, that danger lurks in every discussion in America that employs these terms. Success is not growth, whether it be addition or multiplication. If a church is not engaged in a missionary encounter and in contextualizing the gospel faithfully in all of life, if the church is not being discipled to live as the new humanity in a way distinct from its culture, then church growth may be positively dangerous.

We are reminded of the words of missionary Paul Schutz, who said in his missionary journal in 1930, "The house of the Church is on fire! In our mission work we resemble a lunatic farmer who carries his harvest into his burning barn!"[30] And Newbigin comments on the pruning of the vine in John 15: "Church growth, if it does not mean bearing fruit and growing, is merely providing fuel for the fires of hell"![31]

Joining God in His Work in the World

The GOCN originally focused on three primary points of discussion: church, culture, and gospel. We observed throughout this section that the primary focus of much of the MCC is the first of these. It has been the missionary nature of the congregation and its congregational structures, leadership, and involvement in the neighborhood that have received the most attention. We have also noted that issues of the theological foundation of God's mission and the relationship between gospel and culture, while not absent from the

29. Lesslie Newbigin, *The Open Secret: An Introduction to the Theology of Mission*, rev. ed. (Grand Rapids: Eerdmans, 1995), 127. See pages 121–59 for his discussion of conversion and numerical church growth.

30. Quoted in David J. Bosch, *Transforming Mission: Paradigm Shifts in Theology of Mission*, 20th anniversary ed. (Maryknoll, NY: Orbis Books, 2011), 5.

31. Lesslie Newbigin, *The Light Has Come: An Exposition of the Fourth Gospel* (Grand Rapids: Eerdmans, 1987), 199.

discussion, have not been probed with the same depth. So it was inevitable that there would come a protest. And there has, from Alan Roxburgh.

Roxburgh believes that "the spirit of Lesslie Newbigin" has been lost in the MCC. A primary reason is that the conversation has entered a "church cul-de-sac" and ignored bigger questions of God's mission and gospel engagement of culture. Roxburgh and Scott Boren put it like this: "A missional imagination is not about the church; it's not about how to make the church better, how to get more people to come to church, or how to turn a dying church around. . . . God is up to something in the world that is bigger than the church."[32]

What is this "bigger" something that God is up to? What has the missional conversation ignored? There are three things. The first is the humanistic penchant of American Christianity. We want to fix things ourselves and achieve success by our own planning and strategies. Human agency is prioritized over God's agency. Our imaginations have been shaped by a technocratic rationalism that leads us to look to technique, strategy, effort, and know-how to solve our ecclesial problems. We look to the professionalized class of clergy to lead the way. We reflect the image of the technology that we serve, an image of management and control. We want to "fix the church."[33] What Newbigin stressed, says Roxburgh, was that mission is primarily a work of God. The Spirit goes ahead of us and we follow, joining in the Spirit's works. Roxburgh wants to restore the theocentric focus of God's mission and God's agency.

The second "bigger something" is God's concern for the whole world and the ways in which God is moving in culture and in history. The mission of God is not primarily about forming a religious institution called "church" and adding more adherents. God is concerned for the whole of human life, and our ecclesiocentric focus has lost sight of this reality.

The third missing piece of the bigger picture is the cultural context in which the church finds itself. The primary relationship in the triangle of gospel, culture, and church is gospel and culture, with the church as a subset. The church has forgotten that the good news is about the renewal of cultural life and that the church is an instrument in God's renewing mission.

---

32. Alan J. Roxburgh and M. Scott Boren, *Introducing the Missional Church: What It Is, Why It Matters, How to Become One* (Grand Rapids: Baker Books, 2009), 20, 31–34.

33. Alan J. Roxburgh, *Missional: Joining God in the Neighborhood* (Grand Rapids: Baker Books, 2011), 43–44. See also Roxburgh, *Joining God, Remaking the Church, Changing the World: The New Shape of the Church in Our Time* (New York: Morehouse, 2015), 21; Roxburgh, *Joining God in the Great Unraveling: Where We Are and What I've Learned* (Eugene, OR: Cascade Books, 2021).

What is Roxburgh's solution? He wants to follow Newbigin in making the agency of God primary so that gospel-culture questions become more dominant and church questions become secondary and so that we might learn to discern where God is at work and join God on mission.[34] This leads to a threefold agenda: focus discussion on North America as a missional context; recover the centrality of the *missio Dei* for understanding the gospel so that emphasis is placed on what God is doing in the world, accompanied by a call to discern his movement so that we might join him in it; and reimagine our ecclesiologies along the lines of seeing the church as sign, witness, and foretaste of the kingdom of God.[35]

We have much sympathy with this critique. We too believe that the MCC has focused too exclusively on issues of the local congregation. One of our main concerns in this book is that the deep and broad theological assumptions forged in the twentieth-century discussion that shaped Newbigin's understanding of missionary church have diminished. So we would affirm that the agency of God must be understood as primary, that the breadth of God's mission includes the whole of culture, that the gospel-culture relationship is important for the church, and that the church should be understood as a sign, witness, and foretaste of the kingdom.

But we question whether Roxburgh's agenda really does recover Newbigin's legacy. We can start by affirming his concern that the church be a sign, witness, and foretaste of the kingdom. For Newbigin, it is precisely the fact that the church already tastes the comprehensive renewing power of the kingdom of God that means the church is very important in God's mission. On the one hand, the church must itself be a "pointing people" who by their very life embody the kingdom of God as a community in the midst of an idolatrous culture. As Newbigin expresses it, "The most important contribution which the Church can make to a new social order is to be itself a new social order."[36] It is in local congregations that the first shoots of the new-creation life sprout. Their new life in Christ challenges and subverts the principalities and powers of culture. The congregation must be visible and recognizable as a community that is shaped by the gospel, as a people living distinctively out of a different story.

On the other hand, the gathered church is the place where the new life of the kingdom of God is nourished. The power of God's kingdom to change

---

34. Roxburgh, *Joining God, Remaking the Church*, 33. See also Roxburgh, *Joining God in the Great Unraveling*.

35. Roxburgh and Boren, *Introducing Missional Church*, 65–70.

36. Lesslie Newbigin, *Truth to Tell: The Gospel as Public Truth* (Grand Rapids: Eerdmans, 1991), 85.

lives is channeled to God's people in congregations through the Word, sacraments, prayer, worship, and fellowship. And so a truly missionary church cannot afford to ignore these communal practices but must shape them to equip and empower the congregation for its calling in the world. The more one discerns what God is doing and joins God in the neighborhood, the more one needs to be renewed to take up the difficult task of encountering the powers there. Moreover, since institutional structures will either facilitate or hinder this renewing work and direct it toward the world, it is essential to attend to these issues. In other words, attending to the bigger issues of God's mission to restore his whole world and the idolatrous culture in which we find ourselves will make the church much more important, not less!

We hear echoes of Johannes Hoekendijk in Roxburgh.[37] Hoekendijk's "anti-ecclesiological thrust"[38] was born of a prophetic judgment on and a holy impatience with a preoccupation with the church. He wanted to see the church turned inside out, joining God in establishing justice in the world. The communal life and witness of the local congregation were increasingly eclipsed by the rightful goal of turning the church outward to seek *shalom* in society. The church was to attend to where God was at work and join him in that work. The church had to be defined by its function—it is an instrument in the coming of the kingdom in culture. Hoekendijk describes this functional role of the church as a sign and witness to the kingdom.

Newbigin's fierce critique was to say that the church is a sign of the kingdom not only as an instrument but also—and foremost—as a foretaste or the firstfruits of the kingdom. The church is a hermeneutic of the gospel only insofar as it is a "foretaste of a different social order" and a "sign, instrument, and foretaste of God's redeeming grace for the whole life of society."[39] It must embody this new social order in its life, not only when it is scattered joining God in his mission in the world, but also as a gathered community. It is this neo-Anabaptist tradition, which has been dominant in the MCC, that is now being challenged by Roxburgh.

Roxburgh does repeat the threefold Newbigin formula for the church: sign, instrument, and foretaste of the kingdom. And he has written prolifically and consulted with churches on the leadership of a missional congregation. It is hard for us to square this with the primary thrust of his recent writing, which is to minimize the importance of the gathered congregation and to

---

37. See chap. 4 for an analysis of Johannes Hoekendijk.

38. Jan A. B. Jongeneel, *Philosophy, Science, and Theology of Mission in the 19th and 20th Centuries, Part II* (Frankfurt: Peter Lang, 1997), 90.

39. Lesslie Newbigin, *The Gospel in a Pluralist Society* (Grand Rapids: Eerdmans, 1989), 233.

emphasize the task of joining God where he is at work in the neighborhood.[40] This seems perilously close to Hoekendijk.

Missionary Encounter: Gospel Meets Culture in the Church

The more one stresses the relationship between gospel and culture, the more important the church becomes. Newbigin spoke of the relationship of the gospel to culture most often in terms of a missionary encounter. A missionary encounter is composed of six elements:[41]

1. All cultures have a religious and comprehensive credo at the center of their life together that is incompatible with the gospel.
2. The gospel makes an equally comprehensive claim and demands absolute allegiance.
3. A missionary encounter is the clash between these two incompatible stories, religious visions, and ways of life that compete for the whole of life.
4. The clash between the gospel and the cultural story is socially embodied; the encounter takes place *within* the very life of the church since the church is a community that inhabits both stories.
5. This creates a painful tension that requires an inner dialogue—within each Christian and within the believing community—to be resolved. This resolution is contextualization, which can be faithful or unfaithful.
6. This encounter is "missionary" in that there is *radical* discontinuity between the two stories but not *total* discontinuity; the gospel can be faithfully translated into culture.

It is the fourth point that interests us here. Newbigin asks whether in posing the question of the relationship between gospel and culture we have already implied "an unacknowledged and disastrous dualism." We treat the gospel and culture issue "as though it were a matter of the meeting of two quite separate things: a disembodied message and a historically conditioned pattern of social life."[42]

40. Our confusion is only heightened when we note that the majority of positive comments made about the gathered congregation in Roxburgh's recent book, *Joining God in the Great Unraveling*, are relegated to the footnotes. See the footnotes on pages 60, 81, 104, 141.
41. Michael W. Goheen, *The Church and Its Vocation: Lesslie Newbigin's Missionary Ecclesiology* (Grand Rapids: Baker Academic, 2018), 142–50.
42. Newbigin, *Gospel in a Pluralist Society*, 188.

However, neither the gospel nor the culture exists in abstraction—"out there." Culture is not an abstract entity but a socially embodied pattern of life. The gospel is not a disembodied message but is always socially incarnated and expressed in the concrete words, lifestyles, and patterns of a particular place. The church is part of both communities, inhabits both stories, and participates in both ways of life. Congregants are narrated and socialized into their cultural community, story, and way of life from birth. Then their lives are renarrated and resocialized into the new humanity and its way of life with the biblical story through the hard work of discipleship. And it is precisely in the very life of the church that the gospel and culture meet. It is a meeting of two ultimate and comprehensive religious visions that are socially embodied and demand total allegiance in all of life. For the church to be faithful, there must be an ongoing dialogue, both within the hearts of believers and within the community, that seeks resolution to the painful tension.

This might be illustrated in terms of "living at the crossroads." The church lives in two stories, embodied by two communities, and finds itself at the crossroads between these two stories. The painful tension leads to a dialogue to resolve the tension. Contextualization is the resolution the church ultimately embodies at the crossroads (see fig. 8.1).

The more one stresses the relationship between gospel and culture, the more one must say *church*, since it is there that they encounter each other. Mission is the embodiment and resolution of this encounter, both as a gathered and as a scattered community. The church is also the place where the life of the people of God is renarrated and resocialized with the biblical story through

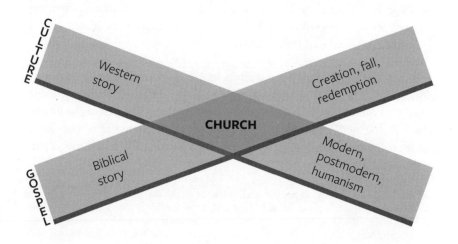

Figure 8.1. Living at the crossroads

the Word, sacraments, worship, prayer, fellowship, discipleship, and formation. This encounter heightens the importance of the institutional church. If we follow Newbigin, to say "gospel and culture" is to say "church."

Biblical Story, New Humanity, and Missionary Encounter

We conclude this chapter by identifying three big areas we believe need to be recovered in the MCC. The first is the *biblical story* as an overarching structure and fundamental framework for the whole discussion. The *missio Dei* reoriented the missiological discussion seventy years ago, but the narrative dimension no longer features prominently. Yet it is precisely the Bible as the story of universal and cosmic history that binds it all together and gives meaning to every aspect of a missionary ecclesiology. The second is taking hold of the missionary nature of the church in terms of being the *new humanity* for the sake of the world. The church is not a religious body but God's purpose to restore humanity to its Adamic role. The more we understand this bigger picture of the church, the more it begins to bind together many of the dimensions of a missionary ecclesiology. And finally, we need to hear again Newbigin's vision of a *missionary encounter* between gospel and culture embodied in the church—an encounter that involves a spiritual battle between two ultimate and comprehensive powers for all of life, the painful tension of living as the new humanity at the meeting point of the battle, the inescapable contextual nature of being a missionary church, and the importance of training leaders and congregations to diagnose the religious nature of their culture if they are to be faithful.

PART 3

The Emergent Church Conversation

9

Modern and Postmodern Cultural Context

There have been rumors of the death of the emergent church conversation (ECC). But, in the words of Mark Twain, those reports have been greatly exaggerated. There is no doubt that the conversation has fragmented into incompatible factions and the name "emergent" does not appear so prominently anymore. Nor is there a central hub for its conversation. So the question can rightly be asked: Why deal with the emergent church conversation?

We write for pastors who are motivated to lead their congregations into a fuller appropriation of their missionary identity and who want to learn from Lesslie Newbigin and the missionary church movements that have developed his legacy. The ECC remains one of those important conversations that raises important issues for becoming a missionary congregation.

Historical Perspectives

The ECC is indebted to Newbigin.[1] Early leaders of the ECC believed that there was a tectonic shift taking place in Western culture that could be described as a transition from modern to postmodern. They sensed that this had significant implications for the church, and a conversation ensued to tackle the

1. Joe Randell Stewart, "The Influence of Newbigin's Missiology on Selected Innovators and Early Adopters of the Emerging Church Paradigm" (EdD diss., Southern Baptist Theological Seminary, December 2013).

question: What might it look like for a church to be faithful in this radically new postmodern context? Moreover, they were deeply concerned about the mass exodus of the younger generation from the church—a generation disillusioned with a church captive to modernity. The ECC grew out of a desire to be missionary in the postmodern context, to be followers of Jesus faithful to their place in a new time.[2] They combed through the work of various authors for resources and insights to negotiate this cultural shift to postmodernism. By their own testimony, many of them found Newbigin's work on a missionary encounter with Western culture to be their most helpful resource.

The leaders of this movement were also influenced early by the missional church conversation (MCC). Months after the publication of *Missional Church*,[3] George Hunsberger spoke at what may have been the inaugural event of the emergent church movement.[4] In founding meetings such as this one, "missional church" was a central item on the agenda. Various leaders in the Gospel and Our Culture Network (GOCN) were involved in the early meetings of the budding ECC. Many of the leaders of the ECC acknowledged their indebtedness to the dialogue on missional church taking place in the GOCN and to the publication of *Missional Church*. Emergent church thinkers believed they were implementing the insights of Newbigin and *Missional Church* in faithfully negotiating the cultural shifts. So it is legitimate historically and theologically to ask to what degree this was true.

Reference to these early days of the ECC leads us to the issue of the subsequent development and growing diversity of the movement. We can discern three historical stages. Initially the ECC began as a movement, particularly in North America, around an emerging generational ministry focus among youth pastors and young church planters of so-called Generation X. In the United Kingdom context, it was alternative worship movements that prompted a new direction. They initially arose as a church within a church—carrying on their youth and worship agendas within the established church. But the movement began to morph into something deeper. As early leaders in the movement attended more closely to the cultural shift from modernity to postmodernity, they realized that this cultural shift encompassed something much bigger than a generational reality or form of worship. What was needed was a deeper encounter with postmodern culture and a wholesale renewal of the

2. Eddie Gibbs and Ryan Bolger, *Emerging Churches: Creating Christian Community in Postmodern Cultures* (Grand Rapids: Baker Academic, 2005), 28.

3. Darrell L. Guder, ed., *Missional Church: A Vision for the Sending of the Church in North America* (Grand Rapids: Eerdmans, 1998).

4. Michael Clawson, "Emerging from What? The Historical Roots of the Emerging Church Movement" (PhD diss., Baylor University, 2017), 165.

congregation. The movement originated as a protest movement against the ways that modernity had taken the evangelical church captive.[5]

The second stage was one of "dismantling and rebuilding."[6] The forms of church disfigured by its captivity to modernity had to be dismantled and rebuilt in a postmodern context. The goal at this stage was not simply protest and critique but reimagining "liturgy, mission, social justice, spiritual formation, leadership development, authority, church structures, connectionalism, interfaith relationships, and more"[7] in light of the dramatic shift to postmodernity.

There was diversity within the movement regarding how "hard" or "soft" the postmodern tendencies were. "Softness" characterized those who were more critical of the postmodern context, while "hardness" characterized those who uncritically embraced postmodernity.[8] But two things held the movement together: the conviction that a tectonic shift was taking place in Western culture from modernity to postmodernity and a common commitment to finding a new way of being church in this setting to appeal to those losing their faith—a dismantling of the modern church and a rebuilding of the postmodern one for a new generation.

The third stage was one of fragmentation and, for many, a slide into liberalism. The ECC faced rigorous criticism from evangelical writers, especially from the so-called New Calvinist stream and the Gospel Coalition, accusing ECC participants of theological liberalism. This critique was motivated by the rightful concern for theological orthodoxy but often was also the fruit of the critics' own captivity to modern culture, of which they were unaware. Rejected by evangelicalism, the ECC moved from an evangelical to a liberal Protestant home and found a champion for its cause in Phyllis Tickle.[9] A new generation of leaders is emerging today as the movement becomes increasingly radicalized within mainline denominations. What began as a search for a "generous orthodoxy" has become, for the most part, simply generous.[10]

5. See D. A. Carson, *Becoming Conversant with the Emerging Church: Understanding a Movement and Its Implications* (Grand Rapids: Zondervan, 2005), 20–36.

6. Gibbs and Bolger, *Emerging Churches*, 28–29.

7. Brian D. McLaren, "Emergence as Conversation, Network and Movement," in *Phyllis Tickle: Evangelist of the Future*, ed. Tony Jones (Brewster, MA: Paraclete, 2014), 104.

8. Scot McKnight, "What Is the Emerging Church?" (paper presented at the Fall Contemporary Issues Conference at Westminster Theological Seminary, October 26–27, 2006).

9. Tony Jones, "Preface to the 10th Anniversary Edition of *The New Christians*," in *The New Christians: Dispatches from the Emergent Frontier* (Minneapolis: Fortress, 2019), xvi–xix; Phyllis Tickle, *Emergence Christianity: What It Is, Where It Is Going, and Why It Matters* (Grand Rapids: Baker Books, 2012).

10. Brian D. McLaren, *A Generous Orthodoxy: Why I Am a Missional and Evangelical and Post/Protestant and Liberal/Conservative and Mystical/Poetic and Biblical and Charismatic/*

Writers within this conversation continue to reimagine the Christian faith, including traditional Christian doctrine. Sadly, much of the present conversation departs from an orthodox Christian tradition.[11] Post-institutional expressions of Christian community continue to emerge as the importance of the church in the ECC recedes.[12] While the movement is no longer organized as such, it has become ubiquitous and its growing presence is evident in multiple forms of media, such as podcasting, blogging, and conferences, as well as in new movements and organizations.[13] Neither has the publishing come to a halt.[14] The questions raised by the ECC remain important for the missionary church today.

The Urgency of an Encounter with Postmodern Culture

The urgency of a missionary encounter with postmodern culture can be highlighted in two ways: our own pastoral experience and the situation of the American evangelical church today. In our congregations we find many who have exposure to the postmodern ethos through university education, news media, social media, and peer influence. And they start to question the Christian faith. They look for a framework to understand the questions and issues that trouble them. They may question certain doctrines, such as the

Contemplative and Fundamentalist/Calvinist and Anabaptist/Anglican and Methodist and Catholic and Green and Incarnational and Depressed-Yet-Hopeful and Emergent and Unfinished Christian (Grand Rapids: Zondervan, 2004).

11. A turning point may be marked by two books: Brian D. McLaren, A New Kind of Christianity: Ten Questions That Are Transforming the Faith (New York: HarperOne, 2010); Doug Pagitt, A Christianity Worth Believing: Hope-Filled, Open-Armed, Alive-and-Well Faith for the Left Out, Left Behind, and Let Down in Us All (Grand Rapids: Zondervan, 2009).

12. See, e.g., Tony Jones, The Teaching of the Twelve: Believing and Practicing the Primitive Christianity of the Ancient Didache Community (Brewster, MA: Paraclete, 2009); Brian D. McLaren, Seeking Aliveness: Daily Reflections on a New Way to Experience and Practice the Christian Faith (New York: Faith Words, 2017); Doug Pagitt, Outdoing Jesus: Seven Ways to Live Out the Promise of "Greater Than" (Grand Rapids: Eerdmans, 2019).

13. Brian D. McLaren lists podcasts, events, bloggers, and networks shaped by emphases of the ECC in Faith after Doubt: Why Your Beliefs Stopped Working and What to Do about It (New York: St. Martin's Essentials, 2021), 231–34. Clawson, "Emerging from What?," 378–79, also provides a list for networks and ongoing influences.

14. In addition to titles cited already, consider Rob Bell, What Is the Bible? How an Ancient Library of Poems, Letters, and Stories Can Transform the Way You Think and Feel about Everything (New York: HarperOne, 2019); Tony Jones, Did God Kill Jesus? Searching for Love in History's Most Famous Execution (New York: HarperOne, 2015); Doug Pagitt, Flipped: The Provocative Truth That Changes Everything We Know about God (New York: Convergent Books, 2015); Brian D. McLaren, The Great Spiritual Migration: How the World's Largest Religion Is Seeking a Better Way to Be Christian (New York: Convergent Books, 2016).

atonement, or difficult parts of the Bible, such as its teaching on sexuality or texts describing violence. They may be troubled by the sexual scandals of church leaders or shaken by issues of science and faith. They may be distressed by the judgmental and sometimes hostile posture of the church toward the LGBTQ community or sense the presence of patriarchy in church leadership structures. All these issues begin to erode their certainty of faith. They want to believe, and so they look for answers and frameworks to engage the issues. Many evangelical churches seem to be part of the problem. The Emergents rightfully feel the burden to evangelize this postmodern generation. Emergents are tech savvy and often communicate well. They address the issues that are rarely being addressed by others; they scratch where this younger generation itches. There is resonance because members of this younger generation feel that finally somebody is answering their cry and helping them with their faith.

The urgency can also be illustrated by the contemporary situation of the evangelical church in the United States. A recent Gallup poll shows the dramatic decline in church attendance in the United States.[15] As you move to younger generations, the numbers who attend church decline more significantly. They are not leaving the faith because the Christian faith conflicts with culture.[16] That was the problem a generation ago: people left because the Bible clashed with cultural beliefs—the naturalism of science, for example. Today they leave because they believe the church itself doesn't believe its own gospel. They detect hypocrisy in the contrast they witness between the Christian faith professed by the church and the church's way of life.

To this can be added an avalanche of news articles that were written during the buildup to and shortly after the 2020 election, mainly by unbelievers but sometimes by believers. These testify to the political influence and allegiances of evangelicals. Many are baffled because in the past few decades the evangelical church seems to have denied its own faith or changed it to fit the shifting political winds. They see a church that is deeply enmeshed in political ideology and has compromised its own Scriptures and Christian faith.[17]

They are confused by a church that has failed to engage white nationalism while it is also unable to see any insights in critical race theory. They read the Prophets and Gospels and are bewildered that so much of the evangelical

15. Jeffery M. Jones, "US Church Membership Falls Below Majority for First Time," March 29, 2021, https://news.gallup.com/poll/341963/church-membership-falls-below-majority-first-time.aspx.

16. Russell Moore, "Losing Our Religion," April 15, 2021, https://www.russellmoore.com/2021/04/15/losing-our-religion/.

17. Kristen Kobes, *Jesus and John Wayne: How White Evangelicals Corrupted a Faith and Fractured a Nation* (New York: Liverlight, 2020). Agree with it or not, the remarkable reception of this book is a clear indicator to any with ears to hear that something is wrong!

church is blind to issues of social injustice. They sense in the evangelical church a syncretism of Christianity and modernity—even if they don't fully understand what that is. Will the voices of the ECC be the voices that growing numbers of younger Christians who sense this turn to in the future? Will a new generation who want to "dismantle and rebuild" evangelicalism turn again to resources of the ECC? We don't know. But clearly a missionary encounter with our culture is an urgent issue. The postmodern option in response to modernity is no better; the Left is as dangerous as the Right. The question is whether the ECC offers the resources to address the issues faithfully.

In counterpoint to the ECC, there is a reactionary movement within evangelical and Reformed circles, sometimes found in certain wings of the Gospel Coalition, that seeks certainty in the dizzying uncertainty of postmodern times by returning to the past. Searching for dogmatic certainty amid relativist uncertainty, members of this movement retrieve older theologians and confessions to revive a better day from the past when there was certainty. While turning to past traditions for resources is important, it is not sufficient to bring about a vibrant faith. This reaction will drive people further from the gospel because it fails to address the burning issues of our day. And this will not bring about a vibrant faith among the next generation. Neither the jellyfish faith of liberalism that is carried to and fro with the waves nor the fossil faith that is a dead remnant of a faith once alive will do: "There are Churches which have so evaded the duty of articulate confession that they have become, like jelly fish, incapable of moving in any direction but that of the tide; but there are also examples of Churches which have so identified faith with blind submission to authoritatively prescribed formulae that they have become but petrified fossils, having the form of the Church but not its life."[18]

Newbigin articulates the challenge to contextualize the gospel afresh today:

> This is always a fresh task in each generation, for thought is never still. The words in which the Church states its message in one generation have changed their meaning by the time the next has grown up. No verbal statement can be produced which relieves the Church of the responsibility continually to re-think and re-state its message. No appeal to ecumenical creeds, to the universal belief of the Church, or to the Scriptures, can alter the fact that the Church has to state in every new generation how it interprets the historical faith, and how it relates it to the new thought and experience of its time. . . . Nothing can remove from the Church the responsibility for stating *now*, what is the faith.[19]

---

18. Lesslie Newbigin, *The Reunion of the Church: A Defence of the South India Scheme* (London: SCM, 1948), 142.
19. Newbigin, *Reunion of the Church*, 138.

The concerns of the ECC are urgent for a missionary church. How can we have a missionary encounter with postmodern culture?

Addressing a New Generation—but Which Culture?

The ECC wants to address the postmodern generation departing the church. The members of the conversation recognize the urgency of the issue—some have even moved down this path to save their own faith. They have responded to Newbigin's urgent call for an encounter with modern Western culture. Yet the question remains: To what degree has the ECC followed Newbigin's approach in answering his call?

We have three closely related concerns and questions about the ECC's diagnosis of the contemporary cultural terrain. The first is that members of this conversation are so ruthlessly critical of modernity that they are unable to see its insights. Newbigin would agree that the modern story issuing from the Enlightenment is an idolatrous story and harbors many dangers. Moreover, he would agree that both the liberal and the evangelical wings of the church are compromised by modernity. A postmodern critique has rightly unmasked modern idolatries that produce the terrible injustices of our world. But we also need to continue to embrace many insights from modernity, as the unraveling of American politics makes clear. The left-wing version of the postmodern voice threatens much that is good in North America. Newbigin believed that more and more it would be the church's task to defend some of the gains of modernity from a postmodern onslaught.

The second concern is that the ECC does not engage in the same prophetic criticism of postmodernity as it does of modernity. This stands in contrast to Newbigin, who saw both modernity and postmodernity as issuing from the same idolatrous source. Both are humanistic and are rooted in human autonomy. Postmodernity is in some ways the unraveling or collapsing of modernity under the weight of its own idols. Postmodernity offers helpful criticisms of *rationalistic* modernity. But postmodernity has hardly left human *autonomy* behind. If anything, human autonomy has been enhanced greatly. It may be that as the house is swept clean from the demon of modernity, seven more postmodern spirits have filled its place (see Luke 11:24–26).

We recognize that there are various postures within the ECC toward postmodernity. There is a more critical stance toward postmodernity, in which the stress is placed on doing ministry *to* postmodern people that emphasizes the dangers of the postmodern situation. There is also a less critical stance, in which we seek to do ministry *with* postmodern people, seeing postmodernism largely as the cultural context within which we are called to live out the gospel. In addition, there are some who seem largely devoid of criticism of postmodernism and instead are seeking to do ministry *as* postmodern people. Yet, even with this more nuanced taxonomy, it remains the case that the majority of the ECC is simply not critical enough of postmodernity.[20]

We can illustrate this problem with Brian McLaren's selective affirmation and critique. In his influential and insightful *The Church on the Other Side*, McLaren highlights five core values of postmodernism, describes fifteen opportunities that postmodernism presents to the church, critiques seven viruses of modernity that the church has caught and that postmodernism can deconstruct, and concludes with ten guidelines for the revolution that postmodernism is able to bring to the church.[21] There is much insight here. Yet we are warned only against modern viruses, not postmodern ones. We are given fifteen opportunities that postmodernity brings the church but none from modernity.

Our third and final concern is the most important. The focus on postmodernism has shifted attention from arguably the two most dominant powers at work both in Western culture and globally. Both of these pose a tremendous threat to the gospel and the church today: the power of economic idolatry in globalization and the rampant consumerism gripping the West. The fixation on the postmodern challenge to the modern story has prevented leaders in the emergent movement from addressing these two greater threats to the gospel.

Newbigin is aware of the dangers of Enlightenment modernity and postmodernity.[22] But the greater threat is what modernity is morphing into—a new globalized and economic form. He saves his harshest criticisms for the "modern, scientific, liberal, free-market culture" that is spreading like a missionary religion across the world, reshaping all Western culture but also increasingly molding a global culture. He believes that we need to dig down deeper than the level of politics and economic systems to the "level of fundamental beliefs, ultimate commitments, in fact of idolatries."[23] And the other side of the coin of economic globalization is consumerism. Global and economic modernity has produced a "meaningless hedonism" and a consumer society that has the "depth and power of a religion whose cathe-

20. Scot McKnight, "Five Streams of the Emerging Church," *Christianity Today*, January 19, 2007, https://www.christianitytoday.com/ct/2007/february/11.35.html.

21. Brian D. McLaren, *The Church on the Other Side: Doing Ministry in the Postmodern Matrix* (Grand Rapids: Zondervan, 2000), 159–201.

22. Lesslie Newbigin, *Proper Confidence: Faith, Doubt, and Certainty in Christian Discipleship* (Grand Rapids: Eerdmans, 1995), 27–28.

23. Lesslie Newbigin, "The Gospel as Public Truth: Swanwick Opening Statement" (unpublished address, 1992), 6.

drals are the great shopping malls and supermarkets where families come week by week for the liturgy of consumerism."[24] Economic globalization and consumerism—these are the central idolatrous threats, not only to the church but to the whole world today.[25]

It is true that many of the early leaders of the ECC have become more sensitive to the global crises of unchecked greed, poverty, economic injustice, and environmental destruction—sadly, more so after finding their new liberal home. They are deeply concerned about these issues, send out a call to activism that often they themselves heed, and bring the prophetic rebuke of Scripture to bear on a Christian community that apathetically ignores these global issues.[26] This is admirable. Yet our concern is twofold: first, postmodernity does not offer the resources to counter these issues, especially as it abandons the Bible as a true metanarrative; second, the attention given to modernity and postmodernity has not been given to the biggest global issues of the day.

Even so, the question of what a missionary encounter with modernity in a postmodern ethos looks like is a critical question for the missionary church in North America.

The Way Ahead

In the remainder of this chapter we deal with culture: How does the ECC critique modernity? In the next chapter we turn to ecclesiology and theology: How does the ECC reimagine the practices of the missionary congregation in a postmodern context? What is the theological foundation on which the participants build their vision of a missionary church? All of this will be carried on in dialogue with Newbigin.

Two further comments are important. First, we will engage the ECC primarily in its second stage of development, which was characterized by dismantling and rebuilding. This is the ECC at its strongest, and it is here we find the best insights. Second, we will not engage specific thinkers or the whole movement in any in-depth way. We enumerate themes that characterize the conversation and its importance for a missionary church. We are interested in hearing Newbigin's voice within this conversation.

24. Newbigin, "Gospel as Public Truth," 6.
25. Lesslie Newbigin, *Signs amid the Rubble: The Purposes of God in Human History*, ed. Geoffrey Wainwright (Grand Rapids: Eerdmans, 2003), 117–19.
26. Rob Bell and Don Golden, *Jesus Wants to Save Christians: A Manifesto for the Church in Exile* (Grand Rapids: Zondervan, 2008); McLaren, *Great Spiritual Migration*.

Dismantling the Church's Syncretistic Blending with Modernity

Newbigin stated famously that the Western church is in an "advanced case of syncretism"[27] living in "cozy domestication with the 'modern' worldview."[28] Certainly, the ECC understands this well: it rightly abhors the syncretism of the North American church and modernity and the rotten fruit of this union that has driven many from the church. Participants in the conversation have set out to dismantle its idolatry.

Critiquing Modernity

What defines modernity? McLaren identifies seven modern viruses that the church has caught:

- The conquest and control virus
- The mechanistic virus
- The objective/analytic/reductionist virus
- The secular/scientific virus
- The virus of individualism
- The organizational virus
- The consumerist virus[29]

His quite popular and very brief treatment defines well some of the main features of modernity. We have put idolatrous faith in reason disciplined by the scientific method to gain conquest over our world. Reason has given us power to control nature by translating science into technology and to control society by translating the social sciences into social organization, especially for the goal of economic wealth. This is modern humanism: humanity becomes the redeemer of the world by its own reason, science, technology, and social organization, especially for the sake of economic growth.

Two important features of modernity emphasized by Newbigin are absent here.[30] The first is autonomy: in fact, this may be the deepest root—the most infectious virus—of modern humanism in the West. Greek rationalism had

27. Lesslie Newbigin, *A Word in Season: Perspectives on Christian World Missions* (Grand Rapids: Eerdmans, 1994), 67; Newbigin, *The Other Side of 1984: Questions for the Churches* (Geneva: World Council of Churches, 1983), 23.

28. Lesslie Newbigin, "Pluralism in the Church," *ReNews (Presbyterians for Renewal)* 4, no. 2 (May 1993): 1.

29. McLaren, *Church on the Other Side*, 191–97.

30. Michael W. Goheen, *The Church and Its Vocation: Lesslie Newbigin's Missionary Ecclesiology* (Grand Rapids: Baker Academic, 2018), 172–78.

been around during the medieval period, but only when it was married to human autonomy in the Renaissance did modernity explode. While modern rationalism is under attack and is retreating before the postmodern onslaught, autonomy has continued to flourish and expand in postmodernity. This shows the deep religious continuity between the modern and postmodern forms of humanism (see fig. 9.1).

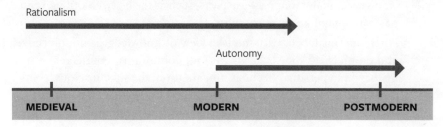

Figure 9.1. Rationalism and autonomy in humanism

The second missing component is the progress story.[31] The eschatological vision of the Enlightenment was to build a better world by reason, science, the control of nature in technology, and the control of society in rational social organization. Modernity claimed to be a true metanarrative, a religious story of universal history with an eschatology of a better world. All the features mentioned by McLaren—reason, science, technology, social organization, individualism, consumerism, and so on—are bound together and find their place in the story of progress toward the new creation built by humanity. Providence, God's control of history, was replaced in the fifteenth century by progress, human control of history. It was this story of progress that replaced the Augustinian story as public truth. It is the failure of the varying humanist metanarratives of progress that has led to postmodernity.

This metanarrative offers a full-scale religion, that of confessional humanism. It is a humanism in the deeply religious sense of faith, hope, and confidence that autonomous human beings are able to save themselves. Humanity is godlike, capable of liberating and redeeming the world from misery and evil.[32] The Enlightenment was the collective conversion to this new religion when the light of the world—autonomous rationality—dawned on Europe.[33]

31. Newbigin, *Signs amid the Rubble*, 5–6; Lesslie Newbigin, *Foolishness to the Greeks: The Gospel and Western Culture* (Grand Rapids: Eerdmans, 1986), 28.

32. Newbigin, *Signs amid the Rubble*, 6.

33. Newbigin, *Foolishness to the Greeks*, 23; Newbigin, *Other Side of 1984*, 7–8.

Postmodernism critiques modernity in the following ways:

- Postmodernism is suspicious that claims to universal truth found in the big progress stories of modernity are inherently imperialistic and oppressive, and thus wants to create space for multiple perspectives, stories, and truth claims.
- Postmodernism rejects the centrality of reason to define humanity and emphasizes many suppressed aspects, such as the body, emotions, senses, passion, imagination, spirituality.
- Postmodernism believes a modern view of knowledge is not objectivist and emphasizes the social (tradition, community, language, culture, history) and personal (feelings, imagination, the subconscious, gender, class, race), subjective factors that shape knowledge. The contextual nature of knowledge should make us much more humble.
- Postmodernism believes our language and concepts are limited and cannot capture reality, and so we must be open to mystery and ambiguity.
- Postmodernism rejects the privileged place of logical, mathematical, scientific reasoning and wants to recover the importance of the arts, imagination, and other nonscientific ways of knowing.
- Postmodernism believes that claims to universal truth constructed for the sake of personal interest, especially by the powerful, are oppressive and therefore need to be deconstructed.
- Postmodernism believes that the modern story has been unjust and wants to rectify the injustices of modernity toward marginalized groups (in terms of gender, class, race, ethnicity, sexual preference), developing nations, the poor, and the environment.
- Postmodernism believes that naturalistic secularism falsifies our world, and it wants to recover the spiritual dimension of human life that has been suppressed.

The ECC movement has led the way in listening to the postmodern critique of modernity, and the church would be wise to follow. Participants in the conversation have rightly seen the danger of modernity, and its idolatries have been exposed by a postmodern critique. If we don't attend to this, even as we do so in a way critical of postmodernity itself, we will continue to harbor idolatry within the church. And we risk losing those who sense this syncretism. The ECC is rightly concerned that these modern viruses have made the church sick. Writing this during the coronavirus epidemic reminds us how deadly a virus can be.

In the remainder of the chapter, we note two major critiques the ECC makes of modernity—critiques of a modern view of knowledge and of the sacred-secular dichotomy.

Postmodern Critique of Modern Epistemology

Modernity has adversely affected the church through its foundationalist and objectivist epistemology.[34] At this point pastors and nonacademic types may be tempted to tune out. After all, this is the talk of the academy. But this is the stuff of the church. There is at the religious core of our culture an idolatrous commitment to autonomous reason,[35] especially as it is disciplined by the scientific method. The ECC is concerned that the enshrinement of scientific reason as the ultimate arbiter of truth has negatively impacted our world and the church in a wide variety of ways: it has led to the abuse of power, to naive claims to truth, to the legacy of colonialism and imperialism, and to the exclusion and often shameful treatment of those who are "other"—sexually, ethnically, and so forth. Thus this is an urgent pastoral and missional issue. A whole generation is leaving the Christian faith because the church does not recognize this and has become complicit in modernity and its injustice. It is the wise leader who attends to this discussion and patiently explores this modern idol and its wide relevance.

Idolatry always brings rotten fruit, especially in terms of oppression. This is the message of the Old Testament prophets, and the ECC has seen this in modernity. This is why its participants address issues of knowledge and truth and seek to dismantle modern forms of knowledge. On the one hand, these ECC authors have turned to many late-modern and postmodern writers, such as Ludwig Wittgenstein, Stanley Fish, Richard Rorty, and Jacques Derrida.[36] On the other hand, they have been drawn to N. T. Wright and to Newbigin, who also critique modern epistemology.

For Newbigin, the attack on modern epistemology was motivated by a concern for a missionary encounter. If there is to be a missionary encounter with Western culture, the church must be confident that the gospel and the biblical story are true. The church must believe its *comprehensive* truth claims: it is the ultimate authority within which everything else must be interpreted. The

---

34. *Epistemology* is concerned with issues of truth and knowledge: How can we know the truth about the world?

35. The word *autonomous* comes from the two Greek words *auto* (self) and *nomos* (law). *Autonomous reason* is the claim that reason is able to give us the truth about the world, and even answer its ultimate questions, apart from dependence on God and Scripture.

36. Tony Jones, *The Church Is Flat: The Relational Ecclesiology of the Emerging Church Movement* (Minneapolis: JoPa Group, 2011), ii.

church must believe its *narrative* truth: it is the true story of universal history, with the End revealed and accomplished in the Christ-event. If there is to be a missionary encounter, the church must believe this gospel and embody it, viewing and living in its congregants' culture within this story, encountering the culture's story.

When there is an encounter between two comprehensive and ultimate stories, only one can be ultimate and comprehensive. Newbigin's concern is that the church has allowed the modern story, with scientific reason as the ultimate arbiter of truth, to be the ultimate and all-embracing story from within which the church has understood its own Christian faith and its own Scriptures. And this is true not only of the liberal wing of the church but also of the conservative wing.

When the ultimate authority of reason is enshrined as the ultimate criterion that judges all truth claims, then the world is divided between facts, which are admitted into the public square as truth that we can objectively know, and values, which must remain in the private realm as mere subjective opinions that we simply believe. When the humanist story is considered ultimate and when autonomous reason is the final criterion of truth, then the gospel and biblical story are consigned to the private realm.

But the church, instead of challenging scientific reason as the filter of truth, permitted this to stand. The liberal tradition allowed the Bible to remain in the private realm, reducing it to a narrative of Israel's religious experience. The conservative tradition, with a rightful concern to protect the truth of Scripture, left the dichotomy intact and refashioned the Bible as a set of inerrant propositions after the model of scientific truth (fig. 9.2). Newbigin

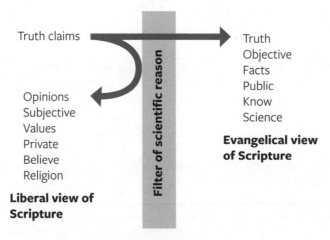

Figure 9.2. Fact-value dichotomy

rejects both traditions, because both envision the modern scientific story as the ultimate story with the Bible tailored to fit within it. The way forward for Newbigin is a resolute attack on the unquestioned epistemology that lies at the foundation of our culture and that has created this dualism. Only in this way can we recover the stance of a missionary encounter by gaining confidence again in the comprehensive and narrative truth of Scripture.

This dismantling of autonomous reason involves, negatively, a critique of autonomous reason in modern epistemology, and positively, showing the rightful creational place of scientific reason. As Newbigin unmasks the autonomy of human reason and its false claims of objectivity, this brings a dual freedom. Not only will the gospel be liberated from the private cage constructed for it by the modern story, but reason itself will be freed to flourish as it was intended to do in creation within the bounds of true religious faith.[37]

The ECC likewise takes up this critique of modern ways of knowing guided by postmodern analysis. But the motivation of its participants is different from that of Newbigin. Their primary concern is to speak to a generation that is leaving the church because of the devastating effects of modernity on our culture. The church has often embraced modernity wholeheartedly and been compromised by the same idols. Thus ECC participants rightly take up a critique of modern scientific reason guided by the insights of postmodernity.

Postmodernity rightly critiques the illusion that our knowledge is objective and neutral. It is mistaken to believe that the knower can gain a neutral vantage point outside the relativities of history and culture to truly understand the world. We cannot achieve neutrality and objectivity by a proper use of the scientific method. The knower cannot transcend the subjectivities that prejudice and distort knowledge.[38] The scientific method is incapable of building a bridge to objective and certain truth or of giving us a God's-eye view. Our knowledge is socially constructed. We stand somewhere. Knowledge is shaped by many social factors (tradition, community, language, culture, history); knowledge is embodied within a communally embodied tradition. Moreover, it is formed by many personal factors (feelings, imagination, the subconscious, gender, class, race). Our minds are not neutral—that is, unbiased mirrors that reflect objective reality—they are creative constructors of the world. There is no universal truth. All truth is limited, contextual, historical, and relative. All truth is carried forward in a communal tradition. Since there are so many factors that influence our reason, there are plural

37. See Goheen, *Church and Its Vocation*, 178–82.

38. Long before postmodernity, the neo-Calvinist tradition launched a critique of modern epistemology. This critique of modern knowledge has led, for example, to the presuppositional apologetics of Cornelius Van Til.

expressions of reality with no way of arbitrating between them. We are no longer certain about what is true. We are left with pluralism and relativism.

Emergents have recognized that there is much truth in this critique and affirm the good insights of the postmodern shifts in epistemology. And since the objectivist epistemology of modernity has had disastrous effects both within culture and within the church, it must be deconstructed. It identifies the source of many of the evils and injustices of the modern story.

Avoiding Relativism

As soon as we critique the illusory objectivism of modernity, the specter of relativism looms large. The question is whether, like Newbigin, participants in the ECC have been able to avoid the corresponding relativism. Why was Newbigin able to avoid relativism and critique postmodernity alongside modernity? Why did so many authors of the ECC embrace postmodernity?

We believe there are two reasons. The first is that Newbigin's cross-cultural experience enabled him to understand the deepest root of human culture as religious. His dismantling of a modern epistemology is a resolute attack on the *autonomy* of reason as part of a bigger soteriological and eschatological metanarrative. Reason liberated from all religious beliefs plays a messianic role to save humanity and usher in a new world. Thus, autonomous reason is an illusion: it is in the grip of the religious commitments—soteriological and eschatological—of the humanist faith. So the deepest commitments that shape reason are not the immanent communal and personal factors of the postmodern critique but the deeper religious beliefs of an ultimate nature (fig. 9.3).

Scientific reason

Social and personal factors influencing knowledge
(Postmodern critique of modernity)

Religious beliefs
(Missiological critique in light of the gospel)

Figure 9.3. Religious beliefs

This allows Newbigin to critique not only a modernist epistemology but also postmodernity itself. He affirms postmodern thinkers' insightful critiques of an Enlightenment view of knowledge but believes that they share in the same humanist autonomy as their modern counterparts.

The second reason Newbigin is able to avoid the relativist trap involves the source of ultimately reliable truth. For the Bible, the source of truth is a narrative series of historical events that disclose and effect God's purpose for the world. Since Jesus has most fully revealed and accomplished God's purpose that will prevail at the End of universal history, he is truth—as a *person* disclosing God and his purpose for the world in the *historical events* of his life, death, and resurrection. This is why Newbigin speaks of the *finality* of Christ. Truth is found in this ultimate disclosure of God's purpose and the meaning of history, which all peoples must ultimately face.

Alternatively, the Greco-Roman stream within Western culture relocates the source of ultimate truth to unchanging ideas that stand above history. This idea has a pagan source in Plato and Aristotle. While this Greek tradition has played an important role throughout Western history, the influence of Augustine's *City of God* kept this tradition from becoming dominant for a thousand years. However, we see a shift beginning in the late Middle Ages with the reentry of Aristotelian rationalism. This shift culminates in the Enlightenment, when this Greek approach moves to an ascendant position in the wake of the scientific revolution. "The Enlightenment . . . was—from one point of view—a shift in the location of reliable truth from the story told in the Bible to the eternal truths of reason, of which the mathematical physics of Newton offered the supreme model."[39]

When this shift takes place, truth is best expressed in eternal and timeless theological statements—ideas, systems, or propositions. The problem comes as Christians embrace this view of truth and impose it on Scripture: thus claiming that the Bible contains primarily timeless theological and moral ideas and propositions. History in the past two or three centuries displays the problem that results. Reformed and Lutheran scholastic theology reduced truth to timeless ideas and theological propositions located in Scripture. The next century saw the rise of higher criticism, which made it clear that these were not timeless and eternal ideas: they could be firmly located within the history of the ancient Near East. So we don't have truth at all; we simply have one more historically relative set of religious ideas and experiences. Fundamentalism reacted to this at the beginning of the twentieth century, returning to the idea of the absolute or unchanging truth of ideas found in Scripture.

39. Newbigin, *Proper Confidence*, 73.

And so today many, including those involved in the ECC, turn from the naive fundamentalist understanding of propositional truth.

The problem is simply that when you locate truth in ideas, they must be eternal and unchanging to be universally valid for all cultures. Yet all ideas can be quickly located in their historical context. Then knowledge becomes enclosed within history; one is left with relativism and uncertainty. This leads to the seesaw between timeless truth and historical relativism.

For Newbigin, the universal validity of truth derives from the fact that God has revealed himself and his purpose for all people in the Christ-event. One way beyond this objectivist-relativist dilemma is to understand a biblical view of truth. Truth is not located in ideas but in historical narrative of the mighty acts of God culminating in the finality of Christ. These events are faithfully interpreted in Scripture, and their authoritative significance is opened up for God's people in many other literary genres in the biblical canon. This gets us off this pendulum and grounds us deeply in scriptural orthodoxy.

Newbigin and, following him, the ECC recognize that fundamentalism and liberalism were two sides of the same modernist coin. Both want to travel a path beyond the dichotomy of fundamentalism and liberalism, certainty and uncertainty, objectivism and relativism. Somehow Newbigin was able to remain orthodox while many in the emergent church movement gradually swerved toward liberalism. Is the reason for this difference that Newbigin had a firm grasp of the fact that both fundamentalism and liberalism shared the common assumption of truth as ideas, and understood that the only way off the spectrum was truth as historical event and universal history? The ECC speaks of the Bible as a story, but is this the same as Newbigin's strong view that the Bible is the true story of the whole world, rooted in historical events, especially the finality of the Christ-event? Would Newbigin's critique of postliberalism—that it is correct in affirming the Bible as a community-forming story but does not take history seriously enough—apply to the ECC? Is there the same deep and unshakable conviction of the finality of Christ—that in the person and events of Jesus, the End of universal history has arrived and will fill the earth one day? With this conviction of the gospel at the center of universal history, one cannot fall into relativism.

Sacred-Secular Dichotomy

The sacred-secular dichotomy has crippled the church's mission. With the rise of modern humanism as the dominant public faith, the church was marginalized, relegated to the private sphere. The church, reduced to its institutional form gathered for worship and fellowship, was sacred or religious or spiritual space. This was set off against the rest of cultural life as secular. In the church, the Bible holds authority, while in the rest of culture, it is scientific reason. A dichotomy formed between church and culture, spiritual and material, private and public, sacred and secular. The church itself succumbed to this dualism. We allowed the humanist story to dictate to us that activities in the church were sacred—that is, related to God and under the authority of Scripture—while the public life of culture was secular and cut off from God and no longer shaped by the gospel. Of course, this is disastrous, and one more way the church capitulated in syncretism to the modern story.

Postmodern humanism began to protest the secular worldview in the latter part of the twentieth century. The suffocating air of scientific naturalism could not satisfy the deepest spiritual longings of the heart. New idolatries were born. Postmodern spiritualities mushroomed, challenging a view of life that reduced the world to a close nexus of cause-and-effect relationships. Postmodern people thirst after a spiritual "dimension" of life.

The ECC rightly recognizes that there is something wrong when a large portion of human life is cut off from God and Scripture. Moreover, its participants believe that the postmodern reaction to secularism and the desire to restore "spirituality" to life is correct. They are concerned to overcome this dichotomy. This moves two ways: they want to transform secular space into sacred space, and they want secularize sacred space.[40]

First, the ECC wants to transform secular space or "sacralize" the world.[41] All of life is sacred space. The sacred-secular dichotomy is perpetuated whenever the church places an emphasis on the sacred practice of corporate worship, and so the solution is to broaden the notion of *worship* and *sacred* to include all forms of Christian service and activity in God's creation. All of life becomes a "secular sacrament"[42] where the whole of life is infused with the spiritual and made sacred. Unfortunately, among some this is accompanied by the sense that there is a need to diminish the sacredness of worship so that the dichotomy is not reinforced. Questions also arise about what is meant by *the sacred* here. But basically, this is a correct concern: all of life must be sacred, consecrated to God and shaped by his Word.

---

40. Jason Wollschleger, "'There Are Not Two Worlds': Transcending the 'Modern' Categories of Sacred and Secular in the Emerging Church Movement," in *Crossing Boundaries, Redefining Faith: Interdisciplinary Perspectives on the Emerging Church Movement*, ed. Michael Clawson and April Stace (Eugene, OR: Wipf & Stock, 2016), 164–78.

41. Gibbs and Bolger, *Emerging Churches*, 65–88.

42. Ray S. Anderson, *An Emergent Theology for Emerging Churches* (Downers Grove, IL: InterVarsity, 2006), 104–5.

So, on the one side, participants in the ECC want to "sacralize" the world—to bring the sacred outside the walls of the church by considering all of life sacred. But, on the other side, the ECC wants to "desacralize" the gathered church and its worship by bringing the secular inside the church—for example, by using culturally mainstream music or art. This is the solution: bring the secular (culture) into the sacred (church) and the sacred (church) into the secular (public life of culture). Or, to put it another way, the solution is a process of "sacralizing the world" and "desacralizing the church."[43]

Newbigin is similarly concerned that the world not be split into the sacred and the secular, the private and the public, the church and the world. On the one hand, he too would affirm that all of human life is sacred. All our vocations, art, sports, politics, economics, popular culture, and so on may be sacred. *Sacred* means devoted and consecrated to God and developed in accordance with his creational intention for that area of life. *Sacred* is not one space in contrast to another space. All of life is either obediently devoted to God or not. All cultural activities may be sacred because they are rooted in creation, where God created humanity to carry out its vocation to cultivate and care for culture in relationship to him and along the normative path he laid out. And they may be sacred because the salvation announced by the gospel of the kingdom restores all human life to its creational intent to be sacred again. The concern of the ECC to see all of life as sacred is important. But this concern needs to be undergirded by a good doctrine of creation and salvation that rejects the dualism altogether.

On the other hand, Newbigin does not want to diminish the sacredness of worship. Precisely because all of life is holy and sacred, the holiness and sacredness of the gathering of the church for worship is of the utmost importance. Newbigin says that worship is "by far the most important thing we do" and "the central work of the church."[44] This is not because the rest is not important. He describes the Lord's Day in this way: there is one day that is holy, but not because the rest are not; one day is consecrated so that all days may be consecrated to God.[45] The meeting of God's people is sacred because humanity offers up their proper worship to God and he meets with them to nurture their new life in Christ. That does not make the rest of time secular. Rather, it is this meeting with God that empowers and centers our lives again, challenging any form of "secularism" and reminding us that all

43. Jones, *The Church Is Flat*, 166.

44. Lesslie Newbigin, "Bishops in a United Church," in *Bishops, but What Kind?*, ed. Peter Moore (London: SPCK, 1982), 156.

45. Lesslie Newbigin, "Ministry" (address given at a conference in Croyden, UK, 1982), 2.

of life is holy. This equips God's people for their mission to live the whole of life *coram Deo*, with every part sacred.

The importance of this for the missionary church is twofold. First, we must increase our efforts to shape worship in which God is honored and glorified, but that also forms God's people for their sacred callings in culture. Second, our discipleship should be as broad as life. How can we have a ministry of formation that equips God's people for living all their lives to the glory of God?

With the ECC's emphasis on the "secular" being "sacred," why is the area of vocation not an urgent priority for the conversation? Why has this concern not resulted in an urgent emphasis on vocational discipleship? For Newbigin, vocation is the primary place where the church witnesses to the public truth of the gospel, because it challenges the notion that humanism and scientific reason have the final word in the life of culture. Living out our vocations under the lordship of Christ demonstrates that the gospel is not private but public and that the church is not a private religious institution but the new humanity. It shows that Christ is Creator—it all belongs to him. It shows that Christ is Lord—he is restoring it all back to himself.

Has the lack of a doctrine of creation and a proper relating of salvation to creation hindered the ECC from accomplishing its intention of breaking down the sacred-secular dichotomy? Is this why it is difficult to find any emphasis on the vocation of God's people to live the whole of life in their work in a distinctive way under his lordship? Is this why the sacredness of the church as the place where such a difficult calling is nourished has been downplayed?

The ECC understands well that there needs to be a missionary encounter with the modern humanist story, and it has challenged the evangelical church for its complicit compromise. Many in the evangelical church, sadly, have rejected this challenge, confusing Christianity and modernity. And many Emergents have simply departed to a new liberal home. Yet the challenge remains, especially in the United States, where modernity is still alive and well in the culture and in the church. If the church does not encounter modernity, the future is grim. However, it is equally important for there to be a missionary encounter with postmodernity—and, even more importantly, with global, economic modernity and consumerism. For this, Newbigin's understanding of the Bible as the true story of universal history and his understanding of the religious nature of culture will be indispensable.

10

The Missionary Congregation in a Postmodern Setting

The emergent church conversation (ECC) has been stamped by its reaction to the deforming effects of modern humanism on the church and by its embrace of postmodernity. It brings insight in its critique of modernity but the potential of a syncretistic alliance with postmodernity. In this chapter we probe how this affects emergent church proponents' understanding of a missionary congregation as well as the theology that underlies it.

Reimagining Practices in a Missionary Congregation in a Postmodern Context

The ECC has exposed modernity's harmful effects on congregational life. The tendency toward bureaucracy and organization has burdened the institutional structures of the church. Hierarchical notions of authority have distorted leadership. Rationalism has impacted preaching, worship, and discipleship. Preoccupation with growth has reshaped criteria for success. Modern epistemology has had a damaging impact on many aspects of ecclesial life, including theology and theological education. Modernity has affected evangelism, the way we seek justice and show mercy, and colonial missions. There is hardly a place where modernity has not insinuated itself into the local congregation. The ECC has reacted against this deformity and wants to reimagine what a church might look like in our postmodern world.

Lesslie Newbigin sensed the urgency of reshaping the missionary congregation to carry out its vocation in Western culture. The structures of the church reflected a Christendom theology and needed to be transformed to nurture and equip God's people for their missionary vocation. Newbigin's concern emerged in the 1960s, when plans for structural renewal were lost in the shift to the secular that marginalized the church. The book *Missional Church* wanted to return to this agenda to discover new structures and practices for a missionary congregation. The ECC stands very much in this historical trajectory.

In the ECC, there are two quite discernable motivations for this renewal. One the one hand, there was a deepening understanding of the missionary calling of the church that needs new structures to cultivate a missionary congregation. On the other hand, there is a reaction to Enlightenment modernity that shapes the evangelical church. Both factors prompt Emergents to pursue new structures and practices.

Hospitality to the Stranger

The ECC emphasizes *hospitality to the stranger*. This emphasis is motivated, on the one hand, by the inclusive practices of Jesus, who welcomed prostitutes, tax collectors, children, and other marginalized folk, and, on the other hand, by a reaction to the exclusive and often unwelcoming practices of the modern evangelical church. For example, when one recognizes the enormous challenges posed by the experiences of those within the LGBTQ community, it is clear this is an urgent issue.

Hospitality is put into practice in various ways. All are welcomed to the eucharistic meal, which becomes the central act of worship.[1] There is an emphasis on eating meals together as a practice of hospitality and welcome to the stranger. Emergents want to create the community as a safe place for the inclusion of the stranger and outsider. There is a softening of boundaries that tend to exclude others. They want to intentionally foster a "come as you are" culture in the local congregation. Those within the LBGTQ community and people from other religions who have been shunned in the evangelical churches are welcomed and invited into a safe space to explore the Christian faith.[2] People are invited to belong before they believe or to become part of the community to wrestle with the claims of Christ. Moreover, this hospitality and welcome is to be part of evangelistic practices where relationship

1. Tony Jones, *The Church Is Flat: The Relational Ecclesiology of the Emerging Church Movement* (Minneapolis: JoPa Group, 2011), 100–103.
2. Jones, *The Church Is Flat*, 111–14.

and presence are emphasized before proclamation. The stranger needs to be loved and welcomed, heard and safe in order to hear the claims of the gospel.

There is much wisdom in this approach. But, of course, the gospel confronts the inclusion that characterizes postmodernity as well as the exclusion evident in modernity. Jesus welcomed the stranger, provided hospitality, safety, and a sympathetic ear. Gently and lovingly he also called for repentance and demanded that people follow him in a sacrificial way. The church must be a welcoming and safe community and a hospitable and humble presence. We must learn to listen and love before we speak. Conversion is also a long process. There is much to be learned here.

But if these practices of inclusion start to break down the boundary between those who follow Christ and those who do not, they depart from the Scriptures. This is precisely the concern of Newbigin in his conflict with Konrad Raiser, who wanted to erase the boundaries between the church and the world. Raiser wanted solidarity to triumph over separation. Newbigin's own practices were deeply hospitable. He was known, for example, as the unofficial bishop of the lepers in India because of his love, solidarity, and welcome toward this marginalized community. But the people of God are those who commit their lives to following Jesus and become distinctive. All must repent and believe the good news and become part of the new humanity that is being transformed by the Spirit. There are those who are "in Christ" and those who are not.

We can and must warmly welcome and love our LGBTQ neighbors and our friends from other religions. The repellent and hostile treatment they sometimes receive from the evangelical church is shameful. But we must call all to repentance and faith, even in a way that humbly acknowledges our own sin and continual need for forgiveness and renewal. We know conservative churches that cannot welcome their LGBTQ neighbors and liberal churches whose welcome and "come as you are" posture demands no repentance. And, sadly, we also know of churches that try to do both in the way of Jesus and become the target of suspicion by both. There is no doubt that solving the problem of exclusion and inclusion, of hospitable welcome and gospel summons, of sympathetic understanding and call to repentance and full discipleship, of solidarity and separation is an urgent one for the missionary church in our postmodern world.

Worship and Preaching

It was recognized early in the twentieth-century discussion of the missionary church that we must give renewed attention to worship. This was a common topic for Newbigin in his sermons as a bishop to the pastors under his care. He believed that worship is "by far the most important thing that we do"[3] and attended to a theology of worship, how worship is connected to the mission of the church, and concrete practices such as music and liturgy, but especially Word and sacrament.[4] Some in the ECC have focused on this area in fruitful ways.[5]

Newbigin challenged a consumerist approach to worship that asks, What do I get out of it? This consumer mentality arises from worship in which the members are merely spectators—a "gazing stock"—instead of participants.[6] "We should work ceaselessly for the full participation of the lay membership of the congregation in the act of worship."[7] This has become one of the central planks in emergent worship. Emergents believe that the modern evangelical church is nonparticipatory in its many established patterns of worship. And the very structure of the congregational space for worship—seating arrangements and the centrality of the pulpit—ensures this nonparticipatory mentality. Moreover, worship services are large events with technology and professional polish. All this fosters a passive and consumerist approach to worship. Worship is led by a few, and the rest look on.

By contrast, for Emergents worship is not about people coming to consume music provided by a professional band or preaching by a polished communicator. Rather, worshipers are invited to become participants in the process. Emergents foster this participation in a variety of ways. They attend to size: large simply doesn't allow participatory worship, and so small is normative. They attend to the space: sitting in circles, for example, allows the congregation to see one another rather than to focus on the person up front. They attend to liturgical and fellowship practices that enable participation: people are invited to tell their stories and share their faith journeys, and an atmosphere of interactivity, and dialogue is encouraged.[8] They attend to inclusivity of many ages: children participate in the service.[9]

In a global, modern world, worship has been standardized and is irrevocably modern in its use of technology, music, and liturgical practice. In contrast,

3. Lesslie Newbigin, *The Good Shepherd: Meditations on Christian Ministry in Today's World* (Grand Rapids: Eerdmans, 1977), 37.

4. Michael W. Goheen, *The Church and Its Vocation: Lesslie Newbigin's Missionary Ecclesiology* (Grand Rapids: Baker Academic, 2018), 110–20.

5. Eddie Gibbs and Ryan Bolger, *Emerging Churches: Creating Christian Community in Postmodern Cultures* (Grand Rapids: Baker Academic, 2005), 156–72; Dan Kimball, *The Emerging Church: Vintage Christianity for New Generations* (Grand Rapids: Zondervan, 2003).

6. Newbigin, *Good Shepherd*, 32–34.

7. Newbigin, *Good Shepherd*, 36.

8. Gibbs and Bolger, *Emerging Churches*, 156–72.

9. We'd better pay attention to this! The earlier children participate in worship, the more likely they are to remain in the faith.

Emergents want worship to be indigenous and creative, involving the members in various ways in the planning, organizing, and practice of worship. Moreover, there is a desire to return to ancient practices, such as *lectio divina*, in contrast to the noise of modern entertainment.

Emergents challenge the rationalism of modernity in worship. Dan Kimball speaks of "experiential, multisensory" worship.[10] Instead of monological preaching dominating the service, the weekly practice[11] of the Eucharist becomes the center of worship. Arts that engage the various senses are incorporated into the worship experience.[12] Various practices with prayer, music, and Scripture reading that engage more of the senses are encouraged.

The ECC has also challenged traditional forms of preaching, moving to dialogical preaching models instead of monologue. Tony Jones notes in particular the important role that the sermon plays in emergent gatherings and the way it has been reimagined.[13] He is concerned to more actively involve members in the hearing of Scripture since the Spirit is given to the whole church. Kimball emphasizes the importance of storytelling and the use of visuals.[14]

There is much to learn here for a missionary congregation. But the questions may be asked: Ancient practices notwithstanding, is there much in the traditional liturgy of the church that needs to be recovered? Is it only modernity that is being critiqued here? And, even so, is every imprint of modernity on worship to be rejected? Is it possible to follow much of this wisdom in smaller groups or missional communities, and to have larger worship celebrations that do not succumb to the consumerist and entertainment cultures? Is it the egalitarianism and democratism of the American culture that is leading us here as much as Scripture?

Leadership

The ECC is also rethinking leadership practices and roles in the local congregation. Modernity stressed authority and a hierarchical form of leadership. Emergents find much of this incompatible with the teaching of Scripture on the gifting of all members by the Spirit to build one another up, on the

10. Kimball, *Emerging Church*, 127–32, 155–70.

11. Newbigin criticizes the "dry Mass" (*missa sicca*), a service of the Word without the Eucharist. See Lesslie Newbigin, "Worship—Cleaning the Mirror," *Reform* (September 1990): 7; Newbigin, *Good Shepherd*, 34.

12. We need to beware of new postmodern idolatries that speak of art as a "holy practice" (Jones, *The Church Is Flat*, 117). If art is prioritized over other areas of creational life as a special channel of God's grace because it bypasses the rational, then a new idol is created.

13. Jones, *The Church Is Flat*, 106–7. See also Doug Pagitt, *Preaching Re-imagined: The Role of the Sermon in Communities of Faith* (Grand Rapids: Zondervan, 2005).

14. Kimball, *Emerging Church*, 171–96.

priesthood of all believers, and on the unbiblical clergy-laity distinction. But the egalitarian and relational nature of postmodern culture, along with its suspicion of authority, also drives the ECC's new practices.

Leadership in emergent churches leans strongly toward nonhierarchical models. Emergents want to dissolve the clergy-laity distinction that has been so destructive of the use of gifts in the church. Leadership shifts to a more facilitative role, with many emerging churches experimenting with leaderless groups. Leaders as facilitators create space for the group to discern its calling together and to embody the practices that arise out of its local context and sense of mission. Power is diffused throughout the group, and decision-making is consensual.[15] Brian McLaughlin summarizes this reimagined leadership: "This type of leadership flattens the typical modern hierarchy and creates a community in which 'all members help make decisions and take turns leading, actions that serve as a counter to the control and oppressive tendencies of modernity.'"[16]

The ECC has rightly discerned some serious problems with structures of modern leadership, forms that stretch back in church history and contributed to the formation of a clergy-class and the institution of ordination. These are huge topics, and Newbigin has addressed some of these issues.[17] He too was aware of the problems with the abuse of power. Yet God gave leaders to the church to do more than facilitate. Newbigin is concerned that a certain kind of radical egalitarianism can undermine the kind of leadership and good creational gift of authority that is needed for missionary congregations. He was a bishop, after all, and wrestled with how the bishopric could serve the church. His reflection on that issue alone is worth considering when coming to terms with postmodern egalitarianism. Moreover, Newbigin is much more sensitive to tradition than is the ECC—he does not want to break with the entire tradition of the church in terms of ministerial order. He has also struggled with how leaders can take individual initiative while also fostering the involvement of the whole community. Leaders are neither dictators who impose their wills on the community nor pollsters who register the desire of the majority.

There is much food for thought from the ECC. Its participants have raised important questions about long-standing distortions of church leadership that have arisen out of Christendom and modernity. As with many issues, the question remains whether they have reacted too strongly and resisted helpful approaches to leadership shaped by past traditions.

15. Gibbs and Bolger, *Emerging Churches*, 192–213; Jones, *The Church Is Flat*, 118.
16. Brian McLaughlin, "The Ecclesiology of the Emerging Church Movement," *Western Theological Seminary* 61, no. 3 (Fall 2008): 109.
17. Goheen, *Church and Its Vocation*, 127–32.

Spiritual Formation

Newbigin stressed the importance of spiritual formation practices for the missionary church. The ECC has continued much further down this road, seeking to implement various practices of formation as well as to recover ancient spiritualities. This is a burning need today. More and more, we have begun to see that the liturgies and practices of a consumer society need to be countered by more intentional spiritual practices rooted in the gospel.

Kimball begins his discussion of spiritual formation with the words of Dallas Willard: "Nondiscipleship is the elephant in the church."[18] Indeed, preoccupation with the Sunday morning event has led to churches lacking strong discipleship. Many within the ECC want to correct this. Their version of discipleship is set over against what they see as wrong with the modern evangelical church. Kimball sets up a table comparing the modern and emerging church, contrasting compartmentalized with holistic, individual with communal, modern with ancient, knowledge and belief with faith and action, education with spiritual formation, presentation and teaching with experience and participation, peripheral ministry with central practice.[19] Sometimes these contrasts feel a bit too simplistic. But there is much truth here on which leaders can chew. The challenge to *do* discipleship and to think about *how* we do it, considering the powerful forces of modern culture, is urgent.

We note again the general absence of discipleship in two of the most critical areas: vocation and family. Most people will spend most of their time at work or school and in their families. Yet most people have no idea how to live under the lordship of Jesus Christ in the public square, where the powerful religious spirit of humanism dominates. In fact, many deeply committed Christians have no idea even that they should. Again, this is an issue of great importance for Newbigin.[20]

Of no less importance is training parents for their task of discipling their children. By far the most important calling of every parent is forming their children. Most parents are struggling with how to disciple their children in a very difficult time. In our ministries, we have found parents at a loss about how to equip their children in the areas of education, media, technology, family worship, gender and sexuality, political ideologies, consumerism, racism, and much more. We submit that vocation and family must take a much higher priority in the discipling ministry of the church.

18. Dallas Willard, *The Divine Conspiracy: Rediscovering Our Hidden Life in God* (New York: HarperSanFrancisco, 1998), quoted in Kimball, *Emerging Church*, 213.
19. Kimball, *Emerging Church*, 215.
20. Goheen, *Church and Its Vocation*, 82–86.

Among the spiritual formation practices addressed by the ECC, of note is the adoption of Celtic and other contemplative traditions, including those of Ignatius, such as *lectio divina* and the *examen*, as practices of discernment, reflection, meditation, and communal listening to God's spoken word. Monastic orders are emerging in many emergent churches, leading to a neomonasticism—a truly eclectic spirituality from a variety of ecclesiastical and theological traditions, most of which are premodern.[21]

Of course, there is always the threat that these spiritualities will be taken up into postmodern spiritualities that are really one more item for consumption that leads to our "spiritual" well-being. But there is also great potential here for nurturing practices that will more deeply root us in the gospel.

Relational Evangelism

We noted above the ECC's strong stress on the importance of hospitality, building relationships, and adopting a listening, welcoming, and humble posture for sharing the gospel. These practices are critical. But there is also much wisdom in the ECC concerning how to proclaim the gospel. We noted in the previous chapter Brian McLaren's discussion of "opportunity maximizers" in a postmodern world that will enable us to seize opportunities to make known the gospel. McLaren also speaks of "designing a new apologetic" and "learning a new rhetoric."[22] Even though we believe there is not enough critique of postmodernity nor an appreciation of the creational insights of modernity, we have found his discussion and the similar approaches of other ECC authors to be full of wisdom. We take from these discussions the following helpful insights for communicating the gospel to a postmodern generation:

- Embody a humble and listening posture.
- Take a dialogical rather than a dogmatic approach.
- Appreciate the spiritual thirst in a postmodern generation.
- Recognize and address the postmodern spiritual predicament.
- Refuse to offer easy answers to tough questions.

21. Gibbs and Bolger, *Emerging Churches*, 217–34; Tony Jones, *Sacred Way: Spiritual Practices for Everyday Life* (Grand Rapids: Zondervan, 2005); Brian D. McLaren, *Finding Our Way Again: The Return of the Ancient Practices* (Nashville: Thomas Nelson, 2008); Doug Pagitt, *Re-imagining Spiritual Formation: A Week in the Life of an Experimental Church* (Grand Rapids: Zondervan, 2004).

22. Brian D. McLaren, *The Church on the Other Side: Doing Ministry in the Postmodern Matrix* (Grand Rapids: Zondervan, 2000), 73–85 (new apologetic), 87–93 (new rhetoric), 171–88 (opportunity maximizers).

- Discern the difference between significant and less significant issues.
- See dialogue partners as friends and potential strugglers.
- Communicate winsomely, with respect and compassion.
- Tell stories and invite them to tell theirs.
- Avoid coercion, pressure, and a defensive posture.
- Listen carefully and with sympathy, compassion, and solidarity.

There is much here to be gleaned. However, a warning is in order. A humble and listening posture can keep us from proclaiming the truth of the gospel. Recognizing our relativity can lead to relativism. A dialogical approach can make us fearful of proclaiming the truth of the gospel as an event in history that accomplished salvation and calls for a total response. A refusal to offer easy answers to difficult questions, such as sexuality, can lead us to where the Bible has nothing to say to these issues. An attitude of sympathetic compassion can hamper us from calling for repentance from sin. A solidarity with the postmodern world can lead us to adopt the humanistic idolatry at the base of that worldview. A Christian tolerance can become a postmodern tolerance. A recognition of the spiritual thirst of postmoderns can lead to treating the gospel as one more spirituality to meet those needs. A "committed pluralism" can become an "agnostic pluralism."[23] Humility may become timidity.

The gospel is a story of what has happened in history for the whole world. This kind of message needs to be announced as truth by witnesses. While arrogant and aggressive approaches to evangelism have been only too real in modernity, this does not abolish the task to tell the true story of the world and to seek to convince others of its truth and to aim at response, conversion, and discipleship. This is not an act of dogmatic arrogance but simply the discharge of the task that we have been chosen to do. Not to discharge this task is betrayal.

A Gospel of the Kingdom for a Postmodern World

Newbigin and N. T. Wright

For Newbigin, the gospel is the good news of the kingdom that Jesus preached. It is a narrative of his life, death, and resurrection, by which the kingdom of God as the culmination of God's renewing work in the Old Testa-

---

23. Lesslie Newbigin, *Truth to Tell: The Gospel as Public Truth* (Grand Rapids: Eerdmans, 1991), 58; cf. Goheen, *Church and Its Vocation*, 193–94.

ment has broken into history. This emphasis on the kingdom continued in *Missional Church*, and the emergent church conversation carries on this tradition.

The kingdom of God as the central theme of the preaching of Jesus has increasingly captured New Testament scholarship. Over against the doctrinalism of modernity, the ECC emphasizes the Gospels and the kingdom.[24] And particularly, early in the second stage of the emergent church, it was N. T. Wright who influenced the leaders of the ECC.[25] Wright's work shifts the interpretation of Jesus and especially Paul from the categories of dogmatics shaped by the Reformation to the eschatological setting of first-century Judaism. One reads Paul through the theological lens of the Judaism of the first century and not through that of Luther. Wright opens New Testament teaching about the kingdom of God for many in the ECC.

When the kingdom of God becomes central, many dimensions of New Testament teaching fall into place—like pieces of a puzzle. The first is a deepening doctrine of *creation*. The kingdom is about the restoration of the whole of creation and all human life from sin and its effects. Thus we need to pursue much more urgently what God's purpose in creation was in the beginning, the "what" that is being recovered. A doctrine of creation is found among some in the ECC, but—compared to Wright or Newbigin—it remains weak.

The second piece is *structural sin*. This is seen in the New Testament language of the "powers" and of the "world." While sin is rooted in the heart of each person, we pattern cultures in the form of the idols we worship together. And idolatry always produces injustice. The gospel of the kingdom is about the renewal of human life, which means an ultimate dismantling of all systemic evil. This understanding of systemic sin is often grasped by the ECC.

The third aspect of New Testament teaching that the gospel of the kingdom leads us to is the *scope and nature of salvation*. Salvation is comprehensive (its scope) restoration (its nature); it is the renewal of creation. So much theology has reduced the Christian faith to the individual person in terms of sin and salvation. The kingdom challenges this reductionism. This reorients our teaching on the cross and resurrection as well. These events are the hinge of universal history. The cross is the defeat of the sin and evil that corrupts the whole world, and the resurrection is the dawning of the new. This cosmic breadth of the gospel is acknowledged by the ECC.

24. Gibbs and Bolger, *Emerging Churches*, 47–48.
25. Michael Clawson, "Emerging from What? The Historical Roots of the Emerging Church Movement" (PhD diss., Baylor University, 2017), 185–96.

A fourth category the ECC has taken from Wright and Newbigin is that mission is as broad as salvation. Our understanding of the gospel and salvation will undergird our view of mission. If sin touches the whole of human life and if salvation does the same, then our mission is as broad as the creation.

A fifth piece of the puzzle is that the gospel is not simply a theological or propositional statement. It is more than that: it is the power of God unto salvation. Emergent leaders call us to push against the ways in which the gospel has been reduced by modernity to doctrinal formulations or theological abstractions. In a vivid metaphor, Jones writes that the gospel is like lava that will burst through all attempts to domesticate it in doctrinal formulations.[26] In contrast to such reduction, the church in the West must recover the claim that the power of God's renewing work is channeled through the gospel.

And a final implication: the kingdom is not simply the gospel of Jesus but is the primary category of the entire New Testament, including Paul. Wright places Paul in his Jewish eschatological context. Some in the ECC have not followed Wright here. McLaren, for example, urges us to move beyond what he caricatures as the "Paulinity" of our understanding of the gospel, with its focus on the doctrine of atonement and the doctrine of justification by faith.[27] Of course, this is not the whole of Paul but a reduction.

Early on, the ECC was schooled by Newbigin and Wright. But there are concerns that the orthodoxy that characterized Wright and Newbigin may have been surrendered by some in the ECC in their revision of biblical teaching. For example, for Wright and Newbigin the atonement stands at the center of cosmic history, but in some voices of the ECC this has been diminished and questioned. Likewise with God's wrath and hell. Both writers affirm God's ultimate judgment and wrath,[28] while Rob Bell proclaims that "love wins."[29] There have been departures from the Christian tradition in other areas as well, including original sin, the exclusivity of Christ, sexuality, and biblical authority.

26. Tony Jones, *The New Christians: Dispatches from the Emergent Frontier* (San Francisco: Jossey-Bass, 2008), 36–37.
27. Brian D. McLaren, *The Secret Message of Jesus: Uncovering the Truth That Could Change Everything* (Nashville: Thomas Nelson, 2007), 91.
28. N. T. Wright, *Surprised by Hope: Rethinking Heaven, the Resurrection, and the Mission of the Church* (New York: HarperOne, 2008), 175–83; Lesslie Newbigin, *Christian Witness in a Plural Society* (London: British Council of Churches, 1977), 24–25. Newbigin has sometimes been accused of being a universalist. His position is fraught with tension, and we are not in full agreement with him. But he is not a universalist. He even says that it may be that the "majority of men . . . may be left outside." *Sin and Salvation* (London: SCM, 1956), 119.
29. Rob Bell, *Love Wins: A Book about Heaven and Hell and the Fate of Every Person Who Ever Lived* (New York: HarperOne, 2011).

Some may ask why this promising start on the kingdom of God moved in a liberal direction. It may well be that the idolatry of postmodern culture has simply caught up with many. That is the danger for all those who rightly want to be relevant and engage the culture to appeal to the church's cultured despisers. But this is not simply intellectual idolatry—wrong thinking—but a realm where the spiritual powers are at work. We are all susceptible to those powers, and we all need ongoing liberation from their grip.

But there might be something else going on as well. We referred above to Newbigin's view of the nature of truth. Newbigin finds ultimately reliable and universally valid truth in historical events, especially in Jesus Christ. Has the ECC grasped the depth of this claim? We can illustrate the problem here with an analogy. In his foreword to Newbigin's book *The Gospel in a Pluralist Society*, Christopher Duraisingh gently calls attention to a tension he sees in Newbigin's thought between "the perspectival and the story character of the gospel" and "the absolute claims that are made for the gospel."[30] Duraisingh believes that the storied character of the gospel of the kingdom leaves far more room for relativity; it is a weaker claim for truth. He is then surprised by the absolute claims Newbigin makes for the gospel. However, Newbigin would no doubt respond that to see the Bible as the true story of the whole world and the historical finality of Christ is not a weaker version of the truth but the strongest version possible. And it is certainly the biblical version. Propositional truth is not a stronger version of truth.

Yet many in the ECC have embraced a more postmodern view of narrative rather than the Bible's view: the historical roots, its intertwinement with all human history, the claim of universality, the finality of Christ. One wonders whether the immersion of the ECC in postmodern thought has hindered its participants from fully following Wright and Newbigin on this point. But it is precisely this point that prevents a slide into liberalism.

The Gospel of the Kingdom and the Church

For emergent leaders, the kingdom of God means two things: first, that our mission in the world is broad; second, that we must rethink our structures to fulfill our mission. A gospel of the kingdom expands our vision for the mission of the church. This expanded vision leads many within the emergent movement to see the church's mission as much larger than the institutional church. Eddie Gibbs and Ryan Bolger comment, "The church is not necessarily the center of God's intentions. God is working in the world, and the

30. Christopher Duraisingh, foreword to *The Gospel in a Pluralist Society*, by Lesslie Newbigin (Grand Rapids: Eerdmans, 1989), viii.

church has the option to join God or not."[31] Emergents see mission primarily as the mission of God to renew all of creational life; therefore, they see that the mission of the church extends as wide as the reign of God.[32]

The church is a people who are sent out into the world seven days a week as witnesses to the kingdom of God, in contrast to the church as a people gathered one day for worship. Emergent churches see the need to deconstruct modern church practices in light of this conviction, asking how communal practices can serve the kingdom mission of the church.[33]

In this process, Emergent churches place emphasis not on numerical growth but on the strength of relationships, connections, interactions, and community bonds—ensuring strong levels of connectedness and community.[34] This often takes the form of de-centralized, smaller gatherings that can more effectively be a visible sign and servant of God's kingdom in a particular place. Emergent leaders see twenty-five to forty people as an upper limit in these communities in order to maintain this strong relational connectedness and kingdom focus. Larger gatherings are suspect and have strong potential to inhibit the kingdom focus. Any community gatherings must be useful to support the life of the community, and they must flow out of the organic connectedness the community experiences together.[35] These are important insights.

We detect, however, two problems: the specter of Johannes Hoekendijk and an anti-institutional spirit. These are especially explicit in Pete Ward's notion of liquid church, which has been popular in emergent circles.[36]

Many within the movement resonate with Ward's small but influential book, *Liquid Church*. His concern is for the renewal of the church in order for it to be an effective agent in changing our culture. He describes "liquid" as a new way of being God's people in worship and in mission, where the emphasis is placed on the church as primarily a network of people and relationships and communications, not a gathering of people who meet at a certain time and place. Emphasis is placed on living as Christ's body in the world, with no weekly gathering together required for this.[37] Ward argues that Paul's view of the church provides us with liquid, organic notions of what the church is that

---

31. Gibbs and Bolger, *Emerging Churches*, 42.
32. Gibbs and Bolger, *Emerging Churches*, 64.
33. Gibbs and Bolger, *Emerging Churches*, 96. See also Tony Jones, *The Teaching of the Twelve: Believing and Practicing the Primitive Christianity of the Ancient Didache Community* (Brewster, MA: Paraclete, 2009).
34. Jones, *The Church Is Flat*, 108–10.
35. Gibbs and Bolger, *Emerging Churches*, 102.
36. Pete Ward, *Liquid Church* (Eugene, OR: Wipf & Stock, 2002).
37. Ward, *Liquid Church*, 2–4.

will move us beyond the static and "solid church" ecclesiologies of the past.[38] With a "liquid reformation" we are free to engage in what God is doing in the world and outside the institutional church.[39]

A liquid church will move us out into the world to seek justice and the healing of creation. We need to see the Spirit of life at work outside the institutional church and beyond the activity of individual believers. The Holy Spirit is the energy of God that creates and sustains life, active in the world and responding to people's searching.[40]

However, Ward has not offered us clarity about how, if at all, one can discern where the Spirit of life is at work in the world.[41] History is littered with claims about where God is at work and summons us to join him, most troublingly in National Socialism in Germany and apartheid in South Africa. Newbigin warns about the difficulty of seeking to identify the work of God in the world throughout history with specific political, economic, social, or cultural processes. In fact, he says, we may attribute the work of the Spirit to pagan spiritual powers![42]

The Hoekendijkian Specter

It is troubling to see history repeat itself. We see repeated the same pattern from the 1960s and '70s. We see it in the missional church movement and now also in the ECC. It begins with a reaction to a church that is introverted, structurally rigid, and captive to its culture. This raises a holy indignation followed by a recovery of the teaching of Scripture in four areas: the missionary nature of the church, the kingdom of God, a broader mission of God's people in the world, and the work of the Spirit beyond the church and the individual. In a prophetic reaction to the self-absorbed and syncretistic church, this teaching is like a drink of cold water in a hot desert. In prophetic (over)reaction, this biblical teaching is itself distorted: there is a diminishment of the church in God's mission; a rejection of the importance of the church community, especially any institutional structure; and a disconnection of the work of the Spirit from Christ and the church. This was the pattern of the secular decades and of some in the ECC.

Newbigin's vigorous clash with this vision, both as he engaged Hoekendijk in the 1950s and as he engaged its new form, championed by Raiser, during

38. Ward, *Liquid Church*, 7–8.
39. Ward, *Liquid Church*, 10–16.
40. Ward, *Liquid Church*, 79–86.
41. Michael W. Goheen, "'As the Father Has Sent Me, I Am Sending You': Lesslie Newbigin's Missionary Ecclesiology," *International Review of Mission* 91, no. 362 (2002): 351–52.
42. Lesslie Newbigin, *Signs amid the Rubble: The Purposes of God in Human History*, ed. Geoffrey Wainwright (Grand Rapids: Eerdmans, 2003), 109.

the 1990s, remains a powerful counterargument. We have noted this argument twice already in this book. Newbigin's primary argument is threefold. First, if we understand the church in terms of the biblical story, then the church must be understood as a sign that points to the kingdom. This pointing comes both as the church experiences a foretaste of the kingdom and as it serves as an instrument of the kingdom. The foretaste is seen in the church as a redeemed community that is distinct and different from the world. The instrumental nature of the church is the way God uses his people as an instrument in the world for evangelism, justice, mercy, care for creation, and so on. The church cannot be reduced to its instrumental role. The Spirit works first *in* the church and then *through* the church.

Second, if this is true then the life of the kingdom must be nurtured within the institutional church. Ward's call for diminishing the importance of the community is suicide. It cuts off the missional means of grace whereby God gives his kingdom life to his people.

And finally, it is true that the Spirit is at work beyond the church and each person. Yet this is not the primary emphasis of Scripture. Christ sends his Spirit on his church to continue his mission in the world through this community. Newbigin is fond of pointing to the story of Cornelius (Acts 10–11) to show how the Spirit works outside the church. But the Spirit then leads Peter to speak the gospel. Cornelius and his household are baptized into the church. Certainly we must demonstrate the kingdom in acts of justice, mercy, creation care, peacemaking, and so on. And further, we will judge where God is at work in the world as we do so. But history has taught us caution about claiming to know where God is at work in the world.

An Anti-institutional Posture

An anti-institutional posture is rampant in emergent church circles. Frustration with church and a tendency to equate the church of Christendom and modernity with the institutional church have moved many in the ECC toward an anti-institutional stance.[43] We have observed this in the missional church conversation, but the anti-institutional spirit is stronger in the ECC.

We can summarize earlier arguments against anti-institutionalism. First, an institutional form of the church is inevitable. This is seen in the many attempts of the ECC to find new ways of forming community and practices

43. See Gibbs and Bolger, *Emerging Churches*, 18–23, 28–29; Jones, *New Christians*, 4–7; Jones, *The Church Is Flat*. 164–65; Doug Pagitt, "The Emerging Church and Embodied Theology," in *Listening to the Beliefs of the Emerging Churches: Five Perspectives*, ed. Robert Webber (Grand Rapids: Zondervan, 2007), 31.

to nourish life in the world. Give the ECC more history, and these ways will either turn into an institution or die. Second, institution does not necessitate institutionalism. Third, if the church wants to have any lasting influence and continue through history, then taking an institutional form is inevitable. Finally, the institutional church is the place where the life of the kingdom is channeled to God's people. The church must organize itself in some way in terms of leadership and practices. A liquid church will die in the long run, and its "members" will not be sustained and nourished in their difficult and painful mission in the world to embody the good news over against the cultural powers.

Theology and the Unity of the Church in a Postmodern World

It can be fairly said that throughout Newbigin's life, one topic he addressed as much as any was the unity of the church. And he closely tied unity to the missionary nature of the church. The church's missionary calling is to be a preview of the new humanity that will inherit the new creation. That new humanity is a reconciled people, one new humankind united in Christ. They provisionally embody God's purpose "to be put into effect when the times reach their fulfillment—to bring unity to all things in heaven and on earth under Christ" (Eph. 1:10), so that the world may believe that the Father has sent Jesus to restore all things (John 17:20–23).

At the end of his major book on ecclesiology, Newbigin concludes that the eschatological nature of the church establishes two fundamental things about the church: the church must be one if the world is to believe, and as the church lives into its missionary nature, disunity is seen as an intolerable scandal.[44] He illustrates scandal in the following humorous way: If there are two rival temperance societies in one town living in conflict, that is unfortunate but not scandalous. If there is a temperance society in which the members are habitually drunk, that is scandalous. This is because the members' life contradicts their message. A church living in disunity is not unfortunate but scandalous, because its disunity contradicts its message.[45] And so Newbigin worked tirelessly for unity.[46]

44. Lesslie Newbigin, *The Household of God: Lectures on the Nature of the Church* (New York: Friendship Press, 1953), 170–74.
45. Lesslie Newbigin, *The Reunion of the Church: A Defence of the South India Scheme* (London: SCM, 1948), 23–24.
46. Michael W. Goheen, *"As the Father Has Sent Me, I Am Sending You": J. E. Lesslie Newbigin's Missionary Ecclesiology* (Zoetermeer, Netherlands: Boekencentrum, 2000), 200–218, available at http://dspace.library.uu.nl/handle/1874/597.

The book *Missional Church* did not take up the topic of unity, and the ensuing conversation on missional church paid scant attention to it. Not so with many in the ECC. Like Newbigin, they rightly see modernity as the culprit for disunity, both in denominationalism and in the scandalous split between liberals and evangelicals.

The ECC recognizes that the root problem of disunity is a modern epistemology that leads to theological division. And so the ECC reflects on the importance of epistemology for the nature of theology. We noted above that a postmodern critique of modernity highlights the historically relative and contextual nature of all human knowledge, the way that individually and socially subjective factors shape our knowledge, the inability of method to rise above our context and give us objective and neutral knowledge, and the need for an epistemic humility that is averse to certainty. It is this postmodern critique of modern epistemology that we must embrace, according to the ECC.[47]

And this will have implications for our theology, argues Jones: an envelope of friendship and reconciliation must surround all debates about doctrine and dogma instead of the modernist claim of right doctrine and correct thinking, which divides. We must place emphasis on the local, conversational, and temporary nature of all our theologizing. We must become increasingly aware of our relative position to God, to one another, and to history in a way that breeds a humility open to dialogue and ongoing discovery. Truth, like God, cannot be definitively articulated by finite human beings. We must be willing to embrace a wider rationality that allows space for the imagination, creativity, intuition, emotions, and dialogue.[48]

There are important insights here about the nature of theology[49] that have implications for the unity of the church. The ECC rightly sees the scandal of a divided and bickering church whose witness has been severely damaged. And many involved in the ECC have correctly observed that a good portion of this scandal is the result of a modern epistemology. Moreover, we must make a distinction between Scripture and theological reflection and not assume that

47. McLaren, *Church on the Other Side*, 162–64. For further exploration and development of this, see Rob Bell, *What We Talk about When We Talk about God* (New York: HarperOne, 2014); and Brian D. McLaren, *Faith after Doubt: Why Your Beliefs Stopped Working and What to Do about It* (New York: St. Martin's Essentials, 2021).

48. Jones, *New Christians*, 78–79, 112–15, 140–42, 153–59.

49. One of the best chapters on contextual theology can be found in Harvie M. Conn, *Eternal Word and Changing Worlds: Theology, Anthropology, and Mission in Trialogue* (Grand Rapids: Zondervan, 1984), 211–60. See also Michael W. Goheen, "Theology in Context: The Changing Landscape," *Christian Courier*, June 25, 2001, 14–15; Goheen, "Theology in Context: Lesslie Newbigin's Contribution," *Christian Courier*, July 9, 2001, 16–17. The combined articles are available online at https://missionworldview.com/wp-content/uploads/2020/06/ea8a85_91cc7e 12f4a447ff9024f7b5b764374e.pdf.

our theological reflection simply mirrors the Bible. The Bible is infallible, but our theological formulations are not. Our theology is always contextual, and it is futile to believe that any biblical hermeneutic or theological method will allow us to transcend our context. This should lead us to epistemic humility that acknowledges that all our theological work is limited and deformed to some degree by cultural idolatry. Dialogue with Christians from other traditions, from other cultures, from other times in history, and from other social locations can enable us to see Scripture's teaching better. And surely, a welcoming hospitality and envelope of friendship and reconciliation should characterize our disagreement, even when we strongly disagree.

Newbigin affirms the need for a critique of theology undergirded by a modern epistemology, as well as many of the insights we have just enumerated. But there are some evident differences between the ECC and Newbigin's thought. In the ECC, often the final authority of Scripture is eclipsed, the history and tradition of the church are minimized, and the specter of relativism arises when the formative power of context is recognized. For Newbigin, there are at least four tributaries that flow into the stream of theology: Scripture; the tradition of the church, especially found in creeds and confessions; current issues and needs of the church in a particular culture; and the theological work of churches from other cultures. Yet these are not equal partners: priority must be given to Scripture, since it is God's revelation.

> Authentic Christian thought and action begin not by attending to the aspirations of the people, not by answering the questions they are asking in their terms, not by offering solutions to the problems as the world sees them. It must begin and continue by attending to what God has done in the story of Israel and supremely in the story of Jesus Christ. It must continue by indwelling that story so that it is our story, the way we understand the real story. And then, and this is the vital point, [it must] . . . attend with open hearts and minds to the real needs of people.[50]

In this statement, the importance of both the primacy of Scripture and the context (real needs of people) is recognized, but Scripture is acknowledged as the final authority.

The importance of Newbigin's insistence on truth located in a narrative of God's mighty acts in history culminating in Christ, rather than in timeless ideas, is evident again here considering the nature of theology. If the gospel is the Christ-event, it can be expressed in a variety of faithful and mutually enriching theologies from various times and places. There will be no search

---

50. Newbigin, *Gospel in a Pluralist Society*, 151.

for a *theologia perennis*, an unchanging, universal theology. Yet all theology must conform to the Scriptures, since its story—centered in the gospel—is universally valid truth.

In addition to the final authority of Scripture for theology, all contextual theology must be done in conscious connection with the "rule of faith" provided in the creeds of the history of the church. Newbigin gives a ringing affirmation of the importance of church history, tradition, confessions, and creeds. "The Bible can only be understood in the fellowship of the Church— and the Church means the whole company of Christ's people in all ages."[51] Theology in dialogue with brothers and sisters in past history is part of understanding the Scriptures "together with all the Lord's holy people" (Eph. 3:18). Newbigin is adamant that all contemporary struggles with Scripture require the guidance of theological tradition. His concern for the importance of context did not bring about an eclipse of the gains of history.

These two affirmations—the final authority of Scripture and the indispensability of theological tradition—put Newbigin at odds with much of the ECC even while he affirmed many of the concerns it has expressed: a critique of modern epistemology, the importance of context for theology, the importance of humility and dialogue, and a fundamental distinction between the gospel and our theological reflection on it. Yet, while affirming all of this, Newbigin was wary and critical of postmodernity.

For Newbigin, both good theology and the unity of the church were based on correctly discerning the nature of truth in Scripture. Scripture tells the true story of God's acts in history, climaxing in Christ. The Bible does not give us eternal theological ideas that we simply rearrange into a systematic theology. Unity is found neither in a modern intellectual agreement to a uniform theology nor in a postmodern relativizing of the truth of Scripture. It is found in the Christ-event and the gift of the Spirit that creates a people who share in Christ's death and resurrection.

Of course, these affirmations do not solve the complex problems of how to discern when one no longer is centered in Christ. But the critique of modernity and the affirmation of truth in the whole event of Jesus Christ is an important starting point.

The ECC has provided an important spur to a missionary engagement with contemporary culture, to be sensitive to those struggling and floundering in our rapidly changing culture, to critique (and love) a church hopelessly domesticated to modernity, to the many insights that come from attending to

51. Newbigin, *Reunion of the Church*, 135.

the postmodern critique of modernity, and to the missionary nature of the church. We have often found its insights refreshing and insightful.

However, Newbigin warns us that the gospel must be contextualized in a way that is both *faithful* to its biblical message and *relevant* as good news to those who hear it. The danger of trying to be faithful is to hold on to older forms of faithfulness out of fear of contemporary spirits and powers. The ECC warns against this as its participants encounter it in much of modernity. The danger of trying to be relevant and engaging the contemporary spirits is that one wades into a spiritual battle fraught with danger. Relevance so easily leads to syncretism, accommodation, and cultural captivity. This is the danger that the ECC faces.

Some in the ECC recognize this danger, and that is why there has been splintering. Our hope is that we might learn from the ECC, as well as from Newbigin's voice, both as it critiques and as it affirms. But ultimately our hope is that the Spirit might shine the light of the gospel on the ECC, Newbigin, and this chapter.

PART 4

Center Church

11

A Missionary Encounter with Western Culture

It is hard to overestimate the growing global influence of Tim Keller and the ministry of Redeemer Presbyterian Church in New York City, where Keller served as founding pastor from 1989 until 2017. Through Redeemer's church-planting center and website of resources, through Keller's speaking and writing ministry, and through the influence of the Gospel Coalition, cofounded by Keller, the scope of his influence has grown significantly.

In his 2017 Kuyper Lecture, Keller makes explicit the significant influence of Lesslie Newbigin on his own ministry in New York.[1] He relates that the year he began to plant Redeemer in New York, Newbigin's book *The Gospel in a Pluralist Society* was published,[2] and that there was no one else at that time who was as helpful as Newbigin as Keller faced the hard secular realities he was encountering as a pastor. For more than thirty years, Keller has wrestled with Newbigin's haunting question, "Can the West be converted?"[3] Newbigin helped Keller see that Western culture had become one of the most challenging and resistant missionary frontiers of our time and what a missionary encounter with Western culture would look like. Keller goes on to articulate seven areas of a missionary encounter inspired by Newbigin.

1. Timothy Keller, "Answering Lesslie Newbigin" (Kuyper Lecture, Princeton Theological Seminary, April 6, 2017), available at https://www.youtube.com/watch?v=V0LG26k6ngs.
2. Lesslie Newbigin, *The Gospel in a Pluralist Society* (Grand Rapids: Eerdmans, 1989).
3. Lesslie Newbigin, "Can the West Be Converted?," *International Bulletin of Missionary Research* 11, no. 1 (January 1987): 2–7.

Keller gave two more lectures about a missionary encounter with Western culture in subsequent years and then, in 2020, published a small ebook about this missionary encounter.[4] There are some minor changes made in these later lectures and the ebook, but what is noteworthy is that even though a heavy debt to Newbigin remains clear, especially if one has listened to the Kuyper Lecture, Newbigin is hardly mentioned or footnoted. What is troubling about this is that if Newbigin was so helpful to Keller in his early ministry as the only one who was addressing the difficult "post-Christian" mission field Keller was encountering, Newbigin may be as helpful to others as well. But if Newbigin goes unmentioned, few will be directed to read and appropriate his insights. Moreover, it is difficult to square Keller's negative characterization of Newbigin in his widely read book *Center Church* with the glowing praise for Newbigin's insight and influence on his ministry expressed in his Kuyper Lecture.[5] We cannot speculate about the reasons. No doubt there are strategic communicative sensitivities one faces when addressing evangelical and ecumenical audiences. We ourselves are aware that all speakers must make strategic choices. But Newbigin's books were significant catalysts for Keller's terminology and understanding of a missionary encounter. We want pastors to read Keller and appropriate much of the insight he gained for a missionary church as he developed Newbigin's vision in the context of New York. But we want them equally to be exposed to the rich work of Newbigin. And we fear that Keller has made it much more difficult for this to happen, especially among his devoted evangelical readers.

While by Keller's own testimony he was shaped by Newbigin, he was also shaped by at least two other traditions, and it is difficult to understand his thought without sensing the tension between them. He was shaped by the neopuritan influence arising from the Westminster Confession and Reformed systematic theology. And he was also formed by the neo-Calvinist tradition. His doctoral advisor was Harvie Conn, who played a role in shaping his vision for urban mission.[6] Conn was the most consistent neo-Calvinist professor at Westminster Theological Seminary, and his cross-cultural experience in South Korea gave that theological tradition a missionary expression. Both of us are also shaped by these two traditions, which jostled at Westminster during

4. Timothy Keller, *How to Reach the West Again: Six Essential Elements of a Missionary Encounter* (New York: Redeemer City to City, 2020).

5. Timothy Keller, *Center Church: Doing Balanced, Gospel-Centered Ministry in Your City* (Grand Rapids: Zondervan, 2012), 252.

6. Keller says, "I would never, ever have been open to the idea of church planting in New York City if it were not for the books and example of Harvie Conn." Quoted in Mark Gornik, "The Legacy of Harvie Conn," *International Bulletin of Missionary Research* 35, no. 4 (October 2011): 215.

our time there, but in our case much more by the neo-Calvinist stream and by Conn in particular. These three streams have converged to bring about a creative tension in Keller's vision for the missionary church.

It might appear initially odd that we have dealt in our first chapters with two church movements or conversations comprising many authors and practitioners, and here we deal primarily with the thought of just one man. This can be justified by the fact that Keller is a prolific author and popular speaker, and his influence in the missionary church conversation has been as great in North America as the missional or emergent conversations, and even greater than them beyond this continent. Moreover, he has placed himself in the historical trajectory of the missionary church conversation that we are tracing. In addition, happily we find Keller addressing crucial issues concerning the missionary church found in Newbigin that are often missing in other conversations. He is closer to Newbigin and to our own missional neo-Calvinism in many points of his missionary ecclesiology than the other two conversations we have addressed.

Yet, while affirming so much, we also find ourselves confounded by Keller's writing and speaking at many points. Most often, we find Newbigin more in line with Scripture. So we again proceed in these three chapters on center church by appreciatively noting how Keller has carried forward the conversation on the missionary church in fresh and helpful ways, and then listen to Newbigin's voice as it affirms, critiques, and enriches the conversation.

In some ways, dealing with the voice of one person might seem easier than encountering the complexity of multiple voices. This is partially true. But Keller is eclectic and, like a magpie, he builds his theological nest from many places. Moreover, he is a busy practitioner who is primarily concerned with ministry and not with systematic exposition. Positively, this gives his thought both ecumenical breadth and ministry relevance. Less positively, sometimes we hear voices from different traditions that are not always consistently unified. But what he has bequeathed to the church, both in North America and beyond, in terms of living out its missionary identity is massively helpful.

A Missionary Encounter with Western Culture

Keller's appropriation of Newbigin's missionary encounter with Western culture is primarily indebted to two books—*Foolishness to the Greeks*[7] and

7. Lesslie Newbigin, *Foolishness to the Greeks: The Gospel and Western Culture* (Grand Rapids: Eerdmans, 1986).

The Gospel in a Pluralist Society. It is the first that Keller explicitly references as shaping his understanding of a missionary encounter, especially the last chapter, on the church's role. Understanding the argument of that book—from the call to a missionary encounter at the beginning of the book to the church's role at the end—is important to understanding Keller.

In the first sentence, Newbigin asks "what would be involved in a genuinely missionary encounter between the gospel and the culture . . . which those of us who share it usually call modern."[8] He opens this up by drawing on his missionary experience in India and articulating a model of communicating the gospel across a cultural frontier. On the one hand, the missionary must enter into the worldview of the foreign culture and employ its language and forms if the good news is to be communicated in a way that is understandable and relevant. On the other hand, since that cultural worldview is formed by a comprehensive religious vision that is to some degree incompatible with the gospel, the gospel must radically call into question the ultimate beliefs embodied in the language. The danger of utilizing the idolatry-laden terms and forms of the culture is that, in an attempt to be relevant, one may take on board the religious vision carried by the language and so fall into syncretism. For example, in India Jesus is proclaimed as Lord (*guru*) and becomes just one of thousands of gurus offering salvation, as understood by Hinduism. Newbigin uses an example of Jesus as one more god in a Hindu temple, worshiped on a special day of the year. In this case, the name of Jesus and the gospel have found a place within the pantheon of gods in the Hindu religion. This is hardly evangelism. However, if the missionary does not embody the gospel in the forms and language of the culture, the message will be incomprehensible. In the very language the missionary uses, there is already an encounter between two different and clashing comprehensive religious understandings—the gospel and the cultural worldview. The goal is to call hearers to repentance—to leave their religious commitment and come to Christ, revealed in the gospel. That radical conversion of turning from one comprehensive religious vision to another in Christ can only be a work of God.

This model of cross-cultural communication is illustrated in John's Gospel, where he freely uses the language and thought forms of pagan culture. But he employs this pagan terminology in such a way as to confront pagans with a challenge to the pagan dualism embodied in the language. "The *logos* is no longer an idea in the mind of the philosopher . . . [but] the man Jesus who went from Bethlehem to Calvary."[9] The religious longing of John's readers to

---

8. Newbigin, *Foolishness to the Greeks*, 1.
9. Newbigin, *Foolishness to the Greeks*, 6.

understand the source of order, revealed in the language of *logos*, is *fulfilled*. Yet the idolatrous worldview that gives expression to that religious longing is *subverted*. This calls for a conversion to Christ to rightly understand and satisfy the desire to know the origin of order in the world.

It is important to understand this dynamic to understand much of what Keller does so well. Newbigin's understanding of missionary communication expressed here is virtually identical to that of Harvie Conn (and J. H. Bavinck), who also influenced Keller. All these men came to this understanding through their missionary struggle to communicate the good news of Jesus Christ in a pagan culture with terms shaped by a religious vision contrary to the gospel. They affirmed the religious longing and insight within the cultural expression, showed the inadequacy of paganism to meet that longing, and offered the gospel as a message that would dismantle paganism but offer the only solution in Christ to the cry of the heart. This model of a missionary encounter—subversive fulfillment—permeates the way Keller engages "post-Christian" culture in New York City.

This model of cross-cultural communication is intended by Newbigin to illustrate more than contextualization in *verbal* communication or evangelism. This is a model that vividly describes the Christian life and witness in its totality. In their missionary identity, Christians must live out their entire lives as a missionary people to make known the gospel in the forms, institutions, customs, and patterns of a particular culture. Their whole lives—family and marriage, economics and politics, art and business, sports and the judicial system, worship and education—are given meaning and form by the neopagan religious vision of the culture. Yet as inhabitants of the culture, we cannot dissociate ourselves from these idolatrous institutions and patterns in which we are embedded. We must live in a way within them that somehow at the same time calls into question the very idolatry that shapes them. In so doing, our lives and words call our unbelieving neighbors to turn from idolatry that cannot meet the deepest religious needs of humanity and to serve the living God, who can. This work of conversion can only be a work of God that enables unbelievers to see and hear things differently in the good news and turn to serve Christ. Their neopaganism is subverted by the gospel even as the gospel meets the deepest longings of their neopagan hearts.

The deadly danger that can derail the whole missionary encounter is the accommodation of the gospel to the idolatry of the culture. If the gospel is reshaped to find a place *within* the cultural religious vision, there is no missionary encounter and no call to conversion. If Jesus is one more god in the Hindu pantheon, he fits nicely into the culture and offers no challenge to radical conversion.

The problem is that this is precisely what has happened, not just in so-called mission fields but in neopagan Western culture. But people led astray by the myth of a neutral culture don't recognize the religious nature of their culture and are vulnerable to syncretism. The gospel has been absorbed into the comprehensive religious vision shaping Western culture. We have understood the gospel from within the religious convictions of the culture rather than understanding the idolatry of the culture from within the comprehensive vision of the gospel. And when our lives and words are captive to culture, there is no missionary encounter and call for conversion to Christ.

It is this logic of a missionary encounter expressed in the opening chapter of *Foolishness to the Greeks* that captured Keller's imagination. Newbigin's book works this out, first, by offering a profile of Western culture that shows that Western culture is not neutral. It is a set of beliefs and practices that seek to grasp and express the ultimate nature of the world, and therefore it claims final loyalty—and so Newbigin rightly designates it as a "religion."[10] It is these religious beliefs that give shape and meaning to the whole of human life.[11] Then, second, if there is to be a missionary encounter, the authority of the Bible must be liberated from its cultural captivity. Scripture is a comprehensive narrative in which God's character and purpose are rendered, and this must be recovered from both liberal and conservative theologians who allow Scripture to be accommodated to modern humanism.[12] With the recovery of the religious nature of Western culture and the comprehensive narrative of Scripture, Newbigin is in a position to elaborate what a missionary encounter between this biblical story and Western culture looks like in two powerful cultural arenas—science and politics.[13] He ends his book with a chapter titled "What Must We Be? The Call to the Church."[14] He asks how the church can be different (separate and distinct) from but also take responsibility (through solidarity and involvement) for our neopagan culture.[15]

Newbigin elaborates seven essential tasks: reclaim eschatology and a gospel of the kingdom; recover a Christian understanding of freedom over against the idolatrous view that shapes the West; pursue a "declericalized theology" that

10. Newbigin, *Foolishness to the Greeks*, 3.
11. "The Profile of a Culture," chap. 2 in Newbigin, *Foolishness to the Greeks*.
12. "The Word in the World," chap. 3 in Newbigin, *Foolishness to the Greeks*.
13. "What Can We Know? The Dialogue with Science," chap. 4, and "What Is to Be Done? The Dialogue with Politics," chap. 5 in Newbigin, *Foolishness to the Greeks*.
14. Newbigin, *Foolishness to the Greeks*, 124–50.
15. For Newbigin, Western culture is a neopagan culture in which "paganism, having been born of the rejection of Christianity, is far more resistant to the gospel than the pre-Christian paganism with which cross-cultural missions have been familiar. Here, surely," he says, "is the most challenging missionary frontier of our time." *Foolishness to the Greeks*, 20.

offers a biblical framework to shape the laity for their callings in the public life of culture; radically critique the modern roots of the denominationalism that destroys the unity of the church; listen to the voices of Christians from other cultures, who can enable us to see the idolatry of our own culture; find the courage to live out and proclaim the gospel that stands in contradiction to the unquestioned beliefs and commitments of our culture; and practice worship and praise that overflows into witness in the life of the world.

We have taken the time to elaborate the logic of Newbigin's vision of a missionary encounter as he develops it in *Foolishness to the Greeks* because it is this logic that has had a shaping influence on Keller's thirty years of ministry. In Keller's Kuyper Lecture, he elaborated his own list of elements of a missionary encounter that would answer the question "What must we be?" In the remainder of this chapter we will sketch the way Keller has worked out a missionary encounter, with appreciation for his rich development but also with an ear to Newbigin's voice.

Elements of a Missionary Encounter with Western Culture

We observe in Keller's writing and work the following elements of a missionary encounter with Western culture: adopting a public apologetic, forming a distinctive community for the common good, bearing witness in the public square, renarrating our lives with the Scripture, and listening to the voice of global Christians.

Adopting a Public Apologetic

Newbigin has recognized that most classical apologetic approaches have simply accepted the religious framework of Western culture and tried to defend the gospel from within that framework.[16] They have ceded the fundamental religious beliefs of our rationalistic culture at the outset and attempted to defend the gospel from within those assumptions. Specifically, classical apologists accepted the assumptions of their humanistic assailants as they embraced the neutrality of scientific reason as the final arbiter of truth and submitted to its canons to defend the faith. The gospel is explained and defended from within the cultural religious vision.

For Newbigin this is not a missionary encounter but the capitulation of the gospel to an alien religion. Apologetics must be the other way around. The cultural religious vision must be interpreted and explained from within

16. Newbigin, *Gospel in a Pluralist Society*, 2–3.

the comprehensive worldview of the gospel. The problem is that the embrace of scientific reason as a final authority has produced a disastrous dualism of the public and private. Scientific reason reigns over the public realm, and the gospel is relegated to the private. Thus it is a category mistake to use the gospel as the final arbiter of truth for areas of public life. The "facts" of public life must be authorized by scientific reason.

To remove this barrier—and we must remember that Newbigin is appealing *to Christians* who have unwittingly accepted humanistic assumptions—we must radically critique the Western epistemology at the foundation of our culture that upholds this dualism and allows scientific reason such ultimate authority. Newbigin critiques this epistemology and offers a more creational one that demonstrates that all knowing is the activity of a community that makes sense of the world by reason in light of its members' ultimate assumptions. The modern scientific worldview employs the ultimate light of science, but the Christian community respectfully declines that authority and begins with the light of the gospel. This clears the way for the Christian community to encounter the issues of Western culture from within the gospel, affirming the creational insights and rejecting its idolatrous distortion.

This "presuppositional" approach starts with the comprehensive truth of the gospel as the final authority and then understands, analyzes, affirms, and critiques the cultural story in its light. This approach characterizes Keller's apologetic engagement. He calls it an "incisive public apologetic" and acknowledges Newbigin's influence.[17] We see this public apologetic in action repeatedly as Keller encounters common objections to the Christian faith as well as pressing cultural longings and baseline narratives.

A missionary approach will welcome skeptics and address their fervent intellectual questions with a respectful and humble apologetic. Keller addresses six heartfelt questions and genuine objections to the Christian faith from Western people:

1. Isn't the Bible a myth? Hasn't science disproved Christianity?
2. How can you say that Jesus is the only way to God? What about other religions?
3. What gives you the right to tell me how to live my life? Why are there so many rules?
4. Why does God allow so much suffering? Why is there so much evil in the world?

17. Keller, "Answering Lesslie Newbigin."

5. Why is the church responsible for so much injustice? Why are Christians such hypocrites?

6. How can God be full of love and wrath at the same time? How can God send good people to hell?[18]

What is important in this context is the way Keller addresses these issues. He demonstrates that these questions do not arise from a neutral place but are the product of an alternate set of ultimate beliefs. He critiques those beliefs, showing that they cannot deliver what they promise. In fact, the Bible offers a better framework to address these concerns.

During the eight years following the publication of *The Reason for God*, Keller became increasingly aware that the objections he had addressed in that book arose out of a general awareness of the Christian faith and out of the objectors' desire to engage the Bible. While the approach he used at that time remains helpful in some situations, in an increasingly secularized world, it had become clear that the cultured despisers were not even interested in engaging the Christian faith. Keller's apologetic shifted to address various themes in American culture that revealed deep religious longing.[19] There is a longing and desire for meaning in life, for finding happiness and satisfaction, for freedom, for identity and self-worth, for hope in the future, for morality, and for justice.

What is significant about Keller's approach is that he is operating with the missionary approach of subversive fulfillment that we saw demonstrated in John's Gospel and articulated by Newbigin. Keller identifies the true longing and spends time articulating and documenting that longing in our culture. He then subverts modern attempts to ultimately fulfill that yearning offered by the Western cultural story. Finally, he offers the gospel as the only true way to fulfillment.[20]

This approach is exceedingly helpful, not just for evangelism but for preaching.[21] What are the deep longings of the heart that the Christian congregation

18. Timothy Keller, *The Reason for God: Belief in an Age of Skepticism* (New York: Riverhead Books, 2008); Keller, "Our New Global Culture: Ministry in Urban Centers," Redeemer City to City, 2010, p. 14, http://www.justinbuzzard.net/wp-content/uploads/2010/04/Keller-Our-New-Global-Culture-Ministry-in-Urban-Centers.pdf.

19. Timothy Keller, *Making Sense of God: An Invitation to the Skeptical* (New York: Viking, 2016).

20. This approach saturates Keller's writing: other good examples include Timothy Keller, *Counterfeit Gods: The Empty Promises of Money, Sex, and Power, and the Only Hope That Matters* (New York: Dutton, 2009); Keller, *Walking with God through Pain and Suffering* (New York: Viking, 2013); Keller, *Hope in Times of Fear: The Resurrection and the Meaning of Easter* (New York: Viking, 2021).

21. See Timothy Keller, *Preaching: Communicating Faith in an Age of Skepticism* (New York: Viking, 2015).

needs to have satisfied? How is our culture trying to satisfy them? How does the gospel satisfy these longings, calling for repentance from seeking fulfillment in the wrong places? Keller masterfully shows us the way foreign missionaries ply their trade in New York City.

Forming a Distinctive Community for the Common Good

Newbigin asks, "How is it possible that the gospel should be credible, that people should come to believe that the power which has the last word in human affairs is represented by a man hanging on a cross? I am suggesting that the only answer, the only hermeneutic of the gospel, is a congregation of men and women who believe it and live by it."[22] The powerful skepticism of Western culture will never be broken by even the best public apologetic. Only when people see the power of the gospel to change a community to be distinctive, a picture of the new humanity, a "new social order,"[23] will the words of the gospel and an incisive apologetic carry power.

Newbigin offers a list of what that looks like if the church is living in contrast with the idols of the culture:

- A community of praise in a culture of suspicion
- A community of truth in a culture of relativism
- A community of selfless involvement in the concerns of the neighborhood in a culture of selfishness
- A community who lives out their vocational callings for the sake of the world in a culture that privatizes the gospel
- A community of mutual responsibility in a culture of individualistic and autonomous freedom
- A community of hope in a culture of despair

Keller runs with Newbigin's insight and calls for the local church to be a "counter-culture for the common good."[24] Being the church today "involves a much more radical break with the surrounding non-Christian culture. The church can no longer be an association or a club but is a 'thick' alternate human society in which relationships are strong and deep—and in which sex and family, wealth and possessions, racial identity and power, are all used and

---

22. Newbigin, *Gospel in a Pluralist Society*, 227.
23. Lesslie Newbigin, *Truth to Tell: The Gospel as Public Truth* (Grand Rapids: Eerdmans, 1991), 85.
24. Keller, *Center Church*, 273.

practiced in godly and distinctive ways."[25] He immediately recognizes that this will not mean withdrawal from culture into a ghetto or a radically polemical or repellant hostility to culture. The alternate society must be set within the culture and not separate from it, serving the culture for the common good. The old missionary dilemma of separation and solidarity is rightly negotiated.

This concern to be a counterculture for the common good drives Keller's thought. One example is the way he uses the language of Larry Hurtado to articulate five distinctives of the early church in the Roman Empire as a "unique, category-defying social project."[26] For Keller, "category-defying" has to do with resisting the paradigms of the dominant culture. This will make the church both offensive and attractive as it challenges cultural norms. The early church was a disruptive social project by being a distinctive community that offered a real alternative in the Roman world. While the disruptive alternative brought suffering, it was also attractive. The early church was a multiracial and multiethnic community in an empire divided by race and religion; it was a community that was committed to caring for the poor and marginalized in an empire devoid of compassion; it was a community whose members did not retaliate but forgave when they suffered in an empire of power and revenge; it was a community that stood against abortion and infanticide on the basis of Scripture and in practice took in exposed infants in a world of callous disregard for human life; and it was a community with a revolutionary sexual ethic in a world of sexual gratification.

Keller translates this into the American setting. The American church needs to be a community (1) that is multiethnic; (2) that is committed to the poor and to justice; (3) that models civility, peacemaking, and bridge-building as a patient, humble, tolerant, gentle, and forgiving people; (4) that is staunchly pro-life; and (5) that offers a sexual counterculture.[27] He notes that the first and second of these characterize the Left in American life (multiracialism, justice) and the last two the Right (pro-life stance, sexual counterculture). And so a category-defying people will reject the deeply held idolatrous ideologies of both wings shaping American culture while affirming the insights of both. This is certainly wise counsel for the missionary congregation in the United States to work out in greater depth.

Bearing Witness in the Public Square

A central feature of Keller's ministry is taking up Newbigin's call to develop the vital missionary role of believers in their vocations in the public

25. Keller, *Center Church*, 273.
26. Keller, "Answering Lesslie Newbigin."
27. Keller, *How to Reach the West Again*, 30–37.

square. For Newbigin, the laity plays a crucial role in the mission of the church in their witness to the public truth of the gospel as the new humanity living under the lordship of Christ. This is more than evangelistic concern for our coworkers; rather, it is being restored to God's original creational intention to cultivate and care for creation by forming a culture that glorifies God. If believers are to live this way, they will be swimming upstream against idolatrous cultural currents. And so congregations must find ways to effectively support and equip the laity in their various callings. The problem is that most congregations have not engaged in the training of the laity for their callings. And so most Christians, even though they are godly and well-meaning, are deeply shaped by the idols of Western culture in their work.

We have noted the general silence and eclipse of this crucial dimension of Newbigin in much of the missional church and emergent church conversations. Not so with Keller: he has developed this in spades. He recognizes that two dichotomies have crippled the church. The fact-value dichotomy has led so many Christians to seal off their faith from their work, relegating their faith to the private sphere. Those who do try to break out of this typically do so by trying to be outspoken about their faith. They lack the resources, certainly not least a doctrine of creation and kingdom gospel, to shape their work. The sacred-secular dichotomy also relegates ministry to the work of the institutional church, and all other work is considered secular. When this happens, we don't see the Christian faith "as a comprehensive interpretation of reality that pervades everything we do."[28]

Keller understands work in the context of the biblical teaching on creation and kingdom. The gospel can shape our work by changing our motivation for work, by changing our conception of work, by giving us an ethic for the workplace, and by giving us a way to reimagine how our work is done.[29]

If the laity are to be faithful, leadership and the ministries of congregational life must equip God's people for their vocations. Newbigin saw the importance of this and articulates four key ways the congregation can take up this task: the congregation can be a fellowship that nourishes the life of Christ through means of grace where Christ himself is present in saving power; the congregation can foster a community that supports believers through encouragement, prayer, and even financial help; the congregation needs to develop ecclesial structures that will equip believers; and the congregation

---

28. Keller, *Center Church*, 330.
29. Keller, *Center Church*, 331; Timothy Keller with Katherine Leary Alsdorf, *Every Good Endeavor: Connecting Your Work to God's Work* (New York: Dutton, 2012).

needs to foster leadership that sees part of its calling as the duty to nourish and equip leaders for their vocation.[30] Keller has taken up this challenge. He says he received this inspiration from *Foolishness to the Greeks*, where Newbigin also notes the importance of the Kuyperian tradition. Newbigin notes especially the servant role of the congregation: it is "important that all its lay members be prepared and equipped to think out the relationships of their faith to their secular work. Here is where the real missionary encounter takes place. . . . However, this line of thinking will be fruitful only if the work of scientists, economists, political philosophers, artists, and others is illuminated by insights derived from rigorous theological thinking. For such a declericalized theology, the role of the church will be that of a servant, not a mistress."[31]

Following Newbigin's lead, Keller looks at ways that the local congregation can serve by nurturing believers for their specific vocations, by being a place where believers develop a Christian worldview to help them do their work distinctively, and by fostering networks and connections to allow for mentoring and encouragement. Keller helped initiate the Center for Faith and Work in New York City and has cast a vision for the importance of this type of ministry in other cities and networks around the globe.[32] Newbigin's vision is being realized and advanced in significant ways through Keller's work in this area.

Renarrating the Church's Life

If the church is to be a countercultural community both in its communal life and in its scattered life in the public square, its life must be shaped by the biblical story. One of the most powerful themes evident in Newbigin's work is that there is an encounter between two stories. From birth we are narrated into our cultural story. But the work of the church in formation is the difficult and intentional task of renarrating the church to live faithfully in the biblical story. Indeed, "if the biblical story is not the one that really controls our thinking then inevitably we shall be swept into the story that the world tells about itself. We shall become increasingly indistinguishable from the pagan world of which we are a part."[33]

30. Michael W. Goheen, *The Church and Its Vocation: Lesslie Newbigin's Missionary Ecclesiology* (Grand Rapids: Baker Academic, 2018), 82–86.

31. Newbigin, *Foolishness to the Greeks*, 143–44.

32. See the Center for Faith and Work website, https://faithandwork.com/, and the Global Faith and Work Initiative website, https://www.globalfaithandwork.com/.

33. Lesslie Newbigin, "Biblical Authority," Newbigin Archives, University of Birmingham (unpublished article, 1997), 2.

The secular narratives of identity, freedom, happiness, science, morality, justice, and progress powerfully shape us as they overwhelm us in a torrent of advertising, music, stories, social media, news media, entertainment, and more. We are daily catechized to live in the cultural narratives by our technology in a digital age. If we are not being intentional to renarrate our lives with Scripture, then it will be these narratives that shape us.

Keller helpfully speaks here of a "counter-catechesis."[34] This will be a catechetical process that "explains, refutes, and renarrates the world's catechisms to Christians."[35] We can note again the deliberate way that Keller employs the missionary approach of subversive fulfillment. The basic narratives of the secular catechism will be identified and illustrated from today's culture. Then they will be both affirmed in their creational truth and critiqued in their idolatrous distortion. Finally, they will be shown to be fulfilled in their best form only by Christ.[36]

We can see a divergence here, with Keller on the one hand and Newbigin and the early church's counter-catechetical practice on the other. Keller speaks here of the secular *narratives* but, when it comes to Scripture, he speaks of the "biblical teachings and *truths*."[37] Newbigin, very much like the early church,[38] speaks of an encounter with the biblical story. While it might appear that this is simply a different way of expressing the same thing, it is not. For Newbigin it is an understanding of the biblical story *as a comprehensive counternarrative* to culture that can catechize us, and not simply theological and moral truths from Scripture. The fundamental authority of Scripture is found in its comprehensive narrative authority. His critique of liberal and conservative theologians in *Foolishness to the Greeks* is precisely to that end. If we lose Scripture as an all-encompassing narrative and if our counter-catechesis is simply truths and teachings of Scripture, that will not be enough. Only the power of a comprehensive narrative can withstand the power of the cultural narrative. Truths and teachings will be discrete bits that will be swept along by the powerful streams of the broader cultural story.

---

34. Keller, *How to Reach the West Again*, 38.
35. Keller, *How to Reach the West Again*, 38.
36. Keller, *How to Reach the West Again*, 40.
37. Keller, *How to Reach the West Again*, 40.
38. Everett Ferguson shows that the catechism of the early church, beginning with Irenaeus's telling of the biblical story in "Proof of Apostolic Preaching," was to renarrate the lives of believers with the biblical story to re-form their identity. See Ferguson, "Irenaeus' *Proof of Apostolic Preaching* and the Early Catechetical Instruction," in *The Early Church at Work and Worship*, vol. 2, *Catechesis, Baptism, Eschatology, and Martyrdom* (Cambridge: James Clarke, 2014), 1–17.

The early church provides a model of counter-catechesis in the biblical story that needs to be recovered today. Living in a pagan environment, the early Christians needed not "truths" of Scripture but the truth of the biblical story, from creation to consummation. Living in a Hindu environment, Newbigin also understood the importance of a counternarrative. This is perhaps one of the most important lessons we need to learn from Newbigin: the church needs to be discipled in the biblical narrative as the true story of the world in order to encounter our culture's story in our lives.

Listening to the Voice of the Global Church

Newbigin quotes a Chinese proverb: "If you want a definition of water, don't ask a fish."[39] If you want to know about American culture, for example, don't ask an American: Americans are swimming in these cultural waters all the time; it is the only environment they know. The problem is when the waters are polluted. Western cultural idols are not readily recognized by folk living in the West. This is dangerous in that it threatens the missionary vocation of God's people to speak and live good news that challenges the West in a way that calls for conversion. If there is to be a missionary encounter with the West, Western Christians must learn to see their own culture through the eyes of Christians shaped by other cultures.[40] Newbigin quotes Ephesians 3:18, which says that the love of Christ is so wide, long, high, and deep that it can only be grasped "together with all the Lord's holy people." If Western Christians are to understand the gospel and see how their lives are compromised by cultural idolatry, they must learn to listen to non-Western Christians.

Keller mentions this in his Kuyper Lecture, even stressing its fundamental importance, but unfortunately, while this does appear a few other times in his subsequent speaking and writing, it does not feature as prominently again.

Contextualization

Underlying all these elements of a missionary encounter is a strategy articulated by Lesslie Newbigin, Harvie Conn, J. H. Bavinck, and Hendrik Kraemer that they learned by trying to communicate the gospel in non-Western missionary settings. Significantly, Newbigin calls attention to the inadequacies of many cultural analyses because they have not been informed by the experience

39. Newbigin, *Foolishness to the Greeks*, 21.
40. Newbigin, *Foolishness to the Greeks*, 146–48.

of a cross-cultural missionary.[41] That is why those of us who have not had this deeply immersive bicultural missionary experience would be wise to attend to their words. Keller has done so, and it has borne rich fruit in North America and beyond. In this last section we highlight more specifically the missionary approach that underlies his encounter with Western culture.

Missionary Encounter

To begin, our encounter with Western culture is a *missionary* encounter. Islam understands well that its religious vision is comprehensive and will inevitably produce an encounter with the equally religious and equally comprehensive vision of Western capitalism. However, for Islam this is not a *missionary* encounter.[42]

An encounter is characterized by the clash of two equally ultimate religious stories: the Christian faith and the religious beliefs of a culture as they are embodied in the various institutions, practices, customs, and patterns of the community. Newbigin employs the imagery of an encounter to curb the widespread assumption that the gospel may be consigned to a private place within the broader culture, and thus to open the way for Christians to bow the knee before other gods and lords in public life. Islam understands this well and has even chastised Christians for not understanding the comprehensive scope and ultimate nature of their own gospel and for their consequent syncretism.

However, in contrast to Islam, this encounter in the Christian faith is *missionary*. That means it is characterized by three things: First, the gospel is translatable and can take on cultural form. There is no need to displace the culture with a Christian culture. Newbigin rejects the notion of restoring Christendom and creating a Christian society. Following Newbigin, Keller says that a missionary encounter means that we do not try to "overtake" the culture.[43] The reason is that while there is *radical* discontinuity between the gospel and the religious vision of culture, there is not *total* discontinuity. The gospel can be translated into every culture in a way that embraces the rich goodness of each culture but rejects its idolatry. Islam wants to displace Western secularism with the Sharia law, while the missionary approach of Christians is to translate the gospel faithfully, embracing what is good and rejecting what is twisted.

---

41. Newbigin, *Foolishness to the Greeks*, 1.

42. See Lesslie Newbigin, "The Secular Myth" and "A Light to the Nations: Theology in Politics," in *Faith and Power: Christianity and Islam in 'Secular' Britain*, by Lesslie Newbigin, Lamin Sanneh, and Jenny Taylor (London: SPCK, 1998), 1–24, 133–65.

43. Keller, "Answering Lesslie Newbigin."

Second, a missionary encounter is noncoercive, loving, kind, gentle, respectful, vulnerable, willing to suffer, and forgiving. Negatively put, this is not an encounter that seeks to coerce the culture to become Christian by using political power. Neither does it stand over against its culture with a repellant sectarianism or arrogant self-righteousness. It does not belittle the beliefs of others. It is willing to be vulnerable and suffer when opposed while responding in a nonretaliatory and forgiving way. All of these characteristics are stressed by Newbigin in his writing, and we find them well expressed throughout Keller's writing and in his practice.

But finally, a missionary encounter remains a bold and uncompromising witness to Jesus Christ. The kind of posture described previously does not lead to a compromised or watered-down witness. There is much at stake: Jesus Christ is Creator of all things and the one who brings salvation and restoration. He is Lord, and all things rightfully belong to him. There can be no *shalom* or justice unless his lordship is acknowledged. He is the final judge. A weak or timid witness will not convert others to bow the knee to Jesus but allow them to submit to other gods. The good news is comprehensive and demands ultimate and comprehensive loyalty to Jesus. A witness that is less than that is not a missionary encounter.

On all these points Keller shares with Newbigin a commitment both to the fact that there must be an encounter and to the fact that it must be missionary.

Subversive Fulfillment

Keller employs a strategy of subversive fulfillment. In his Kuyper Lecture, Keller acknowledges that he has been influenced by Newbigin in a missionary approach he names "subversive fulfillment."[44] This terminology expresses something very important that is intrinsic to Newbigin and undergirds Keller's approach at almost every point of his engagement with secularized Western culture. Indeed, Keller masterfully wields this approach in the Western context.

There are deep religious longings in every human heart. Bavinck describes these yearnings in terms of five magnetic points: groping after God, craving salvation, searching for one's place in the universe, sensing a moral standard or norm, and seeking for meaning.[45] N. T. Wright expresses these religious

44. The exact term is Hendrik Kraemer's but is embraced by Newbigin. Hendrik Kraemer, "Continuity and Discontinuity," in *The Authority of Faith: The Madras Series* (New York: International Missionary Council, 1939), 1:4. Keller acknowledges the influence of Kraemer and Newbigin here. But perhaps the "*possessio*" model of Conn and Bavinck, which is virtually identical, plays a role in shaping his view as well.

45. J. H. Bavinck, *Church between Temple and Mosque: A Study of the Relationship between the Christian Faith and Other Religions* (1966; repr., Grand Rapids: Eerdmans, 1981), 32–33.

longings in terms of the search for justice, the thirst for spirituality, the need for community, and the wistful yearning for beauty. We have noted above that Keller enumerates six desires: to know the meaning of life, to find happiness and satisfaction, to find our true identity and self-worth, to have hope for a good future, to find a true morality, and to see true justice. Perhaps in our consumer society Mick Jagger has expressed it well—albeit with incorrect grammar! "I can't get no satisfaction." This is in spite of having tried, and tried, and tried. Every missionary identifies these deep human longings that need to be fulfilled.

Yet every person has suppressed the truth of God and submitted to the idols of a cultural community to fulfill those needs. Religious systems offer answers to the deepest religious longings. Western confessional humanism is not some neutral, scientifically based culture but a religious vision that offers answers to the deepest longings of the human heart.

A missionary approach takes a sympathetic, insider approach that imaginatively steps inside a rival religious vision to understand it and feel its fundamental religious longings, aspirations, needs, and desires. But at the same time a missionary recognizes the truth of the gospel and therefore takes a critical, outsider approach that brings the gospel to bear on that religious vision. These are brought together in subversive fulfillment. The gospel can offer the answer to the deepest yearnings of the heart. But there must be repentance—a turn from false religion to Christ to meet that need. This is not simply the gospel as an additive fulfillment but a message that contradicts and subverts the very way the need has been expressed as well as unsuccessfully met in another religious vision. John's Gospel leads the way in modeling this approach.

This is the approach Newbigin learned from John's Gospel and from his mentor, Kraemer. This is the approach that Keller has taken. It is an approach learned from cross-cultural communication and is badly needed for the missionary congregation today.

Translation Model of Contextualization

There is a difference between Keller and Newbigin in their approaches to contextualization. This is illustrated by Stephen Bevans's different models of contextualization. In the first edition of his book *Models of Contextual Theology*, Bevan offers five different models of contextualization. In the second edition he adds a sixth, to account especially for the uniqueness of Newbigin's view, which was not captured in the other five.[46] Unfortunately, he

---

46. Stephen Bevans, *Models of Contextual Theology*, rev. and exp. ed. (Maryknoll, NY: Orbis Books, 2002), xvi.

mislabels this sixth model the "counter-cultural model" and groups Newbigin with various other approaches. Keller's approach most closely approximates the first model—the translation model.

The translation model is characteristic of evangelicals and traditional Roman Catholics. It employs the analogy of the translation of literature from one language to another. At the heart of this model is the translation of an unchanging message into various cultures. The gospel has priority and must be inserted into culture. The gospel is somehow supracultural; there is a gospel "core" that stands above culture and is "wrapped" in a cultural expression. The gospel is the essential "kernel," which is encased in a disposable, nonessential husk. Contextualization takes place as the eternal and unchanging truth of the gospel is separated from its culturally bound mode of expression and contextualized within another cultural husk.

This model rightly takes the gospel message with the utmost seriousness; indeed, the Word of God is universally true and cannot be absorbed into any human culture. There is a problem with its view of revelation, however. It is primarily propositional and informational. It is about truths or doctrines that transcend culture and history. It is indebted to the Greek view in contrast to a biblical view, which sees truth as bound up with events in history and a redemptive-historical narrative.

It is here, in their view of biblical revelation, that Keller and Newbigin part ways. Newbigin repeatedly indicates that the source of reliable truth is the narrative of God's mighty acts in history moving to culmination in Jesus Christ, faithfully recorded and interpreted by the biblical authors, that reveal God and his purpose for the world.[47] For Keller, the Greek imprint is discernible, although there seems to be a tension because he has one foot planted in his neopuritan systematic theology and another planted in his neo-Calvinist and missionary biblical theology. For Newbigin, there is consistency in challenging the propensity of Western Christianity to find the source of truth in eternal ideas in Scripture. It is noteworthy that Newbigin spends a chapter in *Foolishness to the Greeks* recovering Scripture as a comprehensive narrative, something Newbigin believes is a prerequisite for a missionary encounter. It is also intriguing that the first item on Newbigin's list for what is needed if there is to be a missionary encounter is the *recovery of eschatology*—a gospel of the kingdom.[48] Interestingly, this is an item Keller does not mention in his elements of a missionary encounter. For Newbigin, contextualization is not the insertion of a gospel core into culture, but the faithful resolution of an encounter between two stories.

---

47. See Bevans, *Models of Contextual Theology*, 120–21.
48. Newbigin, *Foolishness to the Greeks*, 134.

This chapter has sketched important elements of Keller's understanding of a missionary encounter with Western culture. We have read few others who match him on these critical issues. Even though our treatment has been necessarily brief, his emphasis on a public apologetic, a distinctive community, the importance of discipleship that renarrates the church's life with the counter-vision of Scripture, the witness to the gospel in the public square and in the cultural vocation of believers, and the need to listen to the voice of the global church are all foundational to the missionary congregation. His appropriation of a missionary encounter and subversive fulfillment forged in the context of cross-cultural missions is vital. Few take the time to enter so deeply into the cross-cultural missionary experience and learn from that unique experience.

Keller has testified to the influence of Newbigin on his ministry. We wish he had been more explicit about his dependence on Newbigin and more fair in his characterization, so that others could gain the kind of insight he himself received. We also believe that Keller has taken on Greek views of truth and that a deeper dive into the issues Newbigin raises at this point would be beneficial.

This chapter leaves us with two deep impressions: First, we marvel at the way Keller, as a busy practitioner, has been able to appropriate Newbigin's cross-cultural vision and translate it so well into the highly secularized setting of New York City in a way that enables others to follow. Second, we note how often blindness to cultural idols has characterized our ministries and how subversive fulfillment and conversion remain an ongoing process in our own lives—one that is never fully complete. We critique Keller because his vision is impacting many others in the global church, and we do not want it to become a new theological imperialism shaped by Western culture.

12

The Missionary Congregation

One of the significant contributions Tim Keller makes to the notion of a missionary church is to connect a missionary encounter with what a missionary congregation should look like if this encounter is to happen. His deepening reflection on a missionary encounter with the West, prompted by the work of Lesslie Newbigin, led him to reflect further on what this means for the missionary congregation.

This is evident in an unpublished paper Keller wrote several decades ago. The burden of this short paper is that a church in New York City must be a *missional* church. He attributes his growing conviction on this matter to Newbigin. He contrasts "missional" with "evangelistic." An evangelistic church is the product of Christendom, a society that has been shaped by the Christian faith in its public life, its institutions, and its discourse. It "Christianizes" people by making them moral in their outward behavior. The church is one component of this Christendom culture that makes its limited contribution among the constellation of other powers. Like a chaplain, it takes up its task within this setting, and its function is to challenge individual people into a vital and living relationship with Christ while assuming a broader Christian culture.

However, this Christendom setting is disappearing in the West, and the opportunity to evangelize nominally "Christianized and moral" people who are generally favorable toward the Christian faith is rapidly vanishing. We can no longer assume any kind of Christian support system in public life or any interest in the church or some general knowledge of aspects of the Christian faith. The culture has become increasingly indifferent, even hostile, to the gospel and is now a mission field.

Newbigin's four-decades-long missionary experience in India enabled him to see that the church in a pagan setting had to be much more radical than a body that evangelized nominally Christian people. It had to become "completely 'missional'—adapting and reformulating absolutely everything it did in worship, discipleship, community, and service—so as to be engaged with the non-Christian society around it."[1] The posture of a missionary encounter with neopagan culture must pervade everything the church is and does, and the way it organizes itself. It must affect the church's relationship to God in worship, members' relationships to one another in discipleship and community, and the church's relationship to the unbelieving world in evangelism and service. The Western church needs to develop a full-blown "'missiology of western culture' the way it had done . . . for other pagan cultures."[2]

In small-town America, the Christendom situation may still prevail, Keller believes, and the church may still be able to live as an evangelistic church.[3] But increasingly, in the urban setting the United States has become like Europe and Canada. It is no longer tethered to the Christian faith, and its public life is rapidly shedding all traces of Christian influence. New York City is perhaps the most explicit exhibit of this neopagan side of American life. In this context, Keller recognizes the importance of Newbigin's challenge to develop a missional church. The missionary encounter with culture described in the previous chapter must now shape all aspects of the missionary congregation—its inner, gathered life and its outer, scattered life, its worship and its discipleship, its fellowship and its prayer, its leadership and its congregational structures, its relationships to other churches and to other social services in the city, its relationship to the public life of the city and to its injustices, its evangelism and its cross-cultural missions commitment. What Keller rightly grasps is that *missional* is not just about certain activities but about a wholesale reorientation of the church to its missionary vocation. In this chapter, we sketch how Keller tackled this task of helping his church to become a missionary congregation.

Keller's missionary reorientation to the local congregation has led to a breadth and integration of the various aspects of a missionary church that

1. Timothy Keller, "The Missional Church" (unpublished internal document, June 2001), 1.
2. Keller, "Missional Church," 1.
3. Keller might revise this statement today after seeing that small-town America is as deeply shaped by the conservative ideology of the Right as the urban setting is by the progressive ideology of the Left. Both ideologies are incompatible with the gospel. Both threaten the common good of public life and require a missional church.

is unmatched among most contemporary authors on this subject. His rich experience of planting and pastoring a church in the major urban setting of New York City, along with his ability to reflect on his experience in his reading and writing on his ministry, has provided a valuable and rich resource for what a missionary church can look like.

Marks of a Missional Church

Keller offers marks of a missional church in post-Christendom culture. He employed the language of *missional* just a few years after the publication of *Missional Church*.[4] In this first paper, and also from what we have described in the previous chapter, it is clear that he is indebted to Newbigin for some if not much of his fundamental orientation. It seems that he was also familiar with *Missional Church* early, but it was not until later, in *Center Church*, that he reflected more explicitly on the missional church movement.

These later reflections are problematic: Keller shows little awareness of the historical roots of a missionary church in the twentieth century that provide the context for the book *Missional Church*; he seems to collapse missional church into emergent church even though the two, while they may overlap, are different theological orientations; and finally (and most regrettably), he connects Newbigin with the missional church movement with a number of misleading descriptions.[5] While this chapter primarily affirms the rich direction Keller has taken this discussion, our concern here is the way

---

4. Darrell L. Guder, ed., *Missional Church: A Vision for the Sending of the Church in North America* (Grand Rapids: Eerdmans, 1998); Keller, *Missional Church*.

5. See Timothy Keller, *Center Church: Doing Balanced, Gospel-Centered Ministry in Your City* (Grand Rapids: Zondervan, 2012), 252. We must address at least three mischaracterizations of Newbigin in this book even if briefly. (1) Newbigin did claim "to be much more of an evangelical than a liberal" very early during his seminary years, and his evangelical commitment only increased. However, he had more in common with global evangelicals than American evangelicals. See Lesslie Newbigin, *Unfinished Agenda: An Updated Autobiography* (Edinburgh: Saint Andrew Press, 1993), 29. (2) Newbigin was not a universalist. He speaks often of God's final judgment and eternal loss—see, e.g., Newbigin, *Christian Witness in a Plural Society* (London: British Council of Churches, 1977), 24–25—and notes that even the majority of people may suffer eternal loss: Newbigin, *Sin and Salvation* (London: SCM, 1956), 119. (3) Keller seems to group Newbigin with a number of authors whom Keller believes mute the wrath of God (see *Center Church*, 271). In fact, Newbigin speaks strongly of the wrath of God, and quite often. Keller himself quotes Newbigin to this effect in his Kuyper Lecture, quoting one of the *nineteen* places Newbigin speaks of the wrath of God in one tiny book alone: Newbigin, *Sin and Salvation*, 104–5, quoted in Timothy Keller, "Answering Lesslie Newbigin" (Kuyper Lecture, Princeton Theological Seminary, April 6, 2017), available at https://www.youtube.com/watch?v=V0LG26k6ngs.

Keller is raising red flags among his evangelical audience about Newbigin and the notion of a missional church that was so valuable to Keller. These critiques of Newbigin authenticate Keller's own credentials as an evangelical to his readers, but at the cost of unfairly discrediting Newbigin and his missional heirs.

Nevertheless, the burden of this chapter is that Keller was effective in moving from a missionary encounter with culture to its rich implications for a missionary congregation, especially in our global urban context. Moreover, his ecclesiological reflection is broad and has integrated well many important themes. Newbigin's vision for a missionary congregation is greatly developed by Keller's long-term experience in a major American city.

If a faithful posture in Western culture is that of a missionary encounter, then what does a missional church look like? In his early paper Keller offers a list of five elements of a missional church,[6] and Newbigin's fingerprints are clearly discernable. The first element of a missional church is "discourse in the vernacular," in which the church sets aside Christian jargon and learns to speak in a way that is both respectful and comprehensible to unbelievers, as if they are always present. The second is that we "enter and re-tell the *culture's* stories with the gospel." To enter the culture's stories means being familiar with popular culture and the arts, where these stories are told. It also means engaging sympathetically with current issues and concerns—for example, freedom and justice. To retell these stories with the gospel means subversive fulfillment: appreciating the insight and feeling the need expressed in the cultural narrative, deconstructing the implausibility structure to show that the culture cannot fulfill the longing, and—finally—showing that the gospel can meet the need and helping move the unbeliever toward faith.

The third is to "theologically train lay people for *public* life and vocation." The Christendom church could afford to limit discipleship to training people in Bible study, prayer, and evangelism—private world skills. But no longer: a missional church will help people "think Christianly" about work and hold it up as "kingdom work." Helpfully, Keller notes the neo-Calvinist framework of common grace and antithesis for the task of engaging public life. Common grace means that there are areas of truth, justice, and right with which we can engage, and antithesis means that the gospel will clash with every part of culture, since culture is shaped by alternative religious beliefs.

The fourth element is to "create Christian community which is counter-cultural and counter-intuitive." Keller describes a church that exhibits a

---

6. Keller, "Missional Church," 1–3.

biblical sexual ethic, that is generous with money, and that overcomes the power differential created by race and class; a church more deeply and practically committed to mercy and justice than liberal churches, and to evangelism and conversion than fundamentalists; and finally, a church that challenges the liberal and conservative, Right and Left categories of American culture.

The final element is to "practice Christian unity as much as possible on the local level." Unity is far more important in a missional setting than in Christendom, and it is closely connected to the missionary calling of the church.[7] Unity must be displayed in a concrete way at a local level for the common good.

One helpful aspect of Keller's treatment of this topic is the shift throughout his writing from a Christendom-evangelistic church to a missional one, which carries with it the challenge to reorient our whole ecclesiology. His contrasts demonstrate that if we really take hold of a missionary encounter with a neopagan culture, this will change what it means to be church.

Over a decade after the publication of his early paper Keller returns to the topic, enumerating six "marks of a missional church" that are dependent on his first paper but offer increased insight informed by his ministry experience. He opens with a thought that will reorient the whole: a missional church will confront the idols of Western culture—for example, consumerism and expressive, autonomous individualism—through a missionary encounter with culture. This starting point reframes *even better* all aspects of church life, as expressed in the remaining five elements:

1. A missional church will learn to recontextualize the gospel in its evangelistic practices by entering, challenging, and retelling the culture's stories with the gospel.

2. A missional church will equip Christians for missional living in all areas of their lives, including at least three things: evangelizing those in their webs of relationships, loving their neighbors and their cities through acts of mercy and justice, and integrating their faith and work in their vocational callings.

3. A missional church will form a counterculture of those who live distinctively as a "'thick' alternate human society" but who are also deeply woven into their context. In this way, they are a servant community that exists for the common good.

7. Keller, "Missional Church," 1–3. See also Lesslie Newbigin, *The Reunion of the Church: A Defence of the South India Scheme* (London: SCM, 1948), 9–22.

4. A missional church will be "porous" in the sense that the community always expects non-Christians to be present whenever it gathers in worship and in small groups or carries out service projects.

5. A missional church will practice unity in its local place for the good of that place.[8]

Ministry Fronts

For Newbigin, the missionary church "always has two simultaneous duties."[9] The first is worship and prayer, word and sacrament, fellowship and discipleship as a gathered community. If the church fails to fulfill this, "it is liable to become salt without savour." The second is to involve itself more and more deeply in the life of the world, bearing witness to Christ. So "the very first essential" is "the strengthening of our churches in worship" and a "strong liturgical life" so that our eschatological existence as the new humanity in the world might be made "more real and vivid."[10] The "Holy Spirit is present in the believing congregation *both gathered* for praise and the offering up of spiritual sacrifice, *and scattered* throughout the community to bear the love of God into every secular happening and meeting." The "first priority, therefore, is the cherishing and nourishing of such a congregation in a life of worship, of teaching, and of mutual pastoral care so that the new life in Christ becomes more and more for them the great and controlling reality."[11]

We have seen surveyed in earlier chapters the tendency toward a reactionary diminishment of the community and institution of the church that arises out of frustration with an introverted church. Not so for Keller: for him, the gathered life and the scattered life are equally important. He is committed to integrating the many ministries of the church both as a gathered and as a scattered community. He formulates this in terms of four ministry fronts:

1. Connecting people to God (through evangelism and worship)
2. Connecting people to one another (through community and discipleship)

8. Keller, *Center Church*, 271–74.

9. Lesslie Newbigin, "The Evangelization of Eastern Asia," *International Review of Mission* 39, 154 (April 1950): 142.

10. Newbigin, "Evangelization of Eastern Asia," 143.

11. Lesslie Newbigin, "Evangelism in the City," *Reformed Review* 41 (Autumn 1987): 4–5 (emphasis added).

3. Connecting people to the city (through mercy and justice)
4. Connecting people to the culture (through integration of faith and work)[12]

Keller references the influence of Edmund Clowney, who speaks of a three-fold ministry of the church: we minister to and serve God through *worship*; we minister to and serve one another through Christian *nurture*; we minister to and serve the world through *witness*.[13] Keller takes these three ministries and develops them in a more missional way within the urban and post-Christendom setting. He devotes a chapter to each, noting that each deserves at least a book-length treatment. Keller envisions a holistic and integrated ministry for the missionary church. He overcomes a number of dualisms that cripple many churches: worship and witness, word and deed, evangelism and justice, gathered and scattered, diaconal and vocational, incarnational and attractional, institution and movement.

The Church's Outward Face: Holistic Mission

Keller rightly insists that missionary involvement in the world is to be holistic. But he does so in two contexts that shape his discussion: the American evangelical context that is racked by various dualisms and the new urban context of our global world.

Forms of Witness

For Newbigin, mission must be holistic. A careful reading of his literary corpus reveals that he repeatedly returns to five forms of witness:

1. Communal life: As the new humanity, the church in its communal life together must embody God's original creational intentions for humanity and for society, in contrast to the idolatries of culture that vitiate our humanity.
2. Vocation: The new humanity extends to the whole life of the church, including witness to the gospel in the church's scattered and cultural life. In our various vocations, including our work, we are called to be salt and light in the public life of culture.

12. Keller, *Center Church*, 293.
13. Keller, *Center Church*, 294. See also Edmund Clowney, *The Church* (Downers Grove, IL: InterVarsity, 1995), 117–65.

3. Mercy and justice: Both individually as scattered members of the body of Christ and as a community, we must demonstrate the mercy and compassion of the kingdom to alleviate the misery and suffering of people in the world. But we must move beyond the symptoms to the root cause: we must struggle for justice in every part of our culture and global world.

4. Evangelism: We are to give intentional verbal witness to what God has done and is doing in Jesus Christ, summoning people to repent, believe, and follow him.

5. Missions: Every local congregation is to be involved in efforts to cross cultural and social boundaries to extend the gospel to places and peoples who have not yet heard the good news—what has been traditionally called cross-cultural missions.[14]

Undergirding these forms of witness is a helpful distinction between missionary dimension and intention: "Because the Church *is* the mission there is a missionary dimension of everything that the Church does. But not everything that the Church does has a missionary intention. And unless there is in the life of the Church a point of concentration for the missionary intention, the missionary dimension which is proper to the whole life of the church will be lost." While the whole of the gathered and scattered life of the church witnesses to the good news that in Christ God is restoring human life, there remains the important task of intentional activities such as evangelism or church planting, where the "overall *intention* of that action is that they should be brought from unbelief to faith."[15]

Keller's vision for holistic ministry is equally broad. Indeed, all five of these elements find a prominent place in his missionary ecclesiology. First, we have already observed Keller's insistence on the church being a "'thick' alternate human society" and a "unique, category-defying social project"[16]—category-defying in the sense of being a distinctive, countercultural community that resists the idolatrous paradigms of the dominant culture. Second, we have

14. Michael W. Goheen, *The Church and Its Vocation: Lesslie Newbigin's Missionary Ecclesiology* (Grand Rapids: Baker Academic, 2018), 78–101. This exact list of five aspects of mission is enumerated by Harvie Conn two times: Conn, "Teaching Missions in the Third World: The Cultural Problems," in *Missions and Theological Education in World Perspective*, ed. Harvie M. Conn and Samuel F. Rowen (Farmington, MI: Urbanus, 1984), 267; Conn, *Eternal Word and Changing Worlds: Theology, Anthropology, and Mission in Trialogue* (Grand Rapids: Zondervan, 1984), 304–5.

15. Lesslie Newbigin, *One Body, One Gospel, One World: The Christian Mission Today* (New York: International Missionary Council, 1958), 43–44 (emphasis in the original).

16. Keller, "Answering Lesslie Newbigin."

noted Keller's strong commitment to the training of the laity for the vocations in the public life of culture. This dimension of mission, central to Newbigin but neglected by most emergent and missional advocates, is emphasized in Keller's vision. Third, Keller is deeply committed to the ministry of justice and mercy in the world.[17] His book *Generous Justice* makes a compelling case for the importance of justice, with rich exegesis of Scripture and helpful stories that illustrate what it might look like. He keeps his eye on the role of the church in pursuing justice in terms of relief, development, and reform.[18] Fourth, Keller is equally insistent that evangelism be a critical component of the church's ministry. He doesn't have to convince his evangelical audience of this point. Nevertheless, he offers creative, insightful, and practical ways that evangelism may become a lifestyle in our urban world. And, finally, Keller believes that the local congregation must be involved in missions to the ends of the earth. City to City is a ministry that has emerged from Keller's work in New York City with a vision for reaching the ends of the earth by planting churches that are also missional.

Keller's discussion of each of these components of mission is broad. We cannot begin to summarize his insights in this short chapter. Our hope is that pastors will listen again to the rich missionary ecclesiology of Newbigin along with the decades of theological reflection in the missionary tradition of the twentieth century, and then engage with the way Keller has appropriated and implemented much of this discussion in the urban and global world of the twenty-first century. In the rest of this section, we make three general comments and then give a little more space to two areas of importance—Keller's vision for a citywide ministry in an urban context and his creative insights on evangelism in this setting.

First, it is rare to see all five of these aspects of mission integrated into a single theological vision for a missionary congregation. This is one of the things that has drawn us to Newbigin's work. And Keller has integrated these five aspects of mission as well, implementing this vision of holistic mission in fresh, creative, and rich ways in the twenty-first century.

Second, it is especially gratifying to see in Keller at least two areas that were important for Newbigin but neglected in much of the conversation of his ecclesial heirs. The mission of the laity in their various vocations was urgent for Newbigin. One of the primary reasons was that the gospel was wrongly considered to be a private "religious" message and the church a private

17. Keller, *Center Church*, 322–28; Keller, *Generous Justice: How God's Grace Makes Us Just* (New York: Dutton, 2010).
18. Keller, *Center Church*, 326; Keller, *Generous Justice*, 132–33.

"religious" body. But living out the gospel in the public square was a powerful challenge to this degraded understanding and made it clear that the gospel is public truth. For this reason, Newbigin challenged leaders to take seriously their vocation to find ways to equip the laity to take up their role of cultivating and caring for the creation as the new humanity.

Keller has followed Newbigin here and offers significant insight into this area of mission. He elaborates how the gospel shapes and forms our work. He is attentive to the role of the congregation in three ways: "vocation-specific spiritual nurture" that orients the basic means of grace to nourishing believers for their vocation, "worldview development and training" to make sense of what it means for Jesus to be Lord in every area of life, and "mentoring" that connects more experienced and accomplished folk with those who are less so. He has formed structures such as "vocational groups" and the Gotham Fellowship to train young adults in theology, worldview, and formation. He has articulated the importance of both common grace (that recognizes the good and just in culture) and antithesis (that recognizes the encounter between the gospel and cultural idolatry in shaping all of culture).[19]

Missions (with an s) was also important for Newbigin. During the secular decade of the 1960s, mission was becoming very broad and included every political or social endeavor. Newbigin appreciated the breadth of mission that was emerging but was concerned that intentional and deliberate actions to evangelize and call people to faith in Christ might be lost. So he formulated the distinction between missionary dimension and intention, noted above. Further, the embarrassment over the injustice of colonial missions along with the loss of confidence in the truth of the gospel was leading many to give up evangelism and church planting in other cultures. In response, Newbigin formulated the distinction between *mission* and *missions*. *Mission* was the whole vocation of the church to witness to the good news in all of life. *Missions* was one aspect of that vocation, to establish a witnessing presence in places and among peoples who did not have access to such a gospel witness.[20]

Much emphasis on the missional church at home in Western culture has caused the neglect of the important task of missions and has even created a tension between "home-missional efforts" and "cross-cultural-missionary efforts." The Willingen report begins a section titled "The Total Missionary Task" with these words: "The Church is sent to every inhabited area of the

---

19. Keller, *Center Church*, 330–35; Timothy Keller with Katherine Leary Alsdorf, *Every Good Endeavor: Connecting Your Work to God's Work* (New York: Dutton, 2012).

20. Goheen, *Church and Its Vocation*, 97–101. For an attempt to update this for today, see Michael W. Goheen, *Introducing Christian Mission Today: Scripture, History, and Issues* (Downers Grove, IL: InterVarsity, 2014), 401–35.

world. No place is too near or too far. Every group of Christians is sent as God's ambassadors to the people in its immediate neighborhood. But its responsibility is not limited to its neighborhood. Because Christ is King of kings and Saviour of the world, each group of Christians is also responsible for the proclamation of His Kingship to the uttermost parts of the earth."[21] This statement was authored by Newbigin, so we're not surprised to hear him say that "every church, however small and weak, ought to have some share in the task of taking the gospel to the ends of the earth."[22] Keller shares this global vision, and his commitment to being a missionary people in the "neighborhood" of New York City has not choked out a global vision for missions to the ends of the earth, as evident in City to City.

We register a concern here. The City to City movement has the potential to repeat the same imperialist mistakes that were evident in the missionary movement of past centuries. The power of City to City in various cultures of the world because of its wealth of resources harbors real dangers. We know that this goes against Keller's own founding theological vision and against the vision of others who now oversee City to City. But large organizations, especially if they have rich resources to offer, are in danger of theological and ecclesial imperialism.

Our third comment concerns Keller's primary audience: his appeal for a missionary church seems to have primarily in view evangelical listeners. In its early days, the Gospel and Our Culture Network appealed more to mainline churches and sadly neglected the evangelical church, which was more orthodox and alive but just as much in cultural captivity. By contrast, Keller tunes the wavelength of his message to the evangelical receptor. On one hand, this has had a beneficial impact. The evangelical church is weakened by various dualisms that pit word against deed, public against private, secular against sacred. Keller's trusted evangelical voice has offered biblical teaching for the crucial ministries of justice, mercy, and the mission of the laity in public life that deconstructs reigning dualisms. Further, he has challenged a church often suspicious of culture to engage it with an approach of subversive fulfillment. Keller's credentials as an evangelical are usually beyond suspicion.

But there is another side: Keller's approach often reflects the same individualism and doctrinalism of American evangelicalism that has a "love affair

21. *Missions under the Cross: Addresses Delivered at the Enlarged Meeting of the Committee of the International Missionary Council at Willingen, in Germany, 1952; with Statements Issued by the Meeting*, ed. Norman Goodall (London: Edinburgh, 1953), 190.

22. Lesslie Newbigin, *A Word in Season: Perspectives on Christian World Missions* (Grand Rapids: Eerdmans, 1994), 13.

with Enlightenment."[23] Moreover, he repeatedly sets his biblically broad view of mission on the narrow doctrinal foundation of substitutionary atonement and justification. These are certainly biblical, and moreover, they do play a role in undergirding mission, which he helpfully explores. But his focus is reductionistic and far too narrow a foundation on which to build his massive edifice of mission. Newbigin's vision of the gospel of the kingdom (which included substitutionary atonement among other images of the cross and justification among other benefits of the salvation of the kingdom) is a more biblical and theologically robust foundation for mission.

And this understanding of mission is also that of Harvie Conn.[24] For Conn, the gospel is the comprehensive gospel of the kingdom understood against the backdrop of the Old Testament, especially the Prophets. From the gospel he moves to the church as embodiment of this good news of the kingdom. Then, under the word *evangelism*, he outlines both the obligations (love, compassion, moderation, obedience, prayer) and blessings (justification, salvation, new creation) of the kingdom. Conn's vision is gospel-centered but is not limited to the individual, to substitutionary atonement, or to justification. It includes those but also much more. Conn's modus operandi is quite close to the way Newbigin formulates the matter.

While there is much else Keller has written that would be fruitful to highlight in these five areas, we limit ourselves to sketching two noteworthy areas: mission as a citywide movement and a post-Christian evangelistic dynamic.

A Citywide Movement

Newbigin was aware that the future of our global world was urban. He was bishop in the booming urban metropolis of Madras, India, and later ministered in the inner city of Birmingham in the United Kingdom. He addressed the topic a few times briefly.[25] While pastoring at Winson Green in Birmingham, he participated in a commission on urban mission and authored the theological chapter, titled "Christian Perspectives on the City," in its final report.[26] While this is a theologically rich chapter, he does not engage urban

23. George Marsden, *Understanding Fundamentalism and Evangelicalism* (Grand Rapids: Eerdmans, 1991), 122.
24. Harvie M. Conn, *Bible Studies on World Evangelization and the Simple Lifestyle* (Phillipsburg, NJ: Presbyterian and Reformed, 1981).
25. Newbigin, "Evangelism in the City," 3–8; Newbigin, *The Gospel in Today's Global City* (Birmingham, UK: Selly Oak Colleges, 1997).
26. Richard O'Brien, ed., *Faith in the City of Birmingham: An Examination of Problems and Opportunities Facing the City; The Report of Commission Set Up by the Bishop's Council of the Diocese of Birmingham* (Exeter, UK: Paternoster, 1988), 111–29.

mission to the depth and breadth that Keller has. Prompted by Conn's global leadership in urban mission, Keller has made this a central component of his articulation of the missionary church.

Framework for Ministry in Urban Centers

Keller offers a framework for ministry in urban centers in "Our New Global Culture."[27] Here he draws together in summary fashion much that he has addressed separately and more fully in other places. The logic of this paper is helpful to note. He begins with the importance of understanding our *urban context*. Here it is evident that Keller has done the hard work of analysis through both reading on cultural worldview and listening to people in cities. He offers a helpful summary of urban diversity—a macrocultural analysis of foundational Western worldviews (modern and postmodern) along with characteristics of urban people (professionally driven, sexually engaged, consumer oriented, geographically and socially rootless, pragmatic in their thinking, naturally suspicious, ethnically diverse, civic minded). In light of this urban context, Keller asks what is needed in the church to bring the gospel to these kinds of people. He calls these things *ministry marks*. Here he attends to how one contextualizes the gospel, what kind of worship is relevant, how to create a missional mindset in the congregation, and how small groups can aid this process. Then he moves to the five *ministry fronts* that the church must engage in the city. Here we see again his main emphases: engaging secular people with subversive fulfillment, establishing a countercultural community, holistic ministry, faith and work, and planting new churches. And finally, he asks what kind of *theological DNA* is needed to undergird this kind of ministry. His answer is understanding four things: the gospel, cities in light of Scripture, faithful contextualization, and the way cultures are formed.

This offers a helpful framework for being a missionary church in our cities. Hopefully pastors and leaders will not rest on the hard work Keller has done and see it as simply another model that can be imitated in every context. Rather, what is needed is pastors who will do the same hard work in understanding their context and in asking what kind of church is needed, what holistic mission looks like, and what kind of theology will undergird this ministry. This is, of course, important for the various contexts in North America. We can see how this would be done differently in Vancouver and in Phoenix. But even more importantly, it is essential that churches in the global

27. Timothy Keller, "Our New Global Culture: Ministry in Urban Centers," Redeemer City to City, 2010, http://www.justinbuzzard.net/wp-content/uploads/2010/04/Keller-Our-New -Global-Culture-Ministry-in-Urban-Centers.pdf.

South and East do their own hard work and not repeat the mistakes of the missionary movement of the past, where Western forms were simply dropped into very different contexts.

The City and Gospel Ecosystem

A very helpful—and quite rare—focus of Keller's articulation of the missionary church is the role of the church in its urban context in what he calls the "gospel ecosystem."[28] Our own experience in both Hamilton, Ontario, and Phoenix, Arizona, alerts us to the importance of this.[29] In both places we have participated in and seen the impact that churches united together can have in an urban setting. Keller says, "Changing a city with the gospel takes a movement."[30] He sketches three "movement dynamics" that are important for creating this kind of movement: devotion to God's kingdom over self-interest or tribe, unity that creates cooperation across confessional lines, and spontaneous combustion of ideas, leaders, and initiatives that comes from within the network of churches.

Armed with this posture, the congregation can play its role in a gospel ecosystem. A biological ecosystem is made up of various interdependent organisms, systems, and forces that each play their own role and contribute to the health and growth of the whole. Keller uses this analogy to picture a gospel ecosystem in terms of three concentric circles. At the center is a contextualized theological vision that involves a commitment to the gospel, its faithful contextualization in a specific place, and churches that share the commitment to make known the gospel in that context. The next ring is the multiplication of churches planted in the city and churches that are continually being renewed by the gospel. The outside ring is specialized ministries in which the churches cooperate but also work together with various parachurch ministries and public institutions in the city. These ministries involve prayer movements uniting churches in visionary intercession for the city, specialized evangelistic ministries that reach certain groups, many justice and mercy ministries addressing the various needs in the city, faith and work initiatives that gather together professionals from the same public sector, institutions such as schools and counseling centers that promote family life, theological education for ministry leaders, and a network of Christian city leaders united to provide vision and direction.

---

28. Keller, *Center Church*, 368–77.
29. See the TrueCity website (https://www.truecity.ca/) and the Surge Network website (http://surgenetwork.com/).
30. Keller, *Center Church*, 371.

This kind of unity for the common good can have a recognizable impact on the city. But as important is how a united church is a witness to Christ as the one who is sufficient to reconcile people into one new humanity that will inherit the earth. Newbigin calls the disunity of the church "intolerable,"[31] "an intolerable offence against the very nature of the Church," "scandalous,"[32] and a "public denial of the Gospel which we preach, the good news of Him who, being lifted up, will draw all men to Himself."[33] Newbigin does not think "that the world will believe that Gospel until it sees more evidence of its power to make us one. These two tasks—mission and unity—must be prosecuted together and in indissoluble relation one with the other."[34] Yet so many committed to mission show an "astounding complacency" to ecclesial disunity that "so plainly and ostentatiously flouts the declared will of the Church's Lord."[35] Keller offers a compelling model for this unity to be realized among those committed to being missionary congregations.

Post-Christian Evangelistic Dynamic

While Keller's concern for mercy, justice, and vocation in the missionary calling of the church is strong, he remains committed to evangelism. He wants to ignite what he calls a "post-Christian evangelistic dynamic" carried out by every member. Newbigin too is concerned that all Christians speak the name of Jesus. In fact, he uses the very strong language of "betrayal" to describe a position on witness that substitutes presence for evangelistic words.[36] Our evangelizing ministry should be the spontaneous witness of the whole church as an overflow of Pentecost.[37] Evangelism is not an optional task left for a few but the vocation of all who follow Christ.

Keller's goal is to recover the powerful role that "informal missionaries" played in the early church and renew this in our present moment. Following Michael Green, Keller seeks to recapture the ways that "Christian laypeople . . . carried on the mission of the church not through formal preaching but informal conversation—'in homes and wine shops, on walks, and around market stalls

31. Lesslie Newbigin, *The Household of God: Lectures on the Nature of the Church* (New York: Friendship Press, 1953), 173.
32. Newbigin, *Reunion of the Church*, 23–24.
33. Newbigin, *Reunion of the Church*, 21.
34. Newbigin, *Household of God*, 174.
35. Newbigin, *Reunion of the Church*, 9.
36. Lesslie Newbigin, "The Bible Study Lectures," in *Digest of the Proceedings of the Ninth Meeting of the Consultation on Church Union (COCU)*, ed. Paul A. Crow Jr. (Princeton: Consultation on Church Union, 1970), 212.
37. Lesslie Newbigin, "Crosscurrents in Ecumenical and Evangelical Understandings of Mission," *International Bulletin of Missionary Research* 6, no. 4 (1982): 150.

. . . they did it naturally, enthusiastically.'"[38] This can be done by fostering a dynamic within the local congregation that casts a vision for missional living marked by four elements: it happens organically and spontaneously through everyday encounters in the life of believers, it is highly relational and most often takes place within the context of relational networks, it is "Word-deploying" in the sense that we prayerfully seek to bring the gospel and biblical story into connection with people's lives, and it is active, not passive, as each member assumes responsibility to share good news with committed intentionality.[39]

Keller explores what a "missional evangelism through mini-decisions" looks like in a local congregation. Given our post-Christendom context, more and more people journey from unbelief to faith in Christ through a process of "mini-decisions," trying on different aspects of Christian faith and exploring Christianity without a lot of background knowledge of the Bible. He highlights what is needed in this process if such people are to come to faith: they need to gain awareness of the uniqueness of the Christian faith; to see the relevance of the gospel to their lives; to probe the intellectual credibility and integrity of the Christian faith; to experience elements of Christian community, tasting what it might be like to join; to have time to explore what is involved in making a commitment to Christ and his people; and to have time for the truth of the gospel to become reinforced in their lives.[40] Keller addresses the role of pastoral leadership to help believers develop relational integrity and intentionality; to provide concrete pastoral support that casts a vision for, equips people for, and encourages this way of life; and to foster a culture that provides safe venues within the local congregation for people who are in different places on their journey toward Christ.[41]

Given the post-Christendom context in the West, the future of evangelism is not in programs or in church-based curricula. Rather, it will rest heavily on believers missionally engaging their friends and neighbors organically and spontaneously in the rough-and-tumble of life with evangelistic intentionality. To do so, we need to break free from the privatization of the Christian faith that captivates our imagination. As Keller puts it, we need to stop hiding who we are to the people around us. If Christ is at the center of our life, people who are close to us should see him.[42]

---

38. Michael Green, *Evangelism in the Early Church*, rev. ed. (Grand Rapids: Eerdmans, 2003), 243, quoted in Keller, *Center Church*, 277.
39. Keller, *Center Church*, 279–81.
40. Keller, *Center Church*, 281–82.
41. Keller, *Center Church*, 282–89.
42. Timothy Keller, "North American Mission: The Outward Move" (address at the conference "The Gospel and Our Cities: Chicago 2018"), YouTube video, February 28, 2019, 40:01, https://www.youtube.com/watch?v=RitxJ7sodvE.

The Church's Gathered Life

If this kind of comprehensive witness is to be sustained, it demands a vital and thriving Christian community where worship, prayer, fellowship, and discipleship are healthy and vibrant both in congregations and in networks of churches. This was a primary concern for Newbigin. The church has two foci: the inner life of worship, fellowship, and formation in gathered congregations and the outer life of mission in its many modes scattered throughout the world. The danger is that "it is always relatively easy for the Church to do one of these things and neglect the other."[43] Far too often we "allow two things which belong together to fall apart—with consequences which are fatal for the witness of the church."[44] Our inner life of worship, fellowship, and discipleship "is precisely for the sake of the mission to the world" and, for that reason, "these two things must not be allowed to fall apart."[45] A faithful missionary church will "live in the tension of loyalty to both tasks, and in that place, in that tension, . . . bear witness to the gospel."[46]

We have seen that a holy anger with the introversion of the church has moved many to stress the involvement of believers in the world at the expense of the community and institution of the gathered church. Keller's model for mission in the city is certainly one of deep solidarity and profound engagement with the culture. But in his vision, this does not lessen the importance of the church as community and institution or of the activities of worship, discipleship, and fellowship in the gathered congregation.

Institutional Church

Keller affirms the important role of the institutional church in God's mission. He shares Newbigin's concern that the secularization of mission in the ecumenical movement during the 1960s was devastating for the church's mission in two ways. On the one hand, it drastically reduced the church's mission to involvement in social and political issues. The church *discerns* where God is at work in the world in various social changes, and then *participates* with him in pursuit of change.[47] Among other things, this eclipses evangelism and cross-cultural missions. On the other hand, it marginalizes and downplays the central role of the gathered and institutional church in God's mission. Keller recognized this, and so highlights Newbigin's emphasis *both* on what

---

43. Newbigin, "The Evangelization of Eastern Asia," 143.
44. Lesslie Newbigin, "Reflections on an Indian Ministry," *Frontier* 18 (1975): 26.
45. Newbigin, "Reflections on an Indian Ministry," 26.
46. Newbigin, "Evangelization of Eastern Asia," 143.
47. Keller, *Center Church*, 251–52.

is neglected in mission—such as evangelism, conversion, church growth, and communal distinctiveness—*and* on what is needed for that mission—namely, the local, institutional expression of the church.[48] Keller believes that Newbigin, along with David Bosch, "rescued" the whole notion of the *missio Dei* from the secularization of the ecumenical movement.[49] Newbigin helped to restore a more biblical understanding of the mission of God that "sought to avoid the secularization of mission found in the liberal churches. The overarching narrative was still that God is in mission to renew the whole creation, but the new view [Newbigin's[50]] stressed the public proclamation of Christ as Lord and Hope of the world and therefore the necessity of both conversion and the growth of the church."[51]

As we observed earlier in the chapter, Keller calls the church to intimate solidarity and deep engagement in the life of culture. But unlike the secularized model of mission that emerged in the 1960s and continues today, Keller refuses to reduce mission or marginalize the gathered, communal, and institutional life of the church.

The burden of this chapter is that Keller's notion of a missionary encounter has led him to reframe the church as missional—that is, a church that rethinks every aspect of ministry from the standpoint of its missionary vocation. While there is much that is valuable that we could highlight, here we note two further things: worship and catechesis for discipleship.

Keller recognizes that there are two dimensions of worship that need to be reworked as a missionary church. The first is that the whole liturgy must form and shape God's people for their mission. This remains underdeveloped, and thus there is a need for much more thought on this issue.[52] The second is making worship thick enough to nurture believers while at the same time comprehensible to unbelievers. He challenges us to recognize that we should always expect unbelievers to be present and invites us to consider what that might look like liturgically. For Keller, this does not lead to a seeker-sensitive worship. Worship must remain rooted in tradition and a full liturgy. Yet we must also remain attentive to various ways that worship can be comprehensible to unbelievers.[53]

---

48. Keller, *Center Church*, 252.
49. Keller, *Center Church*, 252–55.
50. Keller's term *new view* may be confusing to anyone who knows this history. Newbigin's view is not new; it is the secular view that is new. The view Newbigin holds is the classical and orthodox vision of the early missionary movement formed two decades before.
51. Keller, *Center Church*, 255.
52. See Kevin Adams, *The Gospel in a Handshake: Framing Worship for Mission* (Eugene, OR: Cascade Books, 2019).
53. Keller, *Center Church*, 301–8.

The second thing to note is Keller's insistence on catechesis for formation purposes. He invites congregations to "recover catechesis" in the manner of the early church, where seekers were admitted to a long-term and intensive catechetical process as catechumens. They were taught "basic Christian world-view and ethics." This led to baptism and the Lord's Supper. Interestingly, after beginning with the early church, Keller switches to the Reformation style of catechism that focused on the Apostles' Creed, the Ten Commandments, and the Lord's Prayer.[54]

The style of Reformation catechism was to focus primarily on doctrine and knowledge with a pedagogy of question and answer. This is helpful, but something deeper is needed in our neopagan setting. The early church's practice offers a better way that is also much more in line with Newbigin's stress on story. Alan Kreider argues that the pastoral purpose of catechesis was to "re-form pagan people, to resocialize them, to deconstruct their old world, and reconstruct a new one, so that they would emerge as Christian people who would be at home in communities of freedom."[55] This was done primarily by immersing catechumens in the story of the Bible.

Beginning with Irenaeus, the catechism of the early church was focused on narrative to form identity. That is, it taught the biblical story over against the cultural story and sought to form a new way of life shaped by Scripture. Kreider writes of the catechetical process of the early church, "To enable the catechumen to become ready to join the Christian community, the catechist needed to replace this mythical-historical mix [of pagan Roman stories] by an alternative narrative, by the history of salvation as recounted in the books of the Hebrew Scriptures which culminated in the person and work of Jesus Christ and which continued in the life of the transnational church and the sufferings of the martyrs."[56] The goal of the catechism was to renarrate seekers' lives with the biblical story, re-form their identities, and detoxify them from the dominant Roman story so that they would be an attractive people.[57] As Kreider puts it, "Its rites and practices . . . performed the function of re-forming those pagans who joined the church into Christians, into distinctive people who lived in a way that was recognizably in the tradition of Jesus Christ. As such these people, re-formed, would be attractive."[58]

---

54. Keller, *Center Church*, 316–17.
55. Alan Kreider, *Worship and Evangelism in Pre-Christendom* (Cambridge: Grove Books, 1995), 23.
56. Kreider, *Worship and Evangelism*, 24.
57. The vivid imagery of "detoxification from the dominant [Roman] order" as the purpose of the early church's catechism is William Willimon's in his *Peculiar Speech: Preaching to the Baptized* (Grand Rapids: Eerdmans, 1992), 59.
58. Kreider, "Worship and Evangelism," 10.

The key, as Kreider insists, is the biblical story. This scriptural narrative encountered the pagan stories, renarrating new believers' lives, re-forming them in a new identity, and reshaping them in a whole new way of life that was attractive in the Roman Empire. This stress on narrative and missionary encounter with culture as the way to form believers falls very much in line with Newbigin's own passions.

A huge challenge we face today is to release the biblical story to encounter the neopagan story of our hyper-individualist consumer society, renarrate our lives, form a new identity, and shape a whole new way of life that is attractive. We wish Keller had remained with the early church—it would have contributed even more to this challenge.

Structures

Like Newbigin, Keller is aware that structures in the church will either enable or inhibit the church's mission. Beginning especially in the 1960s, Newbigin gave sustained attention to congregational, leadership, ecumenical, and missionary structures that would facilitate the missionary ecclesiology that had emerged in the two previous decades. Keller is likewise concerned about this area of missionary ecclesiology. The following observations highlight some of the important things Keller contributes to the conversation.

First, Keller is rightly critical of those within the missional church movement who tend to equate "missional church" with a particular ecclesial form. He cites by way of example those who argue that a missional church must be incarnational rather than attractional. Some who emphasize this distinction then go on to indicate that churches that base their ministry on bringing people into a large corporate gathering on a weekly basis cannot be missional.[59] Keller rightly rejects the notion that a missional church cannot take the form of a large church or even a small traditional church centered on weekly worship. He sees that the missionary nature of the church must go deeper than any particular form. The "missional church" is not a church model, nor can it be exclusively tied to any particular ecclesial form—"small or large, cell-group based or midsize community based. . . . The small, organic, simple incarnational church, and the large, organizational, complex attractional church" can all in the end be missional.[60] What makes a church missional are the marks Keller enumerates above. And the exceedingly difficult process of becoming that kind of church is not resolved by one or another kind of structure.

59. Keller, *Center Church*, 265.
60. Keller, *Center Church*, 265–67.

To be sure, Keller advocates the importance of small groups for mission. He speaks of the "critical importance and accessibility of small groups as the infrastructure needed to support Christians living long term in urban centers"[61] and stresses "transforming character through deep community and small groups" as one of the ministry fronts.[62] He develops a concrete case study of how small groups can function in a missional way to engage the city.[63]

Second, Keller is attentive to tradition. He does not peddle novel structures as the hope for the post-Christendom church, nor does he leave behind what has been learned from church history. The bigger issues are whether the church is engaging secular people, living as the distinctive new humanity in a missionary encounter with the idolatry of culture, and engaging in holistic ministry of evangelism, mercy, justice, and vocation. This is what matters, and fresh structures will either facilitate or hinder this calling. But we cannot leave behind tradition. He models this, for example, when he speaks of worship[64] and leadership.[65]

And finally, Keller does not limit structural change to congregational and leadership structures. These are important, and he addresses them. But, like Newbigin, he contends that structural renewal for a missionary church also involves *ecumenical* structures that unite the church in a certain place for mission, *vocational* structures to equip the laity for their callings in public life, and *missionary* structures that enable the church to carry out its cross-cultural missions task to the ends of the earth.

Keller developed a theologically rich notion of a missionary encounter with Western culture and then worked out an equally robust understanding of the missionary congregation that is needed for this encounter. In both cases he was oriented by Newbigin's cross-cultural experience. There is much to learn from his commitment to developing a missional church, both in his broad and integrated forms of missionary engagement in the world and in his reflections on the institutional and communal life of the church. It is especially his experience in a large urban setting that has brought fresh insight. Yet we need to appropriate these fruitful insights in a way that doesn't attempt to mimic Keller's experience in our different settings but rather follows his path of rich theological reflection on a missionary encounter with culture and the kind of missionary congregation that is needed to sustain this vocation.

61. Keller, "Our New Global Culture," 6.
62. Keller, "Our New Global Culture," 13.
63. Keller, "Our New Global Culture," 13.
64. Keller, *Center Church*, 298; Keller, "Our New Global Culture," 9–11.
65. Keller, *Center Church*, 346–47.

13

The Gospel and the Biblical Story

In his book *Center Church*, Tim Keller offers a *theological vision* that has shaped Redeemer Church.[1] A theological vision is "a faithful restatement of the gospel with rich implications for life, ministry, and mission in a type of culture at a moment in history."[2] In that definition we discern the movement from *gospel* to *missionary church* to *contextualization*. In the previous two chapters we have moved in the opposite direction, from contextualization to missionary church. We observed that the notion of a "missionary encounter with culture" shaped Keller's view of contextualization, while "missional church" guided his ecclesiology. In both cases Keller is influenced by the paradigm-shifting nature of Lesslie Newbigin's cross-cultural missionary experience. Thus there is a fair measure of continuity between Newbigin and Keller in these areas.

Yet when it comes to the "gospel," the same cannot be said. Keller wants to distance himself from Newbigin, whom he believes openly repudiates an evangelical doctrine of Scripture.[3] The two share much in common, since they are both committed to the authority of Scripture and an orthodox version of the Christian faith. Yet it is also true that their work reveals important differences concerning the nature of the gospel and the biblical story.

1. Timothy Keller, *Center Church: Doing Balanced, Gospel-Centered Ministry in Your City* (Grand Rapids: Zondervan, 2012).
2. Keller, *Center Church*, 19.
3. Keller, *Center Church*, 252.

We believe that Newbigin's understanding ultimately provides a more biblical foundation for a missionary church and a missionary encounter with culture. So this chapter displays a more critical slant on Keller's theological vision, but hopefully one in the spirit of his "gospel polemics."[4]

Biblical Authority and the Missionary Church

Newbigin believes that if the church is to recover the faithful posture of a missionary encounter with Western culture, there is an "urgent need for the development of a coherent and intellectually tenable doctrine of Scriptural authority."[5] A missionary encounter requires that the church believe that the Scriptures offer the true, ultimate, and comprehensive vision of the world, and that they embody it with their whole lives. They must take a stance *within* this story and interpret their cultural context from inside. If the Scriptures are fitted into the cultural story, a missionary encounter is thwarted from the start.

And this is exactly what has happened. Newbigin asks rhetorically, "Have we got into a situation where the biblical message has been so thoroughly adapted to fit into our modern western culture that we are unable to hear the radical challenge, the call for radical conversion which it presents in our culture?"[6] This is true not only of the liberal tradition but for evangelicals as well. Both have allowed the cultural vision to reshape the Bible. Recovering biblical authority is no academic battle but one of the most urgent tasks required by the Western church if it is to recover a missionary stance. And so he devotes a great deal of time and energy to the struggle to recover "a credible doctrine of biblical authority."[7] His later writings on the matter are profuse. Sadly, a number of them remain unpublished.

Understanding scriptural authority "involves a continual twofold movement: we have to understand Jesus in the context of the whole story, and we have to understand the whole story in the light of Jesus."[8] We begin with the gospel of Jesus Christ as the *clue* to faithfully understanding the biblical story, but we must articulate the biblical story as the true *context* for understanding the gospel of Jesus Christ. Recapturing a credible doctrine of biblical

4. Keller, *Center Church*, 372–73.
5. Lesslie Newbigin, "New Birth into a Living Hope" (unpublished address, 1995), 7.
6. Lesslie Newbigin, "The Bible and Our Contemporary Mission," *Clergy Review* 69, no. 1 (1984): 11.
7. Lesslie Newbigin, *Unfinished Agenda: An Updated Autobiography* (Edinburgh: Saint Andrew Press, 1993), 248.
8. Lesslie Newbigin, *Proper Confidence: Faith, Doubt, and Certainty in Christian Discipleship* (Grand Rapids: Eerdmans, 1956), 88.

authority requires two things: the Bible as the one true story of universal history and the gospel of Jesus Christ as a gospel of the kingdom that is the key to reading the story.

The first is the Bible as the true story of the whole world. "I do not believe that we can speak effectively of the Gospel as a word addressed to our culture unless we recover a sense of the Scriptures as a canonical whole, as the story which provides the true context for our understanding of the meaning of our lives—both personal and public."[9] The problem is that the Western church has lost this comprehensive narrative character of scriptural authority and has allowed the Bible to be broken up into bits—historical-critical bits in liberal biblical scholarship and systematic-theological bits in the evangelical tradition. Newbigin was fond of quoting Chaturvedi Badrinath, a Hindu scholar of world religion, who was surprised that Christians didn't seem to be aware that their Bible was "a unique interpretation of universal history, the history of the whole creation and the history of the human race."[10] This certainly is a "tremendously bold claim,"[11] a "stupendous claim" that is nothing short of "astounding."[12] If there is to be a missionary encounter, this comprehensive authority must be recovered.

The second is that the gospel of Jesus Christ is a gospel of the kingdom. This is the clue to rightly reading Scripture. The Bible tells a story of God's purpose to restore the whole world and the entirety of human life. In the biblical imagery of the kingdom, the Old Testament gives God's promise to one day pour out his power to restore his rule over the whole creation and all human life. When Jesus commenced his ministry, he announced the good news that the story of God's renewing work had arrived at its fulfillment: God's power to restore his kingdom is here. The end of universal history, when God's rule is restored, had broken into the middle. "The original preaching of the Gospel on the lips of Jesus was—precisely—the announcement of the coming of the kingdom."[13] In Jesus, God's purpose is fully and decisively revealed and accomplished. The kingdom as the goal of universal history is present in the middle of history in the Christ-event. God's power to heal and renew has arrived: *this is the good news.*

The importance for mission of recovering the scriptural narrative is evident in the following quotation:

9. Lesslie Newbigin, "Response to 'Word of God?'," *Gospel and Our Culture Newsletter* 10 (1991): 2.

10. Lesslie Newbigin, *A Walk through the Bible* (Vancouver: Regent, 1999), 4.

11. Lesslie Newbigin, "Why Study the Old Testament?," *National Christian Council Review* 74 (1954): 75.

12. Newbigin, *Proper Confidence*, 77.

13. Lesslie Newbigin, *The Good Shepherd: Meditations on Christian Ministry in Today's World* (Grand Rapids: Eerdmans, 1977), 67.

If we take the Bible in its canonical wholeness, as we must, then it is best understood as history. It is universal, cosmic history. It interprets the entire story of all things from creation to consummation, and the story of the human race within creation, and within the human race the story of the people called by God to be the bearers of the meaning of the whole, and—at the very centre— the story of the One in whom God's purpose was decisively revealed by being decisively effected. It is obviously a different story from the stories that the world tells about itself.[14]

We can identify four factors that are closely woven together here. First, the Bible is universal and cosmic history, and therefore encompasses everything, including all human life of all peoples at all times and places. Second, God's purpose that unfolds in this story is fully and finally revealed and accomplished in the person and work of Jesus Christ. This, Newbigin asserts time and time again, is the gospel of the kingdom. Third, the people of God are called to bear the meaning of this universal history and gospel of the kingdom. "The business of the church is to tell and to embody a story, the story of God's mighty acts in creation and redemption and of God's promises concerning what will be in the end."[15] And finally, this story will always encounter all other stories that shape human culture. The story the Bible tells is "the true interpretation of all human and cosmic history and . . . to understand history otherwise is to misunderstand it, therefore misunderstanding the human situation here and now."[16]

Systematic Theology and Individual Salvation

This is not the primary way Keller articulates the gospel and biblical authority. There are times when he sounds this note. He rightly critiques evangelicals who make the gospel about sin, salvation, and heaven, clipping off creation at the beginning and new creation at the end. He is justly critical of the self-centeredness of a personalized gospel that escapes a radical commitment to challenging structural evil and scuttles "the power of the gospel for cultural transformation."[17] There is a need for a gospel of the kingdom

14. Lesslie Newbigin, "The Bible: Good News for Secularised People," Newbigin Archives, University of Birmingham (keynote address, Europe and Middle East Regional Conference, Eisenach, Germany, April 1991), 6.

15. Newbigin, *Proper Confidence*, 76.

16. Newbigin, *Proper Confidence*, 77.

17. Timothy Keller, "Our New Global Culture: Ministry in Urban Centers," Redeemer City to City, 2010, p. 18, http://www.justinbuzzard.net/wp-content/uploads/2010/04/Keller-Our-New -Global-Culture-Ministry-in-Urban-Centers.pdf. Cf. Keller, *Center Church*, 32.

to undergird holistic mission. This critique of evangelicalism is exceedingly important. He counters an "emaciated gospel"[18] rampant in American evangelicalism and prominent among many of his colleagues at the Gospel Coalition.

Keller's "Two Basic Ways"

Yet Keller does not offer an integral gospel. He abstracts two dimensions of the gospel—what he confusingly calls the individual and the corporate—and sets them over against one another, in tension from the outset. He speaks of "two basic ways to answer the question 'What is the gospel?'" The first is about the good news of how an individual can be right with God. The gospel answers the question, "What must I do to be saved?" He commends J. I. Packer's statement that it is only when we discover an answer to Martin Luther's primary question, "How may a weak, perverse, and guilty sinner find a gracious God?" that "*real Christianity*" begins! The second basic way is about the good news for the whole world. The gospel answers the question, "What hope is there for the world?"[19]

The first way is individualistic and is outlined by God, sin, Christ, and faith, stated as propositions.[20] This answer to the question about the nature of the gospel comes by way of systematic theology. The Bible's unity is found in a system of propositions that we construct on the basis that the Bible is the product of a single author. Systematic theology offers the structure of God, humanity, sin, Christ, and salvation, and so is "particularly useful in answering the gospel question, 'What must I do to be saved?'"[21]

The second way is corporate and is outlined by the biblical story of creation, fall, redemption, and restoration. This is expressed in a narrative form. This answer to the question about the nature of the gospel comes by way of redemptive history that "organizes what the Bible says by stages of history or by the plotline of a story."[22] These two ways—systematic theology and redemptive-historical theology, system and story, propositions and historical events—address the question of the gospel. The first answers the question of individual salvation and the second of corporate salvation.

Keller's two ways:

18. This is David Bosch's term in *Witness to the World: The Christian Mission in Theological Perspective* (Atlanta: John Knox, 1980), 202–11.

19. Keller, *Center Church*, 32 (emphasis added).

20. Keller, *Center Church*, 32.

21. Keller, *Center Church*, 40.

22. Keller, *Center Church*, 40. Here he confuses actual redemptive history with a kind of hermeneutical or theological *method* that takes account of redemptive history.

Individual	Corporate
Systematic theology method	Redemptive-historical method
Propositions	Story
"What must I do to be saved?"	"What is the hope for the world?"

There is tension between these two approaches. This comes into relief when Keller says that there is a great "danger" in telling people that the gospel is about the story of God's purpose to save the creation, since this will not tell them how to get right with God. Or when we read Packer's words, quoted approvingly by Keller, that when we view the Bible as a "great metanarrative" it "distracts us from pursuing Luther's question in personal terms" and also "hinders" us from appreciating the gospel.[23] The Bible *is* a metanarrative if by that we mean "an attempt to tell a single story about the whole of human history in order to attribute a single and integrated meaning to the whole."[24] And if stressing the true nature of Scripture is a danger or distraction or hindrance to appreciating the gospel, we have a deeply problematic tension.

The problem with establishing a tension between two aspects of the gospel is that one can never quite hold them together in unity. When one tries to achieve a balance by setting the tennis ball on the net, it will always fall to one side or the other. This is what happens with Keller. So, while his intention to recover a full-orbed gospel and hold various aspects together is admirable, in the end a balance cannot be achieved. What Harvie Conn says about another dualism is true here: "The fact remains that we are far from a holistic solution that integrates the two components. . . . Two abstractions do not make a whole. But two are better than one."[25]

Two Frameworks for the Gospel

Keller rightly recognizes that the gospel receives its meaning from a bigger framework.[26] He proposes two: a propositional framework that comes to us in systematic theology and a narrative framework derived from redemptive history. Indeed, "failing to use both approaches invites danger."[27] In fact,

23. Keller, *Center Church*, 32–33.
24. Richard Bauckham, *Bible and Mission: Christian Witness in a Postmodern World* (Grand Rapids: Baker Academic, 2003), 87.
25. Harvie M. Conn, *Evangelism: Doing Justice and Preaching Grace* (Philadelphia: Presbyterian and Reformed, 1992), 62.
26. Keller, *Center Church*, 32, 40.
27. Keller, *Center Church*, 40.

there is "danger in conceiving the gospel too strictly as a story line of the renewal of the world."[28] One needs a second framework to correct this danger. But, according to Newbigin, this is exactly what the Bible is: the story line of God's purpose to renew the world accomplished, revealed, and made present in Jesus Christ. The gospel must be understood in the context of the narrative framework of creation, sin, Israel, Christ, the church in the power of the Spirit, and consummation. That *is* the shape of the Bible and *is* the very structure of the Christian faith, and therefore the broader context in which the gospel *must* be placed to be rightly understood (fig. 13.1).

Creation ➔ Fall ➔ Israel ➔ Christ / **gospel** ➔ Church ➔ Kingdom

Figure 13.1. Storied context of the gospel

But Keller adds a second framework—God, sin, Christ, salvation, faith—one that ultimately becomes his primary default. The ball will not balance on the net. Where does this framework come from? First, it is typical of an evangelistic presentation within the evangelical tradition. God is holy, and we stand under his wrath as guilty sinners. Only the substitutionary work of Christ can take away the guilt of our sin. When we believe, we are forgiven and justified. This familiar *evangelistic* story line is evident in Keller, and it is quite common to hear evangelicals refer to this evangelistic presentation as "the gospel."

Second, it is Reformed systematic theology. This offers roughly the same kind of structure in a more detailed and nuanced form: God, humanity, Christ, and salvation, with a pronounced individual emphasis. Yet all systematic theologies are human constructions and contextualized attempts to get hold of the biblical story. They have a structure and story line that highlight individual sin and salvation (fig. 13.2).

God ➔ Individual sinner ➔ Christ / **gospel** ➔ Salvation

Figure 13.2. Systematic framework

For Newbigin, the Bible tells the story that is the true story, and all our theological efforts to articulate the "so-called truths" of the Bible in system-

28. Keller, *Center Church*, 32.

atic propositions "are the attempts we make at particular moments in the story to grasp and state how things are in terms of our experience at that point."[29] The Reformation rediscovered the biblical importance of individuals, their responses, and the benefits they receive in salvation, which had been suppressed for a millennium in the tribal contextualization of the gospel in medieval Europe.[30] Luther's urgent question was the wonderful reawakening and recovery of the personal dimensions of the biblical story. Post-Reformation confessions and theologies rightly express this fresh insight.[31] However, this must not become *another* framework that we lay alongside the biblical story as one that carries equal authority. There are not two frameworks for the gospel, but one—and that is the biblical story. All systematic theologies aid us in grasping themes and relationships within that story more fully.

To substitute systematic theology for the biblical story is to be in danger of fatally identifying our theological traditions with Scripture. "Traditions which are good in themselves are evil when they are put into the place which belongs to the Gospel itself."[32] The work of theology is necessary to articulate the gospel in a way that both protects it from the idolatrous currents of culture and leads people into a full and vivid appropriation of the faith.[33] Yet all theological work is a matter of human construction and is therefore limited and contextual. The biblical story is not a human construction or way of organizing what the Bible says. It is the canonical structure and the way scriptural authority functions. The Scriptures alone are the church's "supreme and decisive standard of faith" that comes to us canonically in the form of redemptive history reaching its culmination in Jesus Christ.[34]

Why Two Basic Ways?

There is no doubt that Keller believes that the Scriptures are the "supreme and decisive standard." Yet he has given systematic theology equal weight

29. Lesslie Newbigin, *The Open Secret: An Introduction to the Theology of Mission*, rev. ed. (Grand Rapids: Eerdmans, 1995), 82–83.

30. Andrew Walls, *The Missionary Movement in Christian History: Studies in the Transmission of Faith* (Maryknoll, NY: Orbis Books, 1996), 20–21, 41, 45; Hendrikus Berkhof, *The Doctrine of the Holy Spirit* (Atlanta: John Knox, 1964), 66.

31. See Herman Ridderbos, *Church, World, Kingdom* (Potchefstroom, South Africa: Institute for the Study of Calvinism, 1979), 4–5.

32. Lesslie Newbigin, *The Reunion of the Church: A Defence of the South India Scheme* (London: SCM, 1948), 53.

33. Newbigin, *Reunion of the Church*, 16, 137–38.

34. Newbigin, *Reunion of the Church*, 136.

with the biblical story as the context for understanding the gospel. Why has systematic theology been allowed to take such an authoritative place?

There are two important positive reasons. First, Keller is deeply concerned that emphasizing the Bible as the true story may neglect and even eclipse important themes within that story. He worries that a gospel of the kingdom can downplay the "offensiveness, depth, and destructiveness of sin."[35] Or that it can minimize, if not eclipse, the holiness and wrath of God. Or that the justification of sinners and the substitutionary atonement may vanish. It is true that certain approaches to a "kingdom gospel" have neglected important biblical themes. Yet erecting a second "basic way" is not the only way forward. A more biblical understanding of the kingdom will do the trick. Indeed, each of these missing elements is well integrated in Newbigin's gospel of the kingdom.

Second, Keller is concerned to be faithful as a preacher and an evangelist who addresses the gospel to persons and calls for their response. He is afraid that when we conceive of the gospel as a "story line of the renewal of the world . . . it does not tell them how to actually get right with God."[36] An emphasis on the "corporate dimension virtually eliminates the call for individual repentance, faith, and conversion."[37]

It is this concern for the proper response of faith from each person to the grace of the gospel that motivates Keller to turn to a rather obscure theological controversy in eighteenth-century Scottish Presbyterianism for one of the primary lenses through which he views the gospel. The "Marrow controversy"[38] illustrates a fundamental way the church can misunderstand the gospel because of the constant temptation to fall into two dangers— legalism and antinomianism.[39] "Legalism says that we have to live a holy, good life in order to be saved. Antinomianism says that because we are saved, we don't have to live a holy, good life."[40] Avoiding both of these dangers has become a clarion call for Keller and has given shape to his oft-quoted summary of the gospel: "I am more sinful and flawed than I ever dared believe" and "I am more accepted and loved than I ever dared hope. . . . The former outflanks antinomianism, while the latter staves off legalism."[41] This Marrow-

35. Keller, *Center Church*, 270.
36. Keller, *Center Church*, 32.
37. Keller, *Center Church*, 268.
38. See Sinclair Ferguson, *The Whole Christ: Legalism, Antinomianism, and Gospel Assurance—Why the Marrow Controversy Still Matters* (Wheaton: Crossway, 2016).
39. Keller, *Center Church*, 48.
40. Keller, *Center Church*, 31.
41. Keller, *Center Church*, 48.

controversy-shaped gospel keeps Keller's focus firmly on the individual and their proper response.[42]

This is a great example of how theology can protect the gospel. If we understand the gospel in terms of the benefits of the kingdom, then we receive gifts such as justification, forgiveness, and adoption that change our status *and* gifts such as sanctification, new life, and dying and rising with Christ that change our condition.[43] These benefits are a unity that summarizes various aspects of the entire change that takes place in humanity as we receive God's grace offered in the gospel by faith. All gifts of the one gospel of the kingdom given in Christ by the Spirit in the fellowship of the church restore us to our true humanity. All of this stands against both legalism and antinomianism. Keller rightly discerns this and has found the Marrow controversy helpful in communicating the gospel.

Keller is a master communicator, and he is deeply insightful in understanding how people respond to the gospel. He understands well how quickly and often people fall into one or another of the two dangers of legalism and antinomianism. And he masterfully communicates the gospel in such a way as to show that our response must be one of faith to the grace of God in the gospel for our whole salvation. Keller would enjoy Newbigin's limerick about preaching grace: "There's a preacher I know in Turin, who can preach for three hours about sin; he never has space, for a word about grace; so he doesn't get under my skin."[44] The problem here is not what Keller is affirming. Rather, it is a matter of taking an effective preaching approach that protects a full gospel of grace and then making *that* the good news. This keeps the emphasis decidedly and exclusively on the individual and their response.

Again, there is rightful concern for a proper response to the gospel. Indeed, there is an urgency in the call to repentance, faith, and conversion that we see in Jesus's proclamation of the kingdom. And it is true that certain traditions eclipse this call. The question is whether it is the cosmic and communal dimensions of the gospel of the kingdom that are to blame. Jesus certainly proclaimed the kingdom and called for an urgent response. And Newbigin believed that the gospel of the kingdom always demands a

42. Keller, *Center Church*, 54–83.
43. Lesslie Newbigin, *Sin and Salvation* (London: SCM, 1956), 100–114. This distinction is established exegetically by Herman Ridderbos in *The Coming of the Kingdom* (Philadelphia: Presbyterian and Reformed, 1962), 241–59, articulated theologically by Herman Bavinck in *The Wonderful Works of God* (Philadelphia: Westminster Seminary Press, 2019), 382–84, and expressed missiologically by Harvie Conn in *Bible Studies on World Evangelization and the Simple Lifestyle* (Philadelphia: Presbyterian and Reformed, 1991), 15–30.
44. Lesslie Newbigin, *St Paul in Limerick* (Carlisle, UK: Solway, 1998), 58–59.

response. The "revelation of which we speak in the Christian tradition is more than the communication of information; it is the giving of an invitation. It is more than the unfolding of [God's] purpose . . . it is also a summons, a call, an invitation."[45]

Keller is concerned that a kingdom gospel won't call for a personal response because he associates "kingdom" with the corporate or cosmic pole of his axis. He makes this quite explicit in a section of "Our New Global Culture" titled "The Individual-Corporate Axis: The Gospel of the Kingdom." He concludes, "In summary, if we lose the emphasis on conversion [individual], we lose the power of the gospel for personal transformation. We will not work sacrificially and joyfully for justice. On the other hand, if we lose the emphasis *on the corporate—on the kingdom*—we lose the power of the gospel for cultural transformation."[46] Note this well: "the corporate" is synonymous with "the kingdom"; the individual seems not to be part of that. But, of course, this is not the biblical teaching about the kingdom: the gospel of the kingdom in Scripture feels no such tension.

We tentatively suggest another reason why Keller opts for two basic ways to express the gospel. It may be that Keller is formed by two different expressions of the Reformed tradition. He has one foot in the more neopuritan confessional tradition, which stresses truth as ideas, systematic theology, and a structure that emphasizes the benefits of individual salvation. His other foot is in Dutch neo-Calvinism, which stresses truth as historical events, redemptive and covenant history, and the communal and cosmic dimensions of salvation. The latter tradition is more likely to begin with a more full-orbed doctrine of creation and salvation as restoration to God's creational intention. These two traditions lived in tension at Westminster Theological Seminary during Keller's time there. Moreover, the neopuritan tradition, in the shape of much Reformed systematic theology, has a powerful presence in the United States. We realize it is tricky to understand the traditions at work in someone's theological formation, even if that person is oneself. And these traditions don't organize quite so neatly. Nevertheless, this offers a general description of the differing emphases of two traditions by which Keller was formed. Both are evident and stand in tension in Keller's theology.

But the final reason that Keller opts for two ways is, perhaps, the most obvious. Keller's articulation of the gospel is—necessarily—an American contextualization, and in America the individualism and rationalism of the Enlightenment remain very powerful. Newbigin's missionary encounter with

45. Newbigin, *Proper Confidence*, 65. Cf. Michael W. Goheen, *The Church and Its Vocation: Lesslie Newbigin's Missionary Ecclesiology* (Grand Rapids: Baker Academic, 2018), 33–37.
46. Keller, "Our New Global Culture," 18 (emphasis added).

Hinduism for forty years awakened him to the power of the Enlightenment in shaping the gospel and biblical authority in Western culture. And it was precisely these two things that were often the target of his attack.

New Testament Theology

But these reasons cannot ultimately account for Keller's "two basic ways." For him, Scripture is always the supreme authority, and he is bold to stand against conservative confessionalists in his own tradition for the sake of the gospel. So we must seek a deeper reason in the way he reads Scripture. And, indeed, he briefly sketches his version of a New Testament theology that supports his two ways.

For Keller, the Synoptic Gospels of Matthew, Mark, and Luke give us a gospel of the kingdom. The imagery of kingdom is oriented toward the future and emphasizes the "external and corporate" aspects of the gospel. The kingdom is about the gospel taking corporate shape in a new social order, and this will happen only in the future. The already-not-yet is interpreted in terms of "already = individual salvation" and "not-yet = corporate salvation."[47] In contrast to the Synoptics, the gospel in John is about eternal life, which emphasizes the more individual and inward aspects of salvation. Thus "John and the Synoptic writers reveal complementary aspects of the gospel, stressing both the individual and corporate dimensions of our salvation."[48] But then in Paul we get yet another image that is central to his gospel—justification: "While Paul uses both 'kingdom' and 'life,' he more centrally focuses on the concept of justification."[49] Moreover, Keller calls the book of Romans "the most thoroughgoing exposition of the gospel in the Bible."[50] His reading of the first chapters would run along these lines: the individual sinner is under the wrath of God (Rom. 1:18–3:20), but the substitutionary atonement of Christ has taken the wrath of God and provided justification by faith to anyone who believes (Rom. 3:21–26).[51]

Biblically, then, Keller justifies his approach by assigning the synoptic gospel of the kingdom to the corporate pole of his axis and relegating it to the future as a future-and-not-yet social order. The "already" of salvation in

47. Keller, *Center Church*, 47.
48. Keller, *Center Church*, 39.
49. Keller, *Center Church*, 39.
50. Keller, *Center Church*, 29.
51. For a more redemptive-historical reading of those chapters in Romans, see N. T. Wright, "The Letter to the Romans," in *The New Interpreter's Bible: A Commentary in Twelve Volumes* (Nashville: Abingdon, 2002), 10:405, 413–14.

the present is for the individual, and John and Paul are our guides. And it is especially Romans that offers the path of sin, substitutionary atonement, faith, and justification.[52]

Newbigin's approach to the New Testament is rather different. We find in the Synoptics a gospel of the kingdom as the good news that Jesus preached. However, this cannot be simply associated with the external, the corporate, or the cosmic. The kingdom of God concerns the whole restoration of the creation, including the individual person, the individual's social and cultural context, and the nonhuman creation. The kingdom is about the End of universal history breaking into the middle, and it cannot be reduced to one aspect. Throughout the Synoptics, persons respond to the gospel of the kingdom, and they both receive and enter the kingdom, receiving its blessings and obligations. Nor can the kingdom be pushed to the future.

John's Gospel may display a stronger emphasis on the individual, but it is equally eschatological.[53] John's Gospel is a remarkable example of cross-cultural communication. He employs the terminology of "eternal life" to communicate the gospel of the kingdom to listeners, using familiar categories. Eternal life is eschatological life from the future breaking into the middle. It is imagery that points to the same thing as kingdom. It cannot be reduced to the inner and individual life.

Moreover, the center of Paul's gospel is not justification but is, like the rest of the New Testament, fundamentally eschatological.[54] "The whole New Testament message is set firmly in the framework of this eschatological faith and cannot be understood apart from it."[55] This begins with the Synoptic Gospels and moves through to Paul, who opens up the implications of the gospel of the kingdom for the church. Thus justification itself must be understood in this broader eschatological context. It is one of the gifts of the kingdom— that is why it is good news. Newbigin says, "Justification is an eschatological idea. The Jew who longed for God's kingdom to come longed above all for justification. The righteous were to be justified, and the wicked punished when

---

52. For a contrasting eschatological approach to the New Testament authority of the Synoptics, John, and Paul, see George E. Ladd, *The Pattern of New Testament Truth* (Grand Rapids: Eerdmans, 1968). Herman Ridderbos and N. T. Wright also follow this pattern.

53. Ridderbos calls John's interest in the individual the "personal concept," but goes on to say that eternal life carries the same "'eschatological' all-embracing significance." Herman Ridderbos, *The Gospel of John: A Theological Commentary*, trans. John Vriend (Grand Rapids: Eerdmans, 1997), 125.

54. See "The Redemptive-Historical Character of Paul's Preaching," chap. 3 in Herman Ridderbos, *When the Time Had Fully Come: Studies in New Testament Theology* (Grand Rapids: Eerdmans, 1957), 44–60.

55. Newbigin, *Reunion of the Church*, 73.

God came to end this evil age and reign. The apostles announced a still more wonderful event—that now, 'while we were yet sinners,' Christ had died for the ungodly, and that those who were His were justified *now* by faith."[56] The future eschatological justification of God's people is now present as one of the gifts of the kingdom breaking into history and available by faith.

The New Testament canon is integrated by eschatology. The Gospels announce the coming of the kingdom and the life it brings. God's reign (not just the small component of personal salvation) is already here and will come fully when Christ returns. The Pauline Letters unpack the significance of this announcement both in terms of the salvation that the church now receives and in terms of the mission of God's people in their particular place. The kingdom cannot be associated only with the external and corporate aspects, nor can it be only about the future.

Cross and Kingdom

Both Newbigin and Keller see the events of the cross and resurrection as the center of the gospel. Keller fears that when we take the "basic way" of story, kingdom, and restoration, the cross fades into the background. The cross is disconnected from the kingdom.[57] And his concerns are valid. There are traditions that turn the kingdom into a program to seek justice and the transformation of society. The cross, and its importance for individual salvation, does not feature prominently, if at all. To rectify this rather fundamental distortion of the gospel, Keller moves to the other "basic way," whose story line is God, sinner, substitutionary atonement, faith, and justification. He repeatedly emphasizes the substitutionary atonement, which takes the wrath of a holy God so that we might be justified.

Newbigin would not doubt the truth of what Keller says. And Newbigin certainly cannot be accused of neglecting the cross! In fact, it is hard to think of anyone who makes the cross more prominent and central to everything. Nor can he be accused of neglecting God's wrath, the seriousness of our sin, the atonement as substitutionary, or the importance of justification. Nor has he neglected the importance of the cross for each person and their salvation. However, by comparison, Keller's view of the atonement is reductionist. By placing the cross in the context or "story line" of systematic theology—or by his reading of Romans—and by reducing the image of the atonement to penal substitution,

56. Newbigin, *Reunion of the Church*, 76.
57. Keller, *Center Church*, 269.

and by individualizing and missing the communal and cosmic elements of even that image, Keller has greatly reduced the significance of the cross. Placing the cross in its proper context as well as displaying all the rich imagery of the cross in Scripture heightens, deepens, and broadens its significance. In this we see three fundamental differences between Newbigin and Keller.

First, Newbigin refuses to reduce the cross to the substitutionary atonement. He says,

> Down the centuries, from the first witness until today, the church has sought and used innumerable symbols to express the inexpressible mystery of the event that is the center, the crisis of cosmic history, the hinge upon which all happenings turn. Christ the sacrifice offered for sin, Christ the substitute standing in our place, Christ the ransom paid for our redemption, Christ the conqueror casting out the prince of the world—these and other symbols have been used to point to the heart of the mystery. None can fully express it. It is that happening in which the reign of God is present.[58]

When we focus on one image, we run the risk of missing the fullness of what the cross has accomplished, which can be understood only with the whole multitude of biblical images. For example, the substitutionary atonement allows us to focus on what Christ has accomplished on the cross to take the guilt of our sin. While this is wonderfully true, the military image of the victorious Christ allows us to see how he has conquered the demonic powers that hold us in their grip through evil and unjust structures; meanwhile, the imagery of Christ as the obedience of the second Adam enables us to see how the cross forms a new humanity and ushers in a new creation. All images are needed to point to the fullness of what Christ has accomplished on the cross. But none can by itself fully express what God has done in that historical event at Calvary.

A second difference is that Newbigin sees the significance of the cross in the context of the literary structure of the Gospels. In the New Testament this is the first canonical context in which the cross is placed. The Gospels do not start with the sinful person and move to the cross as the solution. They begin with the announcement of the kingdom and move to the cross as the ultimate victory of the kingdom and the resurrection as its cosmic dawning (fig. 13.3).

A third difference is that Newbigin places the cross in the context of the whole biblical story. The central theme of the biblical story is the restoration of the whole creation. The story of the Gospels is the central moment of that story, culminating in the cross and resurrection. Thus these events ultimately

58. Newbigin, *Open Secret*, 50. See also Newbigin, *Sin and Salvation*, 56–91.

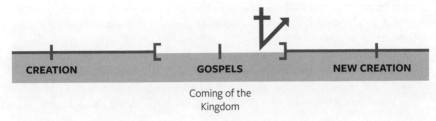

Figure 13.3. Context of cross and resurrection

need to be placed in their cosmic context as the hinge of universal history. The cross defeats the old—the guilt and power of sin, evil, curse, wrath, unjust structures, Satan and demonic power, death, the effects of sin—*all* that belongs to and characterizes the old age. The resurrection ushers in the age to come, the new creation, the kingdom that will one day fill the earth. These events are cosmic in scope.

While Newbigin makes these kinds of statements frequently, perhaps nowhere is his exposition of these events more moving than in two sets of four Bible studies he gave on death and resurrection.[59] He begins with the death and resurrection of Jesus as cosmic events. "At the centre of history, which is both the history of man and the history of nature, stands the pivotal, critical, once-for-all event of the death and resurrection of Jesus. By this event, the human situation is irreversibly changed."[60] Then in following studies he speaks of how the church, individuals, and the whole cosmos participate. The church and each member of that body, as well as the whole creation, share in Christ's death and its victory over the old. "The pattern of cross and resurrection is projected in the Bible, not only on to the personal life, and not only on to the life of the Church, but also on to the life of the cosmos."[61] The church and every individual believer, along with the nonhuman creation, share in the new creation, the kingdom that is coming—already now in foretaste but fully in the consummation. Newbigin emphasizes the eschatological, cosmic, and communal significance of the cross and resurrection, but does not eclipse the personal:

> The Cross of Jesus is the centre of cosmic history. For him who believes that, it is also the centre of his own personal history. Only so does the believer find

59. Lesslie Newbigin, "Bible Studies Given at the National Christian Council Triennial Assembly, Shillong," *National Christian Council Review* 88 (1968): 9–14, 73–78, 125–31, 177–85; Newbigin, "The Bible Study Lectures," in *Digest of the Proceedings of the Ninth Meeting of the Consultation on Church Union (COCU)*, ed. Paul A. Crow Jr. (Princeton: Consultation on Church Union, 1970), 193–231.
60. Newbigin, "Bible Studies," 10.
61. Newbigin, "Bible Study Lectures," 215.

that he can live meaningfully as part of the history of his people, and of the world. . . . He died for me. Sometimes I confess that I become weary of the constant repetition of this "for me." Sometimes we almost come to think that the whole mystery of God's salvation ends up in this little selfish cry "for me." Indeed we must ever remember that the Cross of Christ is the saving of the world and not just my own salvation. And yet there must be a moment when we know that it is not only for the world, not only for us, but also for me.[62]

In these studies, Newbigin's emphasis is on eschatological union with Christ in his death and resurrection. One of the differences between the Lutheran and Calvinist traditions is that for Luther, justification dominated his understanding of salvation. In the Calvinist tradition, it is our union with Christ in his death and resurrection that offers a bevy of eschatological benefits, including justification. Justification is only one of the gifts that enable us to be restored to God and again participate in our full humanity. As Newbigin puts it, "All the benefits which Christ was sent to bring" enable people to be "restored to their true humanity because they are reconciled with their Maker."[63] For Newbigin, this view of the cross and resurrection as the turning point in cosmic history provides the proper narrative context to understand our participation in Christ and all his benefits as members of the new humanity. He says, "by faith, in the Church, and in the Spirit we are made partakers of Christ," and then launches into a discussion of regeneration, justification, conversion, and sanctification.[64]

Keller's primary focus on the substitutionary atonement and the benefit of justification puts him more in line with the Lutheran tradition.[65] To be sure, Keller has not reduced the gospel exclusively to substitutionary atonement and justification. Yet the repeated focus on justification certainly doesn't allow salvation to open up in its breathtaking and expansive panorama that displays *all* the benefits of the kingdom that are ours in Christ and by the Spirit. Newbigin's eschatological version of the recapitulation theory of the atonement offers us this astoundingly rich salvation that restores everything sin, the curse, and God's wrath have taken away, including being put right in our relation to God. Newbigin's vision of the cross is enormous! Everything Keller wants in the substitutionary atonement for each person is there, and so much more.

62. Newbigin, "Bible Studies," 75.
63. Lesslie Newbigin, "The Life and Mission of the Church," in *The Life and Mission of the Church*, ed. C. I. Itty (Bangalore: Student Christian Movement of India, 1958), 7.
64. Newbigin, *Sin and Salvation*, 100–114.
65. Interestingly, Keller mentions Martin Luther at least seventeen times in his section on the gospel, and John Calvin not once.

In this case, as in many others, Newbigin's cross-cultural experience opened him up to the ways our culture has blind spots to scriptural teaching. He shares with René Padilla, the Argentine evangelical leader, new eyes from other cultures to see biblical teaching on the cross that we have often missed in the West. For Padilla (and Newbigin), classical theories of the atonement in Western theology have "concentrated on the salvation of the individual soul but frequently disregarded God's purpose to create a new humanity." Rather, he says, we must "look at the cross, not merely as the source of individual salvation, but as the place wherein begins the renewal of the creation—the new heavens and the new earth that God has promised and that the messianic community anticipates."[66] Here we find the same stress on the communal and cosmic dimensions of the cross without neglecting the fact that "Jesus died for sinners."

Cosmic—Communal—Personal

Keller speaks of the individual and corporate as two aspects of salvation on the ends of an axis to be balanced in the center. For Newbigin, we do not have two aspects or poles: these are abstractions—aspects of a fully integrated salvation lifted out of their fabric and set against each other. Rather, the logic of the Christian faith moves from cosmic to communal to the personal.[67] The Bible is a story of *cosmic* history: it begins in creation and ends in new creation. Christ stands at the center disclosing, accomplishing, and making present in his life, death, and resurrection where universal history is going. That is the gospel. At the center of the biblical story is a *community* that has been chosen to embody and announce God's redemptive purpose to the world. They are to live as the true humanity that the Adamic humanity failed to be. They bear the gospel of the kingdom in their lives, deeds, and words. Together they experience kingdom-salvation and point and witness to the new creation that is coming. Every person—each *individual*, if you will—is extended a personal invitation to become part of that community and experience an ongoing conversion to the fullness of that cosmic restoration of human life accomplished by Christ. They are invited to share in God's accomplished redemption at the cross and in the kingdom and new creation that has begun in his resurrection.

There is no tension whatsoever here between the cosmic and the individual; there are not two basic ways to answer the question "What is the gospel?"

66. C. René Padilla, foreword to *Understanding the Atonement for the Mission of the Church*, by John Driver (Scottdale, PA: Herald, 1986), 9–10.
67. Goheen, *Church and Its Vocation*, 37–38, 201–2, 213.

but one. In Christ—especially in his death and resurrection—God has accomplished his purpose to restore the whole creation. Through the work of the Spirit first *in* and then *through* the church, God forms the true humanity that will inherit the earth. Each person is summoned by this good news to join that community. They will be restored to God (forgiven, justified, adopted, and more) as well as to one another and the nonhuman creation.

Newbigin reflects not only the canonical shape and fundamental structure of the Bible but also the way Paul approaches the proclamation of the gospel. Paul's word *include* is helpful here: "And you also were *included* in Christ when you heard the message of truth, the gospel of your salvation. When you believed . . ." (Eph 1:13). *Included in Christ when you heard and believed the good news. Include* indicates inclusion in something bigger—to "make part of a whole," as the Oxford Dictionary has it,[68] or "to contain something as part of something else," as the Cambridge Dictionary puts it.[69] One was *included* as part of something bigger. What is that "bigger"? In the first twelve verses, it is God's cosmic purpose to unite all things in heaven and earth under Christ and the community that now shares in that salvation. "Individual" salvation is inclusion and participation in "cosmic and communal" salvation by faith in the gospel. "What must I do to be saved?" is not answered with a different framework. Rather, one is saved by believing in the good news of what God has done in Christ for the whole world—which, of course, includes people.

Keeping in mind the danger of using any picture exclusively, perhaps instead of an axis we can picture Newbigin's view in terms of three concentric circles. The outer circle is cosmic salvation, which includes as part of this the new humanity, the community that has begun to taste that salvation even now (the second circle). The inside circle is each person who is included by faith in Christ in the community that enjoys cosmic salvation now (fig. 13.4).

Storied Authority of Scripture

What Does Scripture Do?

Newbigin stresses the need for a coherent understanding of the authority of Scripture if there is to be a missionary encounter. And he expended a great

68. *Oxford English Dictionary*, s.v. "include," https://www.google.com/search?q=include+meaning&oq=include+meaning&aqs=chrome.69i57j0i512l9.3945j1j7&sourceid=chrome&ie=UTF-8.

69. *Cambridge Dictionary Online*, s.v. "include," https://dictionary.cambridge.org/us/dictionary/english/include.

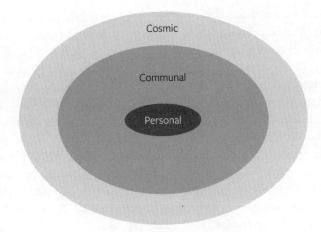

Figure 13.4. The narrative structure of Scripture

deal of energy on the task of fostering such an understanding in the latter part of his life. Yet Keller makes the point that Newbigin "openly repudiated the evangelical doctrine of Scripture."[70] Keller does not seem to be offering a compliment. It is hard to be sure exactly what Keller is referring to, since there are many evangelical models of biblical authority that stress varying elements of a doctrine of Scripture. But we assume that Keller is referring to the way Newbigin critiques both conservative and liberal views of the authority of Scripture as shaped by the idolatry of the Enlightenment story. He targets fundamentalist notions of inerrancy and even has the audacity to tackle the evangelical paragon and champion B. B. Warfield.[71]

While we share certain of Keller's concerns, it is unfortunate that he is not willing to put his own "evangelical doctrine of Scripture" in light of Scripture itself to see whether perhaps it needs to be enriched or even corrected. In fact, we believe that in many ways Newbigin's understanding of the authority of Scripture is stronger than a so-called evangelical doctrine. Moreover, and importantly for this book, it provides a far broader and firmer foundation for a missionary church and missionary encounter, including that which Keller himself envisions.

Newbigin says that "it is less important to ask a Christian what he or she *believes about* the Bible than it is to inquire what he or she *does with* it."[72] It is unfortunate that he sets these two things against each other; in fact, he

70. Keller, *Center Church*, 252.
71. Lesslie Newbigin, *Foolishness to the Greeks: The Gospel and Western Culture* (Grand Rapids: Eerdmans, 1986), 45–46.
72. Newbigin, *Proper Confidence*, 87 (emphasis added).

himself talks a lot about both. But he is on to something that is endemic to the evangelical community: there has been much discussion about inerrancy, often without corresponding attention to how the Bible works, especially as one story. C. S. Lewis says that the "first qualification for judging any piece of workmanship from a corkscrew to a cathedral is to know what it is—what it was intended to do and how it is meant to be used."[73] What Scripture is, what it is intended to do, and how it is to be used are all closely tied together.

Herman Ridderbos distinguishes between the *attributes* and *purpose* of Scripture. Scripture's attributes refer to its inspiration, infallibility, and divine authority. Its purpose tells us what it does and how it is to be used.[74] Evangelicals have rightly spent a great deal of time defending the attributes of Scripture against higher criticism and liberal theology. But often the purpose of Scripture has not received the same attention.

Newbigin seems to be exasperated by all of this. Moreover, he believes much evangelical reflection on the nature of Scripture is already taken up into an Enlightenment framework as evangelicals "apply to the Scripture standards which do not suit it."[75] And this has severely undermined the use and purpose of Scripture. The power of the storied authority of Scripture has been compromised, hobbling us in our use of Scripture to equip God's people to be faithful in an idolatrous context.

We believe Ridderbos is correct when he says that the "*purpose* of Scripture . . . and the use which corresponds to it must always be borne in mind when framing a theological definition of the *attributes* of the Scripture."[76] And so it is a pity that Newbigin does not hold these together. Nevertheless, Newbigin's reflection on what Scripture does, especially as it empowers the church for a missionary encounter, is extremely important. And evangelicals who attend to it—Keller included—will find their views enriched, corrected, and deepened.

Truth in a Record of Historical Events

A prevalent theme for Newbigin is that the biblical story centered in the gospel is an account of *historical events* that disclose the true story of the world. God reveals himself and his purpose first in historical events. Then

73. C. S. Lewis, *A Preface to Paradise Lost* (1942; repr., Oxford: Oxford University Press, 1961), 1.
74. Herman Ridderbos, *Studies in Scripture and Its Authority* (Grand Rapids: Eerdmans, 1978), 20–36.
75. Ridderbos, *Studies in Scripture*, 23. The inerrancy Newbigin denies is of an ahistorical fundamentalist sort.
76. Ridderbos, *Studies in Scripture*, 23 (emphasis added).

those events are narrated in Scripture. There is a distinction between God's revelation in historical events and the authoritative interpretation and infallible recording of those events in Scripture.

One of the fundamental differences between Scripture and Western culture is the source of ultimately reliable truth. For Western culture, from the time of Plato and Aristotle to its culmination in the Enlightenment, truth is to be found in ideas: "The truth about how things are is to be expressed in timeless statements."[77] In the Bible, truth is to be found in a unified narrative of the mighty historical acts of God, beginning in Israel; culminating in the life, death, and resurrection of Jesus; and continuing by the Spirit in the church, which reveals and accomplishes God's purpose to renew the world.[78]

Two further comments need to be made to stave off misunderstanding. First, the meaning of these historical events is given authoritative interpretation in the various books and in the overarching story of Scripture. Newbigin critiques notions of salvation history that locate truth in history apart from their interpretation in the scriptural text.[79] Second, this does not reduce Scripture to the so-called historical books and minimize the plethora of genres. Newbigin says that "the Bible is essentially narrative in form. Its form is that of universal history. It contains, indeed, much else: prayer, poetry, legislation, ethical teaching, and so on. But essentially it is a story."[80] Each of these genres equips and forms us to live in that story out of which they arise.

But the basic structure of Scripture is redemptive history, which is universal history.[81] Newbigin believes that the philosophy of the pagan Greek world has so shaped us that we are predisposed to turn the story of Scripture into the timeless statements of systematic theology.[82] Yet the fundamental truth of God's revelation is revealed in the historical narrative of Scripture. "Revelation is not the communication of a body of timeless truths which one has only to receive in order to know the whole mind of God. Revelation is rather the disclosure of the direction in which God is leading the world and his family. The stuff of the Bible is promise and fulfillment."[83] When we articulate this

---

77. Newbigin, *Open Secret*, 82.
78. Lesslie Newbigin, *The Gospel in a Pluralist Society* (Grand Rapids: Eerdmans, 1989), 1–3; Newbigin, *Proper Confidence*, 3, 14, 72–73, 79.
79. Newbigin, *Foolishness to the Greeks*, 48.
80. Newbigin, *Open Secret*, 81.
81. In Newbigin's critique of salvation history, he is also concerned to emphasize that it is universal history for all people and not simply narrative theology or the religious story of Israel. Newbigin, *Foolishness to the Greeks*, 48.
82. See the powerful critique of this "essentialist" tendency in Harvie M. Conn, *Eternal Word and Changing Worlds: Theology, Anthropology, and Mission in Trialogue* (Grand Rapids: Zondervan, 1984), 211–60.
83. Newbigin, *Good Shepherd*, 117.

story in "so-called eternal [theological] truths," this is, in fact, an attempt we make "at particular moments in the story to grasp and state how things are in terms of our experience at that point." Newbigin does not dispute the importance of theology but stresses that "the reality with which we have to deal is the story." All our theological statements are "provisional and relative to time and place."[84]

When, however, we take our theological statements that express the doctrinal content of the gospel—and such there is—as "timeless truths," in effect, we run the danger of filling the content of the gospel with the theology of our own tradition. It is then difficult to critique that expression of the gospel because it is equated with the divine authority of Scripture. We have the fixed and unchanging content of the gospel as the kernel of truth—which is, in effect, our theological formulation—and now we must translate or contextualize it in different settings. This was precisely the problem in nineteenth- to twentieth-century missionary efforts to communicate the gospel to non-Western cultures.[85]

Keller comes dangerously close to this problem in the first chapter of *Center Church*. He offers a nuanced discussion of a theological vision that is attentive to context. And it is admirable that he wants pastors from other parts of the world to avoid mimicking the "Redeemer model." Yet the book is written to enable these pastors. In the diagram he unfolds in this first chapter, there is a doctrinal foundation made up of "timeless truths" from Scripture.[86] These truths seem to be fixed and are then contextualized in particular ministry settings; they are an unchanging foundation on which we build a theological vision. The unchanging kernel of the gospel sheds its American husk and takes on other cultural husks. Or so it seems.[87]

The danger is that as this book is taken to other parts of the world, Keller's American contextualized expression of the gospel, with all its insights and limitations, is seen as the starting point. And this is not an imaginary concern. Recently a Brazilian leader told us that a proliferation of American church-planting organizations are coming to Brazil and repeating the mistakes of

84. Newbigin, *Open Secret*, 82–83.

85. David J. Bosch, *Transforming Mission: Paradigm Shifts in Theology of Mission* (Maryknoll, NY: Orbis Books, 1991), 449.

86. Keller, *Center Church*, 20. Keller's doctrine of Scripture is far more nuanced and sophisticated than simply affirming "timeless truths" (cf. 107n8). Yet his default description of the gospel is as "biblical doctrines" (31), "gospel truths" laid into the biblical story (33), "propositions" (32–33), "the classic doctrines of the biblical gospel" (11), and a "set of truths" (46). Perhaps it is again one foot in redemptive history and one foot in systematic theology.

87. The rest of the chapter seems more nuanced. But why "timeless truths," and why does contextualization take place only at a later stage?

the cross-cultural missions of the nineteenth and twentieth centuries. He said they are exhibiting a *doctrinal* and ecclesiological imperialism, as each organization has brought its American version of the *gospel* and ministry. He mentioned City to City as one of a number of such organizations.

The Bible as the True Story of Universal History— Its Missional Urgency

The narrative unity of these historical events—God's acts in history—tells us the true story of universal history. Newbigin wants to recover this authority of Scripture, and he believes there is much at stake. Scriptural authority has been vitiated when Scripture has been relegated to the private realm as a religious book concerned only with spiritual, moral, or future matters. Scriptural authority has also been impaired as the Bible is broken up into moral bits, systematic-theological or doctrinal bits, and historical-critical bits. These bits are then easily swept into and carried along by the powerful currents of the Western cultural story. This nullifies a missionary encounter. There is no longer the power of the comprehensive and ultimate scriptural narrative to stand against the overwhelming currents of the equally powerful, equally comprehensive, and equally ultimate narrative of our culture.

The Western church is an "advanced case of syncretism"[88] precisely because it has allowed the gospel to be taken captive by the idolatry of the cultural story. This is a scandalous failure of the church to carry out its vocation to make known the gospel. Over against this syncretism, Newbigin summons the Western church to a missionary encounter. In contemporary Western culture there are "two quite different stories" told as the "real story" of the world: the humanist story and the story that is told in the Bible.[89] A missionary encounter is a clash of foundational stories. It occurs when the church believes the Bible to be the true story of the world and then embodies or indwells its comprehensive claims as a witness in the face of the dominant cultural narrative. Newbigin charges that the reverse has taken place: the Western church has allowed the biblical story to be absorbed into the more comprehensive Western story. The Bible has become a private religious book.

An essential ingredient in reversing syncretism is to recover Scripture as a true grand story: "I do not believe that we can speak effectively of the Gospel as a word addressed to our culture unless we recover a sense of the Scriptures

---

88. Lesslie Newbigin, *A Word in Season: Perspectives on Christian World Missions* (Grand Rapids: Eerdmans, 1994), 67; Newbigin, *The Other Side of 1984: Questions for the Churches* (Geneva: World Council of Churches, 1983), 23.

89. Newbigin, *Proper Confidence*, 2; Newbigin, *Gospel in a Pluralist Society*, 15.

as a canonical whole, as the story which provides the true context for our understanding of the meaning of our lives—both personal and public."[90] Our lives will be shaped by some story; if we are not being formed by the biblical story, by default we will be shaped by the reigning story of culture. As Newbigin puts it, "If this biblical story is not the one that really controls our thinking [and lives] then inevitably we shall be swept into the story that the world tells about itself. We shall become increasingly indistinguishable from the pagan world of which we are a part."[91]

There are three important dimensions of the Bible's narrative authority that need to be recovered if the church is to be faithful in its missionary vocation: the Bible is a *story*—a story rooted in redemptive history; it is a *true* story—it faithfully narrates the purpose of the Creator and Redeemer God in history for the whole world; and it is a true story with *comprehensive* authority over the whole of human life. These elements of biblical authority must be recovered for a missionary encounter.

The importance of Newbigin's constant harping on this point is driven home by Australian sociologist John Carroll, who makes no claim to be Christian. He asks, from the standpoint of a sociologist and historian, why the church in the West—in Europe, the United States, Canada, Australia, New Zealand—is in serious decline. He answers: "The waning of Christianity as practised in the West is easy to explain. The Christian churches have comprehensively failed in their one central task—to retell their foundation story in a way that might speak to the times."[92] Failure to tell our foundation story in our preaching, discipleship, worship, and teaching! Failure to see its all-embracing authority in our world today by interpreting all the issues of contemporary life in its comprehensive light! This has certainly contributed to the waning of the Christian faith in the West. Carroll's solution, however, is to reshape and tailor the biblical narrative to fit into the broader story of the West in order to be relevant. What is needed is the exact opposite: a recovery of the biblical story as true in its sweeping authority to speak to all the issues of our day. Indeed, what is desperately needed is a faithful retelling and rehearsing of this story in the whole ministry of the local congregation[93]—so that the people of God may thoroughly know their foundation story and be equipped for their missionary vocation in their whole lives.

90. Newbigin, "Response to 'Word of God?'," 2.
91. Lesslie Newbigin, "Biblical Authority," Newbigin Archives, University of Birmingham (unpublished article, 1997), 2.
92. John Carroll, *The Existential Jesus* (Brunswick, Victoria, Australia: Scribe, 2008), 7.
93. See Robert Webber and Philip Kenyon, "Ancient-Evangelical Future Call," http://webber center.tsm.edu/about-us/aef-call/. They show the significance of the biblical story for mission, theology, worship, and discipleship in the church.

The way the evangelical church has capitulated to the reigning idolatrous ideologies of our cultural story proves the need to recover the biblical story to withstand their claims and to interpret them aright. The recovery of the biblical story as the one, true, and comprehensive story is urgent![94] And New-bigin's voice—evangelical doctrine of Scripture or not—needs to be heard.

Keller is certainly not blind to this. His own practice and preaching often demonstrate that he has dwelled deeply in the biblical narrative. Yet when he articulates the gospel as the foundation for a missionary church and encounter with culture, this essential narrative dimension receives short shrift. The narrative of Scripture that he offers with his left hand is taken away with his right by a second basic way.

This chapter has offered a strong critique of Keller. This may have obscured both our appreciation for his rich insights into a missionary church and encounter with culture as well as the wisdom he offers on the gospel. We are sure that there are idolatrous tensions in our own work where we integrate aspects of Scripture's teaching. But we believe that Newbigin's cross-cultural experience has offered rich insight into the gospel and biblical story that provides a broad and stable foundation for the missionary nature of the church and a missionary encounter with culture. We believe it is urgent to recover it.

---

94. For the importance of the comprehensive narrative authority of Scripture, see N. T. Wright, *The New Testament and the People of God* (London: SPCK, 1992), 121–44; Wright, "The Bible for the Postmodern World" (Orange Memorial Lecture, Latimer Fellowship, 1999), 9–12; Wright, "How Can the Bible Be Authoritative?," *Vox Evangelia* 21 (1991): 7–32; Richard Bauckham, *Scriptural Authority Today* (Cambridge: Grove Books, 1999), 10–13; Bauckham, *Bible and Mission*, 83–112; Michael W. Goheen, "The Urgency of Reading the Bible as One Story," *Theology Today* 64, no. 4 (January 2008): 469–83.

14

Becoming a Missionary Church

Lesslie Newbigin's Legacy for the Twenty-First Century

T he primary goal of this book is to deepen our understanding of what it means to become a missionary church. We are especially concerned to preserve Lesslie Newbigin's legacy, not for nostalgic purposes but because his theological vision remains exceedingly valuable for our present moment. We conclude by summarizing important elements of that legacy.

Our Situation

Here is the situation in which we as the people of God find ourselves:

- We are born into a cultural community, and our lives are narrated from birth by our cultural story, which forms us and gives meaning to our lives.
- Because we are immersed in this cultural world, its story and its way of life appear to be normal, simply "the way the world is."
- Yet our cultural story is not "normal"; like all cultural visions, it is a religious vision deformed to some degree by idolatry, and thus it shapes us in unfaithful ways.
- We are baptized into another community and given a new identity. We are a people chosen by God to embody a different story and a distinctive way of life as the nucleus and firstfruits of the new humanity for the sake of the world.

• There is thus a continual need to "renarrate" our lives with the biblical story so we can be faithful to our new missionary identity.
• This is an intentional, difficult, and lifelong process of conversion if we are to be faithful to who we are.

This is our situation as the people of God. And in the remainder of this chapter we ask, How can we become a missionary church that is increasingly faithful to our vocation? And, more specifically, what resources does Newbigin offer for this task?

The Gospel Dynamic

To become a missionary church, it is essential that we grasp the proper broader context that gives meaning to our vocation. Every proposal for a missionary ecclesiology involves certain assumptions about the nature of the Christian faith that function, often implicitly, as the broader framework in which it is understood. *Some* more comprehensive framework will shape our understanding of the missionary church, and we are wise to attend to the one offered by Newbigin.

To grasp his understanding of the missionary church, we must accompany him as he digs deeper and asks more foundational questions about the gospel, Scripture, and the nature of the Christian faith. We describe his wider and deeper framework as his "gospel dynamic."[1] By *dynamic* we mean a basic, powerful, and comprehensive theological force that drives his thought. But we also want to communicate the idea, attached to the word *dynamic* in some schools of psychology, that this basic force is an interactive combination of factors. These factors are the gospel, the biblical story, the mission of the church, and a missionary encounter with culture.

Newbigin believes that all thought must begin with the *gospel*—that is, the central events of the biblical story associated with Jesus Christ: his life, death, resurrection, ascension, and outpouring of the Spirit. "If it is really true that God has done what the Gospel tells us that he has done, . . . it must, it necessarily must become the starting point and controlling reality of all thought."[2] The good news is that, in Jesus, God is acting to bring the kingdom of God into the midst of history. Jesus does not need to stop and

---

1. Michael W. Goheen, *The Church and Its Vocation: Lesslie Newbigin's Missionary Ecclesiology* (Grand Rapids: Baker Academic, 2018), 8–9.
2. Lesslie Newbigin, "The Gospel and Modern Western Culture," Newbigin Archives, University of Birmingham (unpublished speech, n.d.), 13.

define the kingdom because the Jews are passionately anticipating its arrival. The kingdom is one image to describe the goal of God's redemptive purpose and the climactic End toward which the whole biblical story has been moving; it is the goal of universal history, when his purpose will be realized. It is the cosmic renewal of the whole creation, including all human life, from the power and effects of sin. The good news is that this renewal is now present in the middle in Jesus and by the Spirit.

The good news of the kingdom necessarily sets us in the middle of a *story* that makes the astounding, even outrageous, totalitarian claim to be the true story of the world. The gospel is a message about the *end* of universal history— the restoration of the creation from sin. The gospel is a message about the restoration of the whole creation, and thus points back to the *beginning* of universal history—the creation of everything. Thus the gospel places us between creation and consummation, the beginning and end of cosmic history. Moreover, the good news is the climactic moment of a long story of what *God the Creator* is doing to direct history to its goal. The story unfolds his work in the nation of Israel, fulfilled in Christ and implemented by the Spirit in the mission of the church. Thus the gospel requires us to read the Bible as universal history that begins in creation and ends with the renewal of the creation, but also as a story of the way God accomplishes his universal purpose through the particular path of Israel, Jesus, and the church. The gospel demands that we read the Bible as a true story of God's redemptive work that gives true meaning to human history.

This story centered in Christ *is the Christian faith*. This is the whole point of Christianity; this is what the Bible is all about; this is the essence of the Christian faith. "The Christian faith *is* a particular way of understanding history as a whole which finds in the story about Jesus the decisive clue."[3] Or again, the "Christian faith *is itself* an interpretation of history."[4] Or once more, "the Christian faith *is* a faith regarding the meaning and end of the human story as a whole."[5] So the missionary church must be understood within this framework.

And, indeed, a central thread of this story is God's work in and through a chosen people. The biblical story is a narrative of God's dealing with a people in whom and through whom he will accomplish his purpose for the world. They bear in their lives the future goal of universal history—the renewal God intends for all. They are blessed: restored to the original creational blessing

3. Lesslie Newbigin, "The Centrality of Jesus for History," in *Incarnation and Myth: The Debate Continued*, ed. Michael Goulder (Grand Rapids: Eerdmans, 1979), 200 (emphasis added).

4. Lesslie Newbigin, *The Finality of Christ* (London: SCM, 1969), 55 (emphasis added).

5. Lesslie Newbigin, *The Open Secret: An Introduction to the Theology of Mission*, rev. ed. (Grand Rapids: Eerdmans, 1995), 89 (emphasis added).

of what it means to be truly human. They are to be a blessing: chosen for the sake of the world to be the means of blessing to all. They are the first place God begins to restore his creational purpose, re-creating them as the true humanity that the Adamic humanity failed to be. As the new humankind, they invite all nations to join them as the people who will one day inherit the earth. It is this outward orientation—"for the sake of the world"—that makes God's people missionary by their very nature.

This chosen people is set to live out their vocation amidst the world to be a sign and preview of where God is taking all of history. They do not exist in a religious vacuum but live out their calling among cultures that serve other gods. The church will always embody and announce the gospel within some cultural context. From the beginning, the primary threat to Israel's vocation was the idolatry of the nations around it. The problem is only exacerbated as the church is sent as a nongeographical and multiethnic people to live *as part of* all the world's cultures. Since each culture is formed and unified by some idolatrous core, the embodiment of God's purposes for the sake of the nations will always involve a missionary encounter.

This is the fourfold dynamic that drives Newbigin's thought: gospel, story, missional people, and missionary encounter with culture. These are not four discrete pieces of his theological vision. Rather, they are closely interwoven and interdependent parts of a story. Each requires the others in order to be properly understood. In sum, if we start with the gospel, we find ourselves in the middle of the Bible as one story where the missionary vocation of God's people is a central thread of that story, a people who necessarily live out their calling in a missionary encounter with culture. This dynamic expresses something intrinsic to the Christian faith. And it shows how central a missionary understanding of the church is to Scripture.

This dynamic offers us, then, a "cosmic—communal—personal" structure of biblical faith. The Bible tells a *cosmic* story of the work of the triune God to renew the whole creation; central to the story is a *community* chosen to embody that renewal for the sake of all; each *person* is invited to believe the good news, join this community, and take their place in the bigger story. This structure is faithful to the Bible as it is given to us in its canonical form. And it gives the importance of the church and the responsibility of each person their rightful place.

Basic Needs for a Missionary Church

The United Nations uses the term *basic needs* to describe the basic resources needed for long-term human health—food, water, shelter, sanitation, clothing, education, work, and so on. In the rest of this chapter, we articulate the "basic needs" of a healthy missionary church. What resources are needed for the long-term health of a missionary congregation? We attend especially to needed resources from Newbigin's missionary ecclesiology.

The Gospel

To become a missionary church, we need to recover a full-orbed gospel.[6] The gospel is about what God has done in the person and historical events of Jesus the Christ. He is the clue to understand everything. But to recover the fullness of the good news we need, first, the *proper context* for these events. There are two fundamental contexts within the evangelical world—often unconsciously assumed—that provide the default background for Christ. The first is an evangelistic message popular in North American evangelism practice: "You stand before a holy God as a guilty sinner deserving of his judgment. But God has provided a way for you to be saved. At the cross Jesus has taken your sin and guilt on himself so you can be forgiven and justified." The truth of this cannot be doubted, and it may be one way to speak of the gospel—provided it is followed in time by a lot more biblical context! But this presentation ignores creation and what it means to be human as the background; it bypasses the fact that God is creating a people; it reduces the power, scope, and gravity of sin and evil in a variety of ways; it speaks only of the cross apart from the rest of Christ's work, and most notably absent is his resurrection; it speaks only of a few benefits, abstracting these from God's purpose to renew human life; it abstracts the human person from their community and the world in which they are enmeshed; to mention a few things! This by itself provides a reductionist version of the gospel.

The second is systematic theology, whether that comes to us in more sophisticated written form or in the belief statements articulated on church websites or in official doctrinal statements. Again, these are important. We will always be guided and shaped to some degree by a doctrinal framework in understanding the Christian faith. The danger is when the story line of our theologies replaces the biblical story line as the fundamental context for understanding Christ. And this is far more common than we realize. Newbigin's warning against the fatal identification of theology with the biblical story is a salutary one.

To be understood, the good news of Jesus Christ must be set in the context of the biblical story. Newbigin speaks of the *finality* of Christ. In this carefully

6. Goheen, *Church and Its Vocation*, 41–65.

chosen word we see that the category of "narrative" has overarching and fundamental significance as the only proper context for understanding Christ. He speaks of the "great divide" among religions.[7] The very nature of religion is that it is concerned with that which is ultimate or that which finally unifies and gives meaning to everything. It is a claim to ultimacy: it claims to make sense of reality as a whole. Ultimate truth can be found in one of two ways. One can find truth in something that lies behind and encompasses all reality. This is the way of Eastern religions—for example, Brahman in Hinduism. Or one can find it in universal history that has an end yet to come. This is the way of Judaism, Islam, humanism, and the Christian faith. The first finds unity and meaning in some eternal and unchanging being and the second in a comprehensive historical narrative. This constitutes the great divide. For Newbigin the Christian faith finds ultimate truth in a story that is centered in Jesus Christ. "To speak of the finality of Christ is to speak of the Gospel as the clue to history."[8] Thus the basic structure of the Bible and the Christian faith is universal history, and this is the context to understand Christ.

The finality of Jesus is found in that he has *revealed and accomplished the end of universal history*. In his life, death, and resurrection, he has finally and decisively disclosed where universal history is going. Moreover, he has fully accomplished it, thereby already making the End present in the middle of history but also assuring its ultimate victory. We see the End revealed in the miracles and parables of Jesus's ministry, for example. His death and resurrection are the turning point in cosmic history: there the old world—dominated by sin, curse, judgment, Satan and demonic power, death, and the effects of sin—is defeated at the cross; the new world, cleansed of evil, begins in the resurrection of Jesus. These events reveal what is coming and accomplish it finally and fully.

The gospel is the gospel *of the kingdom*.[9] This is one of the images of the End. If we are to fill the word *kingdom* with the content that Jesus intended, we must first go back to the Old Testament and set the gospel as the climactic moment of that story. The restoration of God's rule over the world is the goal of the whole story. The gospel of the kingdom is the *power* of God entering human history to accomplish a *cosmic salvation* that restores his rule over all creation and the whole of human life. This kingdom-salvation is made known in the life of Jesus, his mighty works, teaching, and parables. This kingdom-salvation is accomplished in his crucifixion. This kingdom-salvation

---

7. Newbigin, *Finality of Christ*, 65–69.
8. Newbigin, *Finality of Christ*, 65.
9. Lesslie Newbigin, *The Good Shepherd: Meditations on Christian Ministry in Today's World* (Grand Rapids: Eerdmans, 1977), 67.

is inaugurated for the world in his resurrection. This kingdom-salvation is implemented in the world by the power of the Spirit, who gives a foretaste now of the full banquet we await in the future.

Thus we are being renewed in the whole of our lives. Newbigin speaks of four relationships established in creation, corrupted by sin, and restored in the work of Christ. In fact, he sees this—what he calls "the restored relationships"—as one helpful way to tell the whole story of the Bible.[10] The four relationships are our relationship with God, with one another, with the nonhuman creation, and with ourselves.[11] Indeed, "all the benefits which Christ was sent to bring" enable people to be "restored to their true humanity because they are reconciled with their Maker."[12] Forgiveness and justification are benefits that restore us to our Maker, but these are only a few of the benefits that restore us to our true humanity.

This salvation comes to us as we are united with Christ in his death and resurrection. The death and resurrection of Christ are the turning point in cosmic history: his death is the end of the old and his resurrection the beginning of the new. We partake in what Christ has accomplished by faith in the gospel and baptism into his community. Our salvation is eschatological: end-time renewal has broken into the present in the work of Christ and the Spirit. We taste now and dine fully at his return.

But this is not simply a gospel of the kingdom; it is the gospel *of our Lord Jesus Christ*. In Jesus, God's rule is present: "The kingdom of God, his kingly rule, now has a human face and a human name—the name and the face of Jesus from Nazareth."[13] We are invited to follow Jesus, love him, trust him, obey him, serve him, join him in his mission. The gospel is about a "personal relationship." Of course, this "personal relationship" is not solitary; we join a community that loves and serves Christ. Nevertheless, it is fundamentally relational. We enjoy all the benefits only in personal communion.

And so Newbigin addresses two dangers in understanding the gospel: The first is to separate the kingdom from the person of Jesus and turn it into an ideology or program to transform culture. This is the danger of the liberal tradition. However, there is an equal and opposite danger: that is to speak of the person of Jesus apart from the kingdom and to reduce everything to a personal relationship. The announcement of the gospel invites people into a

10. Lesslie Newbigin, "Canon and Mission" (unpublished notes, n.d.), 2.
11. Lesslie Newbigin, *Sin and Salvation* (London: SCM, 1956), 11–15, 21–22.
12. Lesslie Newbigin, "The Life and Mission of the Church," in *The Life and Mission of the Church*, ed. C. I. Itty (Bangalore: Student Christian Movement of India, 1958), 7.
13. Lesslie Newbigin, *Mission in Christ's Way: Bible Studies* (Geneva: World Council of Churches, 1987), 7.

relationship with Jesus—to follow, believe, love, obey *him*. This Jesus embodies the reign of God. The gospel is about the *kingdom* made present in the *person* of Jesus. It is both at the same time.

To recover a full gospel will mean to reclaim the fundamentally eschatological shape of the Christian faith. Newbigin asks what is needed if we are to recover a missionary encounter with Western culture. He lists several essentials and begins: "The first must be the recovery and firm grasp of a true doctrine of last things, of eschatology. The gospel is the good news of the kingdom, and the kingdom is an eschatological concept. A true understanding of the last things is the first essential."[14] The whole of the New Testament is eschatological: it is an announcement that the end of universal history has broken into the middle in the work of Christ and the Spirit. The New Testament canon works out the implications of this shocking announcement, elaborating the salvation it brings and the new calling of the church in this new redemptive-historical period within its cultural setting.

The eschatological nature of the Christian faith requires us to ask where universal history is going. What does the new humanity look like? Our vocation is to be a preview of just that. We are a people who are a sign that points to the reconciliation that will one day fill the earth. It leads us to reject an individualistic and otherworldly future since our salvation is interwoven with community, culture, and nonhuman creation. It also leads us to reject the progress story of the West since the End will come only when Christ returns.

We also need to recover a sense of the gospel as the power of God unto salvation. Our rationalism has caused us to reduce the gospel to its doctrinal content. To be sure, the gospel does have doctrinal content—after all, there may be a false gospel. But it cannot be reduced to that any more than pudding can be reduced to milk because it has milk as an essential component. The gospel is the powerful means or channel by which God's kingdom-salvation comes into the world. And this is why Newbigin would repeatedly say that "everything depends on a recovery of confidence in the gospel."[15]

This gospel should shape everything! It is the power of God unto salvation. Christ comes to us in love and power clothed in the gospel. And so if we want Christ to be present to form us, the gospel must be at the center of our church—what we preach, celebrate, make known, and live.

14. Lesslie Newbigin, *Foolishness to the Greeks: The Gospel and Western Culture* (Grand Rapids: Eerdmans, 1986), 134.
15. Lesslie Newbigin, *A Word in Season: Perspectives on Christian World Missions* (Grand Rapids: Eerdmans, 1994), 187.

The Biblical Story

To become a missionary church, we need to be immersed in the biblical story as the story in which we live our whole lives. "The business of the church is to tell and to embody a story, the story of God's mighty acts in creation and redemption and of God's promises concerning what will be in the end. The church affirms the truth of this story by celebrating it, interpreting it, and enacting it in the life of the contemporary world."[16]

This is the context in which we understand our missionary calling. Back in the middle of the twentieth century the language of the *missio Dei*, or the mission of the triune God, was coined to capture this biblical story as the bigger context for the mission of the church. However, the fundamental narrative structure of God's mission has not always been the primary way that this is understood. Reducing God's mission to a formula of sending, along with theological reflection on the triune nature of God that bypasses or ignores the structure of the Bible as a story, offers a different comprehensive framework for the mission of the church. For Newbigin, the Bible as *story* was fundamental: God's mission was theological terminology, one way to capture the way the triune God worked out his redemptive purposes in the unfolding of the story told in Scripture.

Story must not be reduced to a redemptive-historical *method*. Story for Newbigin was not a redemptive-historical hermeneutic or a method for doing theology. Story offered the overall shape of the Christian faith itself. And all theology—biblical, systematic, historical—is second-order human activity that opens up and deepens our understanding of this basic structure of the Christian faith.

Neither is story simply a religious narrative that forms our distinctive Christian identity. It certainly is and does that. But it is more: it is public truth. The Bible infallibly records the historical events by which the creator God reveals and leads the whole of human history toward its goal. "The biblical story is not a separate story. It is not a special history ('salvation history') apart from human history as a whole. The whole story of humankind is one single fabric of interconnected events, and the story the Bible tells is part of it."[17] As part of human history, the events of Scripture give meaning to the whole. This is a historical story that reveals and accomplishes where God is leading the whole world, and this includes all peoples and cultures as well as the nonhuman creation.

16. Lesslie Newbigin, *Proper Confidence: Faith, Doubt, and Certainty in Christian Discipleship* (Grand Rapids: Eerdmans, 1995), 76.
17. Newbigin, *Open Secret*, 87.

And this story does not need to be "strengthened" in its truth claims by theological propositional statements. There is no stronger expression of the universally valid truth of the Bible than to claim that it tells the true story of the whole world. The redemptive-historical events that precede Scripture are authoritatively interpreted in the narrative of the Bible and reveal to us where God is taking human history. It is especially in the *finality* of Jesus Christ where God fully and finally reveals and accomplishes his purpose for the world. All doctrinal and theological statements can only enable us to grasp something of this truth.

This is urgent and has significant implications for our congregations. Our discipleship must take seriously this shape of the Christian faith. How can we disciple God's people to know and live in the biblical story? Attending to three resources might be helpful. The first is the way the early church formed new believers in their catechetical process.[18] The second is the call to an ancient-evangelical future that invites us to think of ways we can renarrate our lives with biblical narrative in worship and discipleship.[19] There are growing numbers of discipleship tools to this end. The third is a resource that tells the story of the Bible simply and clearly. *The True Story of the Whole World* has been widely used in small group Bible studies to understand the biblical story as a whole.[20]

Our Identity

To become a missionary church, we need to know who we are. We have learned well in the past decades that identities are always formed by a story. And so this reminds us again of the importance of recovering the biblical story. There are three aspects of that identity Newbigin can help us recover.

The first is that we are the *true humanity*. We tend to understand the church in terms of a "religious community," with the term *religious* defined by the cultural story. Thus our identity becomes a private, voluntary society made up of individuals who believe the same kind of "religious" beliefs. Yet the Bible tells us a story of God restoring humanity to be again what he intended in the beginning. He created humanity as a cultural and social community in the beginning. The failure of Adamic humanity to be and do what God intended

---

18. See Everett Ferguson, "Irenaeus' *Proof of Apostolic Preaching* and the Early Catechetical Instruction," in *The Early Church at Work and Worship*, vol. 2, *Catechesis, Baptism, Eschatology, and Martyrdom* (Cambridge: James Clarke, 2014), 1–17; Alan Kreider, "Worship and Evangelism in Pre-Christendom" (Cambridge: Grove Books, 1995).

19. Robert Webber and Philip Kenyon, "Ancient-Evangelical Future Call," http://webbercenter.tsm.edu/about-us/aef-call/.

20. Michael W. Goheen and Craig G. Bartholomew, *The True Story of the Whole World: Finding Your Place in the Biblical Drama* (Grand Rapids: Baker Academic, 2020).

led to his redemptive work to restore a new and true humanity to be what God purposed for human life. He set out on the long road of redemption to restore a people, not as individuals assembled like so many marbles in a bag or beads on a string, but in the integrity of their social and cultural nature. Abraham is the beginning of Israel, the restored humanity. In his death and resurrection, Jesus is the second Adam, who is the source of this new humanity. The gathering that characterizes this eschatological period is the gathering into this true humankind re-created according to its original integrity.

Perhaps his notion of the church as the new and true humanity is most clearly seen in the way Newbigin speaks of the centrality of election. To speak of the "election" of a people is to challenge an individualistic and spiritualistic notion of salvation as a one-to-one relationship of the individual soul to God. In Scripture salvation is social and cosmic: it is about knitting together the human race again in reconciliation with God, with one another as a social and cultural community, and with the nonhuman creation. It is a restoration of the harmony and *shalom* of the original creation and a restoration of the way God made the human community in the context of the nonhuman creation at the beginning. Newbigin describes salvation this way:

> God, according to the Bible, is concerned with the redemption of the whole human race and of the whole created world. The goal of His purpose is not a collection of individual spirits abstracted one by one from their involvement in the world of matter and in the human community and set in a new and purely spiritual relation to Himself. Such a thought is irreconcilable with the biblical view of God, of man, and of the world. The redemption with which He is concerned is both social and cosmic, and therefore the way of its working involves at every point the re-creation of true human relationships and of true relationship between man and the rest of the created order.[21]

The *only* way of proceeding in accomplishing cosmic salvation is to choose a community as the nucleus of his renewing work. God begins to restore this community as the true humanity, knitting them back together and restoring the creational relationships fractured in the fall. Then he incorporates others from outside. In short, God's people have been chosen to be the true humankind: reconciled to God, to each other, and to the nonhuman creation and sent to draw others into that reconciliation. The election of a people is the "only principle congruous with the nature of God's redemptive activity."[22]

21. Lesslie Newbigin, *The Household of God: Lectures on the Nature of the Church* (New York: Friendship Press, 1953), 109.
22. Newbigin, *Household of God*, 111.

In election we see that God moves along the channels he cut at creation, restoring humanity as the image of God, as a social and cultural community to accomplish his universal purpose.

The second aspect of our ecclesial and missional identity is that we are a *sign, foretaste, and instrument* of the kingdom. This places the church squarely in the context of the kingdom. God's rule is broader than the church; it is over the whole creation and all human life. The church is the community where that rule is acknowledged and experienced. The church is a picture and the firstfruits of that reign that will one day extend to all things.

The relationship of the church to the kingdom may be defined in the following statements. First, the church is the place where the eschatological kingship of God in Jesus Christ becomes visible. Second, the church serves the kingdom by embodying and announcing the good news that Jesus is Lord over all. Third, the church is engaged in the struggle of Christ's kingdom in this world against the destructive powers of darkness in all areas of life as a witness to Christ's all-embracing lordship.

Keeping the broader kingdom context for the church keeps us from a host of distortions and reductions in our identity. It keeps us from the sacralization wherein the church defines its life within the boundaries of the institutional church, and we focus on the church's institutional forms and practices, becoming introverted and self-absorbed, with little concern for the world. It keeps us also from secularization, which has been so seductive as a reaction against sacralization by stressing the importance of solidarity with our communities. Secularization has been a healthy corrective, but the danger of breaking down the distinctiveness of the church as the new humanity is very real: we are reduced to an instrument and forget that we are the new humanity, the nucleus of God's coming new creation. The people of God immersed in the world are in danger of being assimilated to its spiritual currents if they forget their identity as the new humanity who have a foretaste of the coming kingdom.

A final aspect of our identity is that we are the new humanity both *gathered and scattered*. The church is the new humanity both when it is gathered for worship, discipleship, fellowship, instruction, and prayer *and* when congregants are scattered throughout their various cultural callings during the week. As a community, the church must embody what the new humanity will look like one day. In our communal life, we must embody generosity and concern for the poor and stand against all economic injustice; we must embody a reconciled diversity and stand against all political and economic ideologies; we must embody communal responsibility and stand against individualist and selfish notions of "rights"; we must be a multiethnic and multiracial community and stand against all traces of racism; and so on. But we must also be a people who embody the lordship of Jesus Christ in our marriages, families, work, use of technology, leisure, citizenship, creation care, and so on. The church is the new humanity—gathered and scattered.

How can our worship, preaching, discipleship, sacraments, and fellowship form communities that understand, embrace, and embody this identity?

Our Culture

To become a missionary church, we need to know our culture. "If you want to know about water, don't ask a fish." If you want to know about Canadian culture, don't ask a Canadian. We are immersed and swim in the water of our culture with all its institutions, customs, rhythms, practices, assumptions, and beliefs. And if the water is polluted by idolatry, we swim on, blissfully unaware as we ingest its pollution.

This is true for the church in all cultures. But Newbigin alerts us to the urgency of a missionary encounter with Western culture in particular.[23] Western culture is the most *powerful* and *pervasive* global power, the most *dangerous* foe the church has faced in its history, the most *resistant* to the gospel because of a long intertwinement that makes it immune to the critique of the gospel, and where the church is most *syncretistic* in its accommodation to its idols. If this is anywhere near the truth—and we believe it is spot on—then knowing our Western cultural context is urgent, even a matter of life and death.

Knowing our culture requires four things. The first is to understand its *religious core*. Newbigin argues that "incomparably the most urgent missionary task for the next few decades is the mission to 'modernity.'" Central to that task is to "probe behind the unquestioned assumptions of modernity and uncover the hidden credo which supports them."[24] Lying beneath the practices of Western culture like tectonic plates is an unquestioned and hidden credo, a religious confession of beliefs. This religious credo is a "set of beliefs, experiences, and practices that seek to grasp and express the ultimate nature of things, that which gives shape and meaning to life, that which claims ultimate loyalty."[25]

The problem is not only that these beliefs are hidden from view but that there is a powerful myth that masks their religious nature: the myth of a neutral secular culture. "Modernity pretends to have no creed. . . . It applies to itself the adjective *secular*, with the implication that it is neutral in respect

---

23. Goheen, *Church and Its Vocation*, 164–66.
24. Lesslie Newbigin, "Gospel and Culture—but Which Culture?," *Missionalia* 17 (November 1989): 214.
25. Newbigin, *Foolishness to the Greeks*, 3.

to beliefs that come under the name 'religion.' In this way it conceals from its adherents the fact that it is itself based on a particular view of the human situation, a view that is open to question."[26] The secular society is "not a neutral area" but "an area already occupied by other gods. We have a battle on our hands. We are dealing with the principalities and powers."[27]

These religious beliefs are ultimate and comprehensive, shaping and giving meaning to the whole of human life. But they also have spiritual power. The myth of secular neutrality cloaks all of this. It is urgent that we expose this myth and understand the religious power shaping our lives.

The second thing knowing our culture requires is to understand our *cultural story*. One way to expose these religious beliefs is to tell the story of our culture. "One way to gain a perspective on our culture is to look at it from the angle of history. European culture was not always so."[28] Telling the story of the formation of the religious beliefs of our culture shows that the assumptions and axioms of our culture are not an objective account of "how things really are" but have been formed historically and are therefore questionable.

The third is to know the *current spirits* shaping our culture. Correctly identifying the religious spirits animating our culture today is essential. For Newbigin, while the postmodern ethos is strong, it is not the biggest threat to the gospel. Rather, it is the new global and economic form of modernity that is sweeping the world, along with its flip side: the consumer culture. He describes the first as a "modern, scientific, liberal, free-market culture"[29] that is rooted in the economic vision of Enlightenment modernity. This has produced a "liturgy of consumerism"[30] in the West. To rightly understand this reality, we need to dig down to a deeper level than the political and economic systems, to the "level of fundamental beliefs, of ultimate commitments, in fact of idolatries."[31]

And finally, the fourth is the *voices of Christians from other cultures and from other times in history*. We are like fish in water; this is the only environment we know. We don't have critical distance, and the Christian faith has been part of this culture for so long we are captive to it. It is for this reason that Newbigin frequently stresses "the necessity for help in seeing our own culture through Christian minds shaped by other cultures." Our culture-bound

26. Newbigin, *Word in Season*, 194.
27. Newbigin, *Word in Season*, 150.
28. Lesslie Newbigin, "The Gospel and Modern Western Culture," Newbigin Archives, University of Birmingham (unpublished article, 1990), 2.
29. Newbigin, *Word in Season*, 188.
30. Lesslie Newbigin, "The Gospel as Public Truth: Swanwick Opening Statement" (unpublished address, 1992), 6.
31. Newbigin, "Gospel as Public Truth," 6.

vision of the Christian faith can be corrected only by those who can see it with other eyes. "We need their witness to correct ours, as indeed they need ours to correct theirs. At this moment our need is greater, for they have been far more aware of the dangers of syncretism, of an illegitimate alliance with false elements in their culture, than we have been."[32]

But it is important to hear the voices of Christians not only from other cultures but also from other times in history. The rejection of enormous chunks of church history robs the church today of the insights, critique, and enrichment of voices from the past. We may not neglect brothers and sisters from the past. As Paul says, we need all the saints to comprehend the richness of the gospel (Eph. 3:18).

How then do we relate to culture? Newbigin's notion of a missionary encounter, subversive fulfillment, and contextualization is insightful. We live as part of two communities shaped by two incompatible stories. There is a clash of stories that produces a painful tension within each of us and within the Christian community. We struggle in that tension to discern the creational good in our culture and how it has been deformed by idolatry. We embody an alternative that stands against the idolatrous distortion that produces injustice and incarnates the creational good within that idol. This ongoing dialogue between stories is a continuing process of conversion toward faithfulness.

If this is true, on the one hand, it requires that far more time be given in theological education to training leaders to read their culture. This is an enormous gap that needs to be addressed. On the other hand, it requires that far more time be given in the discipleship and formation ministry of the local congregation to enabling God's people to understand the cultural spirits that are shaping them.

Our Calling in the World

To become a missionary church, we need to understand our calling in the world. The logic of mission is that the end of universal history has been revealed and accomplished in the good news of Jesus. The nucleus of the new humanity has been formed to inherit the kingdom. Now this good news must be made known and all invited to join the new humanity. Mission to the ends of the earth characterizes this eschatological period. Now is the time of gathering. This missionary vocation characterizes our very identity—the new humanity sent to gather in others between the resurrection and the return of Christ.

32. Newbigin, *Foolishness to the Greeks*, 146–47.

There are a number of dimensions of Newbigin's understanding of mission that are important. The first is the significant distinction he makes between the missionary dimension and the missionary intention. One of the significant characteristics of his missionary understanding of the church is that it is the church's being as the new humanity that is at the heart of the church's mission. There is a missionary dimension to the whole life of the church: that is, every part of human life is being restored to God's original creational intention and so all of life witnesses to God's renewing work. But at the same time there are specific and intentional activities that cross boundaries to the unbelieving world and invite all people to follow Christ and join the new humanity: activities such as evangelism, church planting, and missions. These are essential to mission.

Yet too often a comprehensive vision of mission seems to squelch intentional evangelistic activities or, alternatively, such deliberate outreach activities become the total sum of what mission is. This distinction maintains something central to the missionary vocation of the church. Our whole lives point to God's renewing purpose. But there remains an evangelistic task to intentionally witness to Christ as the one in whom salvation is found. Both are essential to the missionary calling of the church.

Newbigin repeatedly articulates five elements of this missionary vocation in his writings: (1) new being and communal life; (2) the vocation of believers in public life; (3) deeds of justice, peace, and mercy; (4) evangelism; and (5) missions.[33] The foundational and central role of the church in the biblical story is its new being—to be and live out the distinctive life of the new humanity in a world that serves other gods. This distinctive life shaped by the gospel is embodied in the community as well as in the scattered life of the church, particularly in the vocations of believers in the public life of culture. From this new being flow deeds of mercy and justice that witness to the coming kingdom and evangelistic words that summon others to follow Christ and become part of the new humanity. And finally, this mission is to the ends of the earth and all peoples: communities that witness to the coming kingdom in life, deeds, and words must be established amidst every people group so that all may see, hear, and believe.

Have each of these elements found an organic place within our churches? There are two neglected aspects of the missionary vocation of the church that need to be emphasized. The first is the vocation of the laity.[34] This is the primary place where our witness to the lordship of Christ over all is given.

33. Goheen, *Church and Its Vocation*, 78–101.
34. Goheen, *Church and Its Vocation*, 82–86.

This is where we spend most of our time. This is where a witness to the gospel challenges the privatization of the gospel in a humanist culture. And this is the dimension of mission that is least understood by the church and most sparsely treated in much literature of the missionary calling of the church.

Most believers, well-meaning and sincere as they are, are shaped by the humanist story in most of their lives in the public square. This reinforces the public-private dichotomy, ensuring that the gospel will remain sequestered in the private realm. Sadly, many Christians working in their vocations "in politics, commerce, education, industry, scientific research and so on . . . behave as though their work in farm or factory from Monday to Friday were not 'the Lord's work.' . . . That is, in effect to deny Christ's cosmic Lordship." It is to turn over to the powers these creational structures God has created. Rather, we are to "challenge the existing structures and witness to the true purpose for which God created them."[35] It is essential for us to recover this area of mission and for the local congregation to address the question of how it might equip God's people to witness to Christ's rule in their vocations.

The task of each local congregation is to concern itself with a witness to the ends of the earth.[36] Where in the world is there no communal witness to Christ where people may see and hear the gospel in their own cultural setting? How can we establish a faithful witness in that place? Sadly, in much literature on the missionary vocation of the church, this aspect of mission has been abandoned. Perhaps this is owing to embarrassment because of the oppressive colonial ties that shaped missions, or perhaps it is simply owing to neglect. For whatever reason, mission in our own neighborhood has often eclipsed missions to the ends of the earth. This not only fails to embrace an essential aspect of mission, it also blocks from view the ultimate horizon of our mission.

Missional Means of Grace

To become a missionary church, we need to attend to the missional means of grace that equip us for our calling in the world. God has given us channels whereby the power of the gospel might transform our lives as we gather in community. If we do not devote ourselves to these channels, we are vulnerable to the powerful spiritual currents of our culture.

Newbigin indicates the importance of this issue by asking how we may become partakers in the eschatological life of Christ. He asks, "How does what Christ has done for men become mine?" and answers, "It becomes

35. Lesslie Newbigin, *Trinitarian Doctrine for Today's Mission* (1963; repr., Carlisle, UK: Paternoster, 1998), 62.
36. Goheen, *Church and Its Vocation*, 97–101.

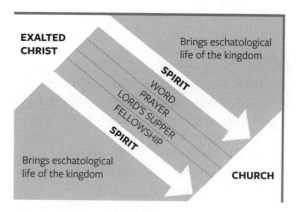

Figure 14.1. Missional means of grace

mine when I become part of this society, this fellowship, He left behind Him to be a continuation of His life on earth."[37] He turns to Acts 2:42 and unpacks the importance of four channels of grace: the apostles' teaching, the breaking of bread, fellowship, and prayer. "These four visible marks are four links by which the continuing fellowship is bound to Christ and His work, continually renewed and re-directed by Him."[38] But these missional means of grace are effectual only by the work of the Spirit that gives this new life (fig. 14.1).

We need to return to the traditional means of grace—Scripture, worship, baptism, the Lord's Supper, prayer, fellowship, ministry—and ask how those channels can be cleared of all debris that hinders the flow of the new life in Christ to us today. By way of example, it is noteworthy to see the way Newbigin struggled with the sacraments to ask how they could nourish the church for its missional calling. In an address to an ecumenical meeting of Anglican and Reformed leaders, he said that he returned "to the New Testament and went through its entire text," making notes on sacraments and ministry. He concluded that both traditions are significantly different from the New Testament. The contrast arises from the fact that "the New Testament assumes a missionary situation in which the Church is a small evangelizing movement in a pagan society, while both of our traditions have been formed in the 'Christendom' era, in a society presumed to be Christian."[39] Baptism is inclusion in a community committed to mission, and the Eucharist is the continual renewal

37. Newbigin, *Sin and Salvation*, 93.
38. Newbigin, *Sin and Salvation*, 96.
39. Lesslie Newbigin, "How Should We Understand Sacraments and Ministry?" (unpublished paper, 1983), 1.

of that commitment. What follows is a reframing of the sacraments that offers to take hold of tradition in ways that are missionary. We also need to return to our worship, preaching, teaching, sacraments, and prayer to ask how we can reframe them in light of Scripture to equip us for our missionary vocation.

One of the important elements to recover in this process will be the authority of Scripture. During the latter part of the twentieth century, the evangelical church rightly battled to maintain the divine authority of Scripture against the naturalistic spirits that encroached on it. Yet evangelicalism has not always been aware of how it too has allowed the Enlightenment to reshape its view of Scripture as it diminished Scripture's narrative authority. Scripture's authority is found in the cosmic story it tells, centered in the person of Jesus Christ. All parts and genres of the canon of Scripture incorporate us more deeply into that story.

Only the Bible as a comprehensive story can re-form us as the true humanity and keep us from being deformed by our cultural story. We repeat two of Newbigin's fundamental convictions we quoted earlier in this book because of their importance: "I do not believe that we can speak effectively of the Gospel as a word addressed to our culture unless we recover a sense of the Scriptures as a canonical whole, as the story which provides the true context for our understanding of the meaning of our lives—both personal and public."[40] Our lives will be shaped by some story, and if we are not being re-formed by the biblical story, by default we will be deformed by the reigning story of culture. "If this biblical story is not the one that really controls our thinking [and lives] then inevitably we shall be swept into the story that the world tells about itself. We shall become increasingly indistinguishable from the pagan world of which we are a part."[41]

Allowing the Bible to be broken into bits—systematic-theological, devotional, and homiletical—will hamstring the church, depriving it of one of the most important resources it has for faithfulness. We need to give attention to the question of how our preaching, teaching, and discipleship can enable the church to understand the whole story and how each part of the canon can enable us to take our place in this story.

Our Institutional Structures

To become a missionary church, we need to shape the institutional church in a way that equips God's people for their calling in the world. We need to

40. Lesslie Newbigin, "Response to 'Word of God'?," *Gospel and Our Culture Newsletter* 10 (1991): 2.
41. Lesslie Newbigin, "Biblical Authority," Newbigin Archives, University of Birmingham (unpublished article, 1997), 2.

know how to organize ourselves to faithfully administer the missional means of grace God has given us so that our lives can be renarrated and empowered for our missionary calling.

The only way we can be a missionary people, making known the kingdom in our lives, is if we receive the life of the kingdom through these channels in the community of God's people. Thus the institutional church is exceedingly important. We have seen again and again the minimization of the gathered church, beginning in the secular decades of the 1960s and continuing in many places since then, in both the ecumenical and the evangelical traditions. This path will ultimately undermine a true missionary church. The holy impatience with an introverted, rigid, and institutionalized church is understandable. But the way forward is not to abandon the church as institution, but to renew it to carry out the task of empowering God's people for their missionary vocation.

To this end the creative work done in the missional, emergent, and center church literature is excellent. Much work moves far beyond Newbigin's own proposals. But there remain at least three helpful emphases in his writing that we need today—beyond his stress on the importance of the institutional church. First, we may not abandon the history of the church. Newbigin stressed the importance of bold and fresh initiatives and experiments in congregational and ministry structures. He wasn't afraid to challenge the status quo: telling both the Anglican and Reformed traditions that their views of ministry were inadequate when compared to the missionary perspective of the New Testament was certainly bold! Yet he never took the path of writing off the confessional traditions that contained much biblical wisdom.

Second, the majority of the work in structural and institutional renewal has been in the areas of the congregation and leadership. The challenge Newbigin brings is that we need to think in three other areas: missionary, ecumenical, and vocational. We need new missionary structures. Our structures still reflect a time when mission was reduced to cross-cultural activity during the colonial era. We need structural renewal in a world where the missionary task is a task of the whole global church. We also need ecumenical structures that will enable the church to be a united body in particular places for the good of each place. And we need structures and leadership that will equip the laity for their callings in the public life of society. Throughout our journey in this book, we have seen the importance of these structures and how they have not been a priority for most of the discussion today of a missionary church.

A final insight that Newbigin offers us today is a caution to take account not only of the promise of small groups but also of their dangers. Newbigin's concern for the renewal of congregational structures was concerned with size and flexibility. In terms of size, he believed that the primary need was for smaller groups. He suggested neighborhood groups, work groups, frontier groups, and action groups.[42] And his fruitful suggestions continue to challenge us to think of the many ways small groups can function to equip the church for its calling. The promise of small groups is a frequent theme in the missional and emergent church literature. But the dangers that accompany them, not so much.

Newbigin warned against three things. First, there is a danger that small groups may become either introverted or activist. They may become places where all the benefits of salvation are selfishly enjoyed, or they may become simply more action groups or programs for social change. The second danger is that novel experimentation is vulnerable to the "real danger that we lose the great essentials which have been preserved and handed on through the ordered life and liturgy of the great churches."[43] And finally, small groups can become disconnected from the broader body of Christ, both locally and globally.

The Glory of God

Perhaps one of the most important things we can recover from Newbigin is his strong emphasis on the glory of God as the ultimate goal of a missionary people. He asks, "What, then, is the point of missions?" Is our ultimate concern the need of all people for salvation? Is it the renewal of society? These are valid concerns, but they are not our primary goal. So what is? "The answer I believe quite simply is the glory of God." If God has done what the Bible says he has done, then our response should be to witness to his love and ask "How can I glorify God" so that there "may be throughout the world those who turn their faces to God and give Him thanks and glorify him. The glory of God is the purpose, the goal of mission, and our one aim is that we should praise and glorify Him."[44]

Mission has been "terribly Pelagian," says Newbigin. "Whether the emphasis was upon the saving of individual souls from perdition, or on the righting of social wrongs, the overwhelming emphasis has been upon missions as our program."[45] In the evangelical tradition, mission has been a narrow concern with "the individual and his or her need to be assured of ultimate happiness,

42. Goheen, *Church and Its Vocation*, 125.
43. Lesslie Newbigin, "Cooperation and Unity," *International Review of Mission* 59, no. 233 (1970): 73.
44. Lesslie Newbigin, *Signs amid the Rubble: The Purposes of God in Human History*, ed. Geoffrey Wainwright (Grand Rapids: Eerdmans, 2003), 120–21.
45. Lesslie Newbigin, "Mission in the 1990s: Two Views," *International Bulletin of Missionary Research* 13, no. 3 (1989): 102.

and not with God and his glory." We talk "as if the whole cosmic drama of salvation culminated in the words 'For me; for me'; . . . But this is a perversion of the gospel."[46] In the ecumenical tradition, mission has centered on our task to renew society. But this too detracts from the ultimate goal. "The center of the picture is not the human need of salvation (from sin, from oppression, from alienation) but God and God's immeasurable grace. So the central concern is not 'How shall the world be saved?' but 'How shall this glorious and gracious God be glorified?' The goal is the glory of God."[47] Mission must "begin with the mighty work of grace in Jesus Christ and asks, How is he to be honored and glorified? The goal of missions is the glory of God."[48]

46. Lesslie Newbigin, *The Gospel in a Pluralist Society* (Grand Rapids: Eerdmans, 1989), 179.
47. Newbigin, "Mission in the 1990s," 102.
48. Newbigin, *Gospel in a Pluralist Society*, 179–80.

Index